SCREENS FADE TO BLACK

SCREENS FADE TO BLACK

Contemporary African American Cinema

DAVID J. LEONARD

PRAEGER

Westport, Connecticut
London

Library of Congress Cataloging-in-Publication Data

Leonard, David J.
    Screens fade to black : contemporary African American cinema /David J. Leonard.
        p.   cm.
    Includes bibliographical references and index.
    ISBN 0–275–98361–7 (alk. paper)
    1. African Americans in motion pictures.   2. African Americans in the motion
picture industry.   I. Title.
    PN1995.9.N4L46 2006
    791.43'652996073—dc22   2006003336

British Library Cataloguing in Publication Data is available.

This book is included in the African American Experience database from Greenwood
Electronic Media. For more information, visit www.africanamericanexperience.com.

Library of Congress Catalog Card Number: 2006003336
ISBN: 0–275–98361–7

First published in 2006

Praeger Publishers, 88 Post Road West, Westport, CT 06881
An imprint of Greenwood Publishing Group, Inc.
www.praeger.com

Printed in the United States of America

The paper used in this book complies with the
Permanent Paper Standard issued by the National
Information Standards Organization (Z39.48–1984).

10 9 8 7 6 5 4 3 2 1

To Anna, for loving me and seeing the value in my work
To Rea, for reminding me of the importance of social justice
To the victims of Hurricane Katrina, for reminding me of the importance
of cultural studies grounded in struggles for social justice
To Tookie Williams, for your efforts to redeem yourself and this nation,
which in the end reminded us that racism does kill

CONTENTS

ACKNOWLEDGMENTS

Like most books, this work is the outgrowth of many conversations, experiences, and influences. While it formally began to take shape after several conversations with Eric Levy—my initial editor at Praeger—this project probably began as a child who was encouraged to critically examine film and the world that informs and learns from these cinematic productions. Of course, my parents and siblings—who like to argue and recite the lines of films—instilled not just a passion for movies, but a certain level of media literacy that made this project possible. Subsequent experiences, from my African American film course at University of California, Santa Barbara, to numerous intellectual debates about film while attending the University of California, Berkeley, pushed me further toward the completion of this project.

Many people have served as a source of education about the history of African American film or helped me become film literate. I thank Kofi Hadjor, Otis Madison, Douglas Daniels, Cedric Robinson (who constructed a foundation), Jared Sexton, Oliver Wang, Dylan Rodriguez, Sara Kaplan and Liz Lee, each of whom has pushed me in significant ways to grow as a scholar and film "critic."

I also have to thank my many high school friends, whose opposition to my readings of film and whose refusal to watch films with me because "I was just too critical," forced me to think about representation, specific productions, and the presentation of my own analysis in new ways.

The many people and intellectual influences who shape my understanding of film deserve credit for the completion of this project (Robin Kelley, Mark Anthony Neal, Todd Boyd, Craig Watkins, Patricia Hill Collins, and Cynthia Fuchs). Some I have had the opportunity to learn from directly, and others have provided insight through the reading of their works.

Likewise, Eric Levy, Daniel Harmon, and the rest of the staff at Praeger deserve much credit for their constant support and their patience.

Much thanks to C. Richard King, my mentor, my biggest fan and supporter, and a person who has been a tremendous influence on me professionally, intellectually, and personally. He is most certainly the cinematographer of this work and a person who has gone to great lengths to assist in the development of this project.

Finally, Lisa Guerrero, Carmen Lugo-Lugo, Jose Alamillo, Kim Christen, Rory Ong, Marcie Gilliland, and John Streamas, who form my current intellectual and pedagogical community, not only directly encouraged and assisted in the completion of this work, but have inspired me through their work and commitment to social justice, and they all deserve credit in the development of this project.

Less obvious, but no less important, have been the all too often invisible efforts of the faculty, students, and staff of the Department of Comparative Ethnic Studies at Washington State University. Whether posing questions that led me to rethink things in class discussion or managing finances, this book would look much different, and undoubtedly be inferior, without them. In particular, I wish to thank Alicia Mackay, Martin Boston, Kelvin Monroe (who introduced me to a new film every week), Kristal T. Moore, Heidi Harting-Rex, Nicole Higgins, Jessica Hunnicutt, Cameron Sparks, and Walter Washington.

Much thanks (big props) to Jessica Hulst, who not only served as a research assistant, copy editor, motivational speaker, and spiritual advisor for the project, but also provided a needed conscience that kept the project moving toward its logical end. This book is a testament to your assistance and your cinematic spirit of intellectual critique.

To my family, I owe a special and significant debt of gratitude that these words can only begin to repay. Their love, support, tolerance, and patience (especially watching the same scene over and over again) have meant more than they know to me. To Rea Jadyn Leonard for bringing the joys of life to me each and every day with cookies, smiles, and kisses; to Elmo and Dora the Explorer, I thank you and your creators for providing entertainment that is educational and allowed me time to write about films that are neither entertaining nor educational (and most certainly not oppositional). And finally, to Anna Chow, thanks for the encouragement, the love, the respect, daily insights, and for tolerating multiple screenings of so many movies and our debts to Amazon.com.

As with the production of a film, this book is the work of many individuals, whose love and influence, whose commitment to social justice and media literacy, resonates in these pages.

1

SCREENS FADE TO BLACK, BUT
LITTLE HAS CHANGED

CELEBRATING THE 2002 OSCARS

In 2002, Hollywood celebrated the "end of racism" in the movie industry with awards to Halle Berry, Denzel Washington, and Sidney Poitier. As with America's larger discourse surrounding race, Hollywood insiders and critics alike cited this supposedly historic moment as a sign of America's racial progress. No longer reduced to maids or clowns on screen, blacks in the twenty-first century had access not only to increased opportunity within Hollywood but also to all the prestige, financial compensation, and opportunities available to white actors. Although there certainly has been change within Hollywood, as recent decades have not only seen a growth in the visibility of actors of color as well as with the diversity of roles available within contemporary Hollywood, recent years have also seen advancement concerning the numbers of and relative power from directors, writers, producers, and executives of color. Without a doubt, black Hollywood does not resemble its past incarnations. As a result of these changes, which also include more awards, more million-dollar contracts for African American stars, and a greater diversity of representations, social commentators, and film critics ubiquitously speak of progress at the expense of discussions around the presence of racist images.

Screens Fade to Black: Contemporary African American Cinema enters this discussion through an examination of several recent African American films to question: how far have we come with representation and opportunity? How far have the representations and ideological orientations of such representations departed from those connected with America's past? More important,

Screens Fade to Black: Contemporary African American Cinema questions the usefulness of a discussion that focuses exclusively on demographic shifts and neglects the issues of politics and ideology, arguing instead that the shifts in representations, from those grounded in explicit racialized ideologies and imagery to those reflective of a new racist project and in the visibility of black artists have not facilitated a new racial politics, nor have they contributed to an erosion of the manifestations of white supremacy and white privilege within American society. Focusing on the ways in which contemporary African American films engage race, racism, the American Dream, state violence, cultural commodification, and difference, *Screens Fade to Black* questions the basis of such celebrations given that just as Step 'n Fetchit, Rochester, and Mammy reified dominant racial discourses and naturalized inequality, today's representations and celebrations contribute to the ubiquity of racial inequality at the dawn of the twenty-first century.

To fully understand the scope of this project as it relates to contemporary African American films, it is important to understand the unique nature of the project. In fact, there are seven distinct features that not only reflect its point of departure from much of the literature, but also reveal the specific approach to contemporary African American film taken in this work:

1. It frames its discussion of African American film around the most recent wave of productions—*Antwone Fisher, Baby Boy, Training Day, Prison Song, Brown Sugar, Drumline, Love and Basketball, Good Fences, Soul Plane, Bringing Down the House, Barbershop, Barbershop 2, Undercover Brother,* and *Bamboozled*—most of which were written, directed, and starred black artists; were well received by a majority of black audiences; and supposedly chronicle elements of the contemporary black experience.

2. It examines African American film at a textual level, exploring plot, ideology, character development, and racial imagery (stereotypes).

3. *Screens Fade to Black* incorporates discussions of context, as to elucidate critical reception, audience reaction, and historical moment of release.

4. It explores a spectrum of genres, including comedies, ghettocentric, and "middle class positivity," which I link together through discussions of their engagement with dominant discourses, ideologies, and racialized tropes, ranging from new racism and state violence, to the American Dream and racial progress.

5. This effort attempts to bridge the gap between film analysis and popular audiences through a sophisticated, but accessible prose.

6. Although much of the text focuses on those films that reify and naturalize dominant racial discourses toward the perpetuation of persistent racial inequality and white privilege, all while noting the complexity, contradiction, and possibilities in virtually every film discussed, I also offer discussion of several films that offer counter-narratives that seek to challenge hegemonic representations and ideologies.

7. Finally, and most important, *Screens Fade to Black* situates this recent cinematic moment within a broader context of new racism, arguing that in spite of the

presence of black artists and the popularity in a commodified blackness, the cinematic representations of blackness continue to perpetuate inequality, poverty, and state violence. Exploring the ways in which the American Dream, racial progress, racial difference, blackness, whiteness, class, capitalism, and a host of other issues are addressed within contemporary films, my effort here seeks to examine how contemporary films teach about race at the millennium.

Screens Fade to Black critically examines a number of films, telling their stories on the screen and off, in an effort to elucidate larger trends within Hollywood and the United States. In providing accessible critical analysis, as opposed to the existing literature that offers either uncritical celebrations or inaccessible academic posturing, this text engages the themes, plots, and narrative structures of a number of popular films. It examines the ways in which characters are constructed and the manner in which ideas of race, gender, sexuality and class are conceived, as well as how race relations, history, and social issues are explored by this recent wave of African American films.

DEFINING AFRICAN AMERICAN CINEMA

In virtually every class I have taught on African American cinema and every conversation regarding this book, debates have taken place as to the defining elements of African American cinema. That is, there is no clear definition or understanding of what constitutes the genre of African American film, nor a transparent set of characteristics that define the cinematic products. As Stuart Hall rightly points out, there are no guarantees with these films in terms of ideology, politics, or aesthetics, regardless of the racial identity of their producers. Academic and popular discourses are thus not helpful in generating a clear definition (which is not desirable) or even providing succinct rationale as to the types of films included within this book.

Many people eschew the desire to categorize films through a broad understanding of racial identity, but it is important to examine black cinema as a phenomenon in its own right—as something having its own history, cultural traditions, and expressive norms (Africanism, oral tradition, narrative style, spirituality, syncretism, hybridization). Such a perspective relies on the idea of an African American perspective or ethos (a world view, which is a very slippery term). Such a practice raises the risk of denying the multiple voices and influences within any cultural production, while running the possibility of overdetermining race at the expense of other variables of difference (gender, class, sexuality, geography, nationality, ethnicity, age, etc.). Although this project illustrates the problems behind such categorizations, given the tendency of contemporary black films, regardless of a filmmaker's racial identity, to advance a new racist project, we must recognize the shared sense of identity/community and linked experience (sometimes imagined) that binds

African Americans regardless of class, gender, sexuality, nationality, color, or geography.

According to Gladstone Yearwood, race or blackness is most certainly a constructed and extremely heterogeneous concept, but it remains significant: "For many people blackness is less a color than a metaphor for political circumstances prescribed by struggles against economic exploitation and cultural domination: a state of consciousness that peoples of various pigmentations have experienced, empathized with, and responded to" (Yearwood 1999, p. 5). Yearwood, Mark Reid, and others specifically link these ideas to the history of African American cinema, arguing that cinematic productions from the black community reflect a cultural expression embedded in a survival impulse of African American cultures—that the history of black cinema is a story of resistance against dominant imagery in and outside of Hollywood. In *Screens Fade to Black,* I most certainly don't question the significance of this history, rather I focus on how commodification, incorporation, and the realities of new racism complicates the preceding discourse and the overall attempt to characterize a cinematic black aesthetic.

At a certain level, given the realities of new racism that uses the presence of black artists to repel and deny analysis or accusations of racism, I do see an importance in understanding this debate as a point of departure. One conclusion of this book is that we need to talk less about representation and inclusion and more about politics and ideology, given that numerous contemporary films that appear to be in the tradition of black cinema are ostensibly a continuation of Hollywood's efforts to legitimize and sanction white racism.

This project does not seek films that offer an authentic glimpse into black life, but it does engage the question of what constitutes African American cinema with its selection of films. Although no definition is sufficient, as all have significant contradictions, Thomas Cripps offers a good starting point for understanding the orientation of this work: "Those motion pictures made for theater distribution that have a black producer, director, and writer, or black performers; that speak to black audiences or, incidentally, to white audiences, possessed of preternatural curiosity, attentiveness, or sensibility toward racial matters; and that emerge from self-conscious intentions; whether artistic or political, to illuminate the Afro-American experience" (1978, p. 3). Mark Reid offers a similar definition, differentiating between black independent and black commercial films (I discuss only commercial films within this project) and also pushing the definition beyond a single author to reflect the transnational corporate realities of contemporary image making:

Black Commercial film is limited here to any feature-length fiction film whose central focus is the Afro-American community. This film is written, directed, or produced by at least one black person in collaboration with non black-people. Films included in this category are distributed by major American film company.

The Black independent film is defined as any feature-length fiction film whose central focus in the Afro-American community. Such films are written, directed and probably produced by people of African ancestry who reside in the United States. These films are not distributed by American film companies. (1993, p. 4)

Both Reid and Yearwood go beyond simple questions of authorship that reduces black films to a simple formula, concluding that, in essence, there are three different types of black film, especially as we look at black independent films: (1) films that deal with racism and its legacy, (2) films that reveal blacks' resistance against white assumptions of black inferiority, and (3) films that attempt to recode the black experience. Although wishful in their thinking and more reflective of an independent black cinematic tradition, which is outside this point of focus, *Screens Fade to Black* argues that processes of commodification, the nature of new racism, and the nature of contemporary racial politics have resulted in a betrayal of each of those principles of black cinematic focus. Indeed much of contemporary black Hollywood erases the contemporary presence and legacy of racism, deny black resistance to racist representations and institutional organization, and most significantly naturalize and legitimize dominant white narratives of blackness and American race relations.

Although these competing discourses offer myriad explanations and definitions, its discussants consistently identify black directors and writers as the defining element of African American cinema. This perspective is understandable and even sensible, but the reduction or limiting of the genre to films written and directed by black men and women is problematic and shortsighted. The images and representations of blackness are determined by a number of factors, none of which stands alone. According to Ed Guerrero, "No Hollywood film of any black image is the result of a single individual's inspiration or effort, but is a collaborative venture in which aesthetics, economics and politics share influences" (1993, p. 5).

Beyond questions of authenticity, the complications of class, color, sexuality, and gender (especially given the scant opportunities afforded to black female cinematic artists), and the limited (or contained) power afforded to writers and directors (studio executives, producers, editors, etc. affect form and contents of every film), history has shown too many holes in this definition to accept it without question. For example, both *Sounder* (1972) and *Foxy Brown* (1974), not without their own problems (especially *Foxy Brown*), were written and directed by white men, yet they also offered a representational field that challenged dominant black cultural imagery. In fact, *Sounder* offers a powerful cinematic narrative on the history of American racism and exploitation within the Jim Crow South. Although written and directed by a white male (Martin Ritt), it is often lauded as a great African American film. Compare that to *Glory* (1989), also written and directed by a white male (Edward Zwick), has received much critical praise for its historical treatment of the 54th Massachusetts Infantry (albeit from the popular press rather than academics or African American cultural organizations). Although at the surface of *Glory* as with a film like *Rosewood* (1997; directed by John Singleton) appears to tell a story about the African American community, it ultimately chronicles the heroism of white masculinity as the source of redemption and salvation for the black community. A film like *Glory,* unlike *Rosewood,* does not meet the definitional requirements of a black director or writer, yet both films deploy similar narratives, strategies, tropes, and ideologies reflective of a Hollywood cinematic model.

To define African American cinema is messy and contradictory. Think about *The Color Purple* (1985), a film based on the novel by Toni Morrison, and directed by Steven Spielberg. Some critics have long denounced the film as racist, as another stereotypical inscription of black masculinity. Others have praised the film, but even more have criticized it for its simplistic construction of black femininity and its failure to bring Morrison's story to the big screen. Reflecting the messiness of a definitional discourse, *The Color Purple, Glory,* and *Sounder* all bring questions of politics, ideology, identity, resistance, blackness, and opposition into discussion, demonstrating the problems of focusing exclusively on authorship or ideology.

Are African American films inherently oppositional, challenging not only Hollywood aesthetics and content, but the normative values and ideologies of white supremacy? Do the films cited here offer resistance to dominant representations or advance a politics beneficial to the black community? Are the comedies discussed within this work, from *Soul Plane* and *Bringing Down the House* to *Barbershop 1* and *2,* all of which were written and/or directed by black artists, voices of opposition? Are they specific to a black cultural or cinematic experience? Do they challenge long-standing representations of African Americans as Toms, Coons, Mammies, and Bucks, or challenge the persistent inequality that defines contemporary America? Such questions do not necessarily provide a greater understanding of what constitutes an African American film, but these questions about politics, ideology, and connections to new racism, guide this project. This project avoids such questions not only because of the messiness and inherent futility of a debate about what constitutes African American cinema, but because of the persistence of racism within and beyond Hollywood, the ascendancy and visibility of black cultural producers notwithstanding.

Our examinations should not fixate on whether or not something is an African American cultural production, but on how particular cultural formations and projects serve the interest of a heterogeneous black community. Do they challenge persistent levels of poverty, violence, segregation, and incarceration; or do they naturalize, justify, and facilitate a white supremacist agenda? How they teach about race, race relations, the African American experience, state violence, the American Dream, and resistance guides our examination here; we are merely using films often described as African American to document the power and ubiquity of colorblind racism.

As evidenced from our discussion here, especially as we begin to think about widespread commodification of blackness, the predominance of discourses that reduce race to cultural signifiers, and the massive scope of contemporary cinematic productions, the challenge of defining African American cinema is a difficult one. In fact, it is outside the scope of this project, which instead focuses on politics and how the films of contemporary Hollywood advance a reactionary, conservative politics, that define a new racist moment.

Likewise, this project does not simply "hate on films" for the sake of hating, nor does it attempt to enter conversations about whether or not a film is authentic or inauthentic, and whether a particular film is an example of good or bad black film. According to Yearwood, such debates are difficult at best:

There are many strong opinions on what constitutes a good black film and which films represent good black cinema. In film classes, students are often eager to establish a neat definition, which specifies a set of rules for classifying and excluding particular works in the black film canon. This reminds me of the story of a student who travels far and wide across the earth to find the meaning of life. After an arduous journey, the student finally reaches a village deep in a Central African forest. In a small clearing in the forest, he finds an old Griot who gestures wistfully with his open hands and whispers that the secret of the meaning of life is a deep well. For a moment, the student is speechless, thinking of many perils and treacherous experiences of the journeys. Disappointed and in disbelief, the youth leaves mumbling the words of the sage. The lesson we learn from the old Griot echoes a point of view articulated by the filmmaker Melvin Van Peebles, who believes that black film should be as rich and varied as the black experience. Van Peebles argues that the public should not expect black filmmakers to all make the same kind of films, speak from the same voice with the same point of view and use the same stylistic devices. "You don't ask Pushkin why he doesn't sound like Dostoevsky or Tolstoy," Van Peebles says. Black film is capable of articulating the rich plurality of the black experience so that we, in the African Diaspora and the world, will come to a deeper understanding about the soul of black culture. (1999, pp. 16–17)

Although in agreement with Yearwood, *Screens Fade to Black* moves beyond such questions focusing on the politics, ideological and discursive orientation, and the pedagogy of particular films, thinking about how they advance or challenge hegemony. Recognizing that such questions are not totalizing or simple, the focus goes beyond whether or not something is good, seeing greater importance in understanding how films naturalize poverty, state violence, and inequality (all bad) rather than challenging, forcing conversations, and resisting dominant institutional and cultural development (all bad). To truly talk about contemporary black cinema is not to limit discussions to definitions, questions of authenticity, and debates of good versus bad, but rather to begin to talk about how films in our contemporary moment reflect the realities of new racism, given that these other questions embody the old realities of an overtly racist system of representation that denied voice and visibility to communities of color. Those days are over, meaning that we must begin to approach our discussions of film in new ways, toward a greater understanding of colorblind and new racism.

A NEW RACISM: POPULAR CULTURE AND COLORBLIND DISCOURSE

Although ideologies of colorblindness emanate from a spectrum of state institutions, ranging from the media to the academy, popular culture represents a crucial site in the deployment of frames of colorblindness. It has become a site of celebration, whereupon American discourses pay tribute to progress and possibilities, thanking popular culture for what various individuals have described as the "browning of America," a "racing of American culture" or an "explicit darkening, blackening and coloring of American culture, at least in terms of operation of its dominant institutions of cultural production and legitimation" (Gray 2005, p. 18). In other words, popular culture does not merely embody a changed or colorblind moment for America; it is simultaneously facilitating greater advancements toward a more equitable racial politics given that popular culture breaks down barriers whether through artists or shared adoration experienced by fans.

As a source of the rhetoric of progress, the entertainment world exists as one of the most powerful disseminators of colorblind ideology, employing and deploying "evidence" of both structural and individual transformation toward a colorblind society (Collins 2004; Bonilla-Silva 2003; Cole, 1996, 2001; Boyd 1997). Herman Gray, in his recent book, *Cultural Moves: African Americans and the Politics of Representation,* laments the ways in which the visibility of blackness on America's screens, televisions, airwaves, and sports fields contributes to a discourse of progress, as part of maintaining hegemony.

Indeed, these representations of black people can just as easily be used to support political project that deny any specific claim or warrant on the part of black folks to experiencing disproportionately the effects of social justice, economic inequality, racism, and so on. As state and national campaigns for 'color blindness' and against affirmative action indicate, black visible is often the basis for claims to racial equality, the elimination of social and economic injustice, and the arrival of the time for racial invisibility. So, liberals use media representation of black achievement (rather than images of, say, criminality) to persuade constituents of the importance of diversity, while conservatives use the same representations to celebrate the virtues of colorblindness and individual achievement. (2005, p. 186)

That is, where politicians, commentators and educators have failed in selling Martin Luther King's dream, entertainers have broken down the walls of racism, demonstrating the merits of people of color to whites, while facilitating an erosion of the social, cultural, and racial distance that has long helped to maintain racism. Despite others' failures, the rest of society has caught on, appropriating the message that popular culture has not only provided opportunity, but serves as a virtual space of integration, whereupon whiteness meets the other. Leon Wynter, in *American Skin,* encapsulates this discourse, arguing that the last 30 years has seen a major transformation in American identity. "We live in a country where the 'King of Pop' was born black and a leading rap M.C. is white, where salsa outsells ketchup and cosmetic firms advertise blond hair dye with black models. Whiteness is in a steep decline as the primary measure of Americanness. The new, true American identity rising in its place is transracial, defined by shared cultural and consumer habits, not skin color or ethnicity" (Wynter 2002, front jacket). In other words, the shifting definition of American identity, as well as the manner in which race fits within American society, is heavily linked to popular culture and consumption. The increasing popularity of celebrities of color is thus both a sign and an instigator of racial discursive shifts. According to this view, something had to give and that thing was the systematic naturalization of whiteness as the defining cultural element of American life. "It's taken a long time, but American identity has finally begun to reach the truth of its composition. The artificial walls between American and being like an African or Hispanic or Asian American are coming down faster than anyone imaged even ten years ago," writes Leon Wynter. "Today, we wouldn't think of trying to describe 'American' by first excluding what is 'nonwhite'" (2002, p. 7). Ellis Cashmore concurs, arguing that through popular culture whites embrace difference, thereby limiting antipathy and hatred.

Before the rise of the Civil Rights Movement, whites were taught to fear difference. The sight of a black man in a suit was enough to cause alarm in some areas. Although similar projects exists today, through differences messages and messengers, the ubiquity of Jim Crow and its corresponding levels of violence define this pre-1960s historical moment.

One of the purposes of segregation was to prevent the potential contamination that might be caused by contact with "others." The others in question were not only different in appearance, language, and lifestyle: they were inferior. Neither the moral nor the constitutional imperative behind the separate-but-equal idea had any force at all.

Today, whites embrace the differences that once disturbed them: appreciation and enjoyment have replaced uneasiness. The images whites held of black have charged in harmony with changes in aesthetic tastes. What was once disparaged and mocked is now regarded as part of legitimate culture. Any residual menace still lurking in African Americans practices and pursuits has been domesticated, leaving a black culture capable of being adapted, refined, mass-produced, and marketed. Whites not [only] appreciate black: they buy it. Having appropriated music, visual arts and the literature traditionally associated with African Americans, they have put it on the market. Black culture is now open for business. A great many blacks have become rich on the back of it. An even greater number of whites have prospered. (Cashmore 1997, p. 1)

This traditional narrative locates the last 50 years of American popular culture as one of progress, setting the standards for race relations and integration. The predominance of black artists and artists of color, from J-Lo to Beyonce, within consumer culture, as well as their personal and financial successes, overshadow the realities of segregated schools, police brutality, unemployment, and the white supremacist[1] criminal justice system. The deployment of evidence that purports to affirm colorblindness obfuscates those many institutions and occurrences that demonstrate the continued relevance of race. Worse yet, as argued here, dominant cinematic discourse not only erases present-day inequities and persistent color lines, but also facilitates, naturalizes, and justifies contemporary racism and white privilege. Both denying and reaffirming the relevance of race, all while maintaining a façade of colorblindness, contemporary popular culture exists as a powerful vehicle of our racial status quo.

The scope of the Civil Rights Movement focused on the importance of integration not only as a means to secure a fulfillment of equality or reach Martin Luther King's dream, but as a step toward lessening the effects of American racism. That is, the advancement of people of color would result in a declining significance of race, whether inside police stations, Fortune 500 companies, or Hollywood. The logic stood that people of color, who inherently lack prejudice and hold an investment in helping "their community," in positions of power would usher in a new racial era of equality defined by the absence of police harassment within communities of color, an elimination of job discrimination, and an end to racist representations. This attitude has been commonplace within both scholarly and community-based efforts focused on ridding Hollywood of racism. Take Clayton Riley, who states that: "The most negative black films of the past were not made by blacks. We must remember that, putting the image of black Americans into the hands of other Americans is like asking management to paint a flattering portrait of workers on strike" (Riley 1973, forward).

Although the history of Hollywood has been one of white supremacist renderings (imagination) of blackness and moments of resistance primarily emanating from the work of artists of color, the ascendance of black filmmakers (just as the emergence of black police officers, mayors, or CEOs) has not resulted in dramatic restructuring of Hollywood image making. Nor has the work of those artists of color, or their close proximity to white artists (some argue that racism is a result of social distance that can be eradicated through breaking down boundaries) dramatically altered the cultural landscape of Hollywood. Whether because of the lack of continued power within Hollywood, or the power of racialized discourses, the presence of people of color has not lead to antiracist films or even projects that offer more humane representations. Rather these films have continued to serve the interest of a white supremacist status quo. Notwithstanding the persistence of racialized representations that serve the interests of a white supremacist agenda, dominant discourses of race consistently cite the presence of people of color inside institutions of popular culture as evidence of racial progress and the arrival of an America where colorblindness and not color consciousness define the historical moment. The visibility of artists of color and of films presumed to be black productions are evidence of a new racial politics where white kids don the jerseys of black athletes while listening to white rappers on their way to work where their boss is Latino and their co-worker is Asian. Both visibility and upward mobility of a segment of a few individuals of color sit at the center of this racial project, one that we call colorblindness.

The logic beyond these discursive assumptions within Hollywood are pretty basic. It assumes that racist representations are a result of prejudiced white executives exerting their power within Hollywood. Subsequently, in the wake of the Civil Rights Movement, the arrival of black filmmakers and voices thus signifies a reversal of this process embodying change while also facilitating hegemony. In other words, not only will the success and visibility of Spike Lee, Robert Townsend, John Singleton, Queen Latifah, and others signal a certain amount of racial progress, but their presence inside Hollywood will further advance the cause of equal opportunity, colorblindness, and "positive-image" making.

The problems, if not absurdity, of this facet of a colorblind discourse in regard to image making are extensive. First and foremost, it privileges a single author or a filmmaker as the source of representations. To understand the continued history of popular representations of blackness must go beyond writers, directors, and actors to include producers, production and distribution companies, editors, advertisers, and the entire institution of Hollywood. What appears to be a "black production" is most certainly misleading given the multiple influences and voices on every film.

Second, this logic works from a very narrow understanding of racist representations, one that focuses exclusively on repressive stereotypes and caricatures. Thomas Bogle (1994) describes the history of black cinema as one limited by the constructions of blacks as Tom, Coons, Mammies, Mulattos, and Bucks. William Grant, in *Post-Soul Black Cinema,* concurs arguing that the "fundamental problem with the American film industry is that 'blackness' as a film construct has a long history of being confined to stereotype caricatures typically used to establish supporting character" (2004, p. 5). By limiting racism to overt stereotypes, much of the literature and those who see today's Hollywood as one of progress erase the ways in which racial codes, common sense understandings of race, and colorblind racism infect contemporary black productions. Instead of examining the ways in which representations of films perpetuate or challenge a racist state or racial inequality, the power of colorblind discourses limits conversations to stereotypes so that in the absence of overt stereotypes, racism is rendered invisible and meaningless within contemporary America.

Third, the focus on stereotypes (in their absence) and the presence of people of color within Hollywood as evidence of colorblindness work from the assumption that racism does not affect people of color—that people of color cannot articulate or even subscribe to racist ideologies, tropes, or representations. So often within colorblind discourses proponents cite or give voice to certain people of color as a way to deny racism. Claims that a policy cannot be racist because its author is a person of color resemble those arguments that deny racism within popular culture because of the visibility and popularity of celebrities of color. While the logic of colorblindness, or better said, the reactionary myopic claims of colorblindness, cite the absence of overt stereotypes, the visibility of people of color within dominant institutions, or the prominence of voices of people of color within the American mainstream as evidence of the arrival of colorblindness, or the existence of a postrace (racism), post-Civil Rights America, such a discourse works from a flawed understanding of racial formation and the nature of contemporary articulations of racism.

Whereas the production and consumption of film in the years before and immediately after the Civil Rights Movement are best understood in the context of racial apartheid—Jim Crow, lynchings, and overt discrimination—recent films grow from a presumption of colorblindness. In other words, rampant stereotypes of 1930s and 1940s, whether the Coon or the Mammy, are believed to have been washed away by American racial progress, struggle, and increased levels of tolerance (and intolerance for intolerance) for racism inside and outside of Hollywood. The idea that racism no longer stains popular culture and that artists can attain stardom regardless of color has achieved significant acceptance in the late 1990s and early twenty-first century amongst both popular and academic discourses. In fact, artists and others have praised popular culture in facilitating colorblindness, in ridding future generations of racism. Charles Barkley, in his recent conversation-based book, *Who's Afraid of a Large Black Man,* not only celebrates the colorblind and diverse realities of contemporary popular culture that demonstrate immense racial progress, but the transformative possibilities. "You had a generation, the one before mine, who are now in their forties, who are in positions of power and influence in their companies in the music industries," writes Barkley. "Now you have a brother in a movie like XXX, you know what I'm saying. Just because rap has kind of churned the soil. The kid who might have been a total racist without rap is like, "Yo, I like this, I like this. I like everything has to do with rap culture. I like Spike. I like Jordan. I like Jay-Z. You know it's not so hard to accept" (2005, p. 131). Reflecting a colorblind discourse, Barkley links progress to ascendance of people of color into dominant institutions and the visibility of celebrities of color. In his estimation, the popularity of hip-hop or black cinematic productions is evidence of a new racial politics. Ice Cube follows suit during his interview with Charles Barkley, surmising this celebratory vision of popular culture one that does not account for the complexity of race and racism within contemporary America:

I think three things transcend race: music, entertainment, and athletics. After that you've got natural disasters and tragedies and accidents, things that happen where people don't think about race, where something is bigger than what somebody is and where somebody's form, where it's just teamwork because there's an emergency and we have all get together. If everybody's house is burning down, then nobody cares what race you are. We're all going to go help, you know? Race truly goes out of consciousness too, in sports. A dude makes a spectacular play and at the instant you don't care what color he is.

It's pretty much the same in the entertainment industry. In a certain instance you could care less who it is because you saw something and you loved it. Or in music. You hear a song you like and you just like it because it appears to something in you and you don't give a damm who the artist is. . .not what race the person is, anyway. I think there are things that, on a day-to-day basis, transcend race and put us all on the same plane, you know? But to me, it's also natural for people to root for their own kind to succeed, no matter who it is. (Barkley 2005, p. 132)

Although immensely problematic on many counts, Ice Cube captures the widespread sentiment regarding race within contemporary America and hegemonic understandings of race as an individual act or taste. Of course, the media reaction to Hurricane Katrina, as well as the larger societal factors that demonstrated the unnatural elements of "natural disasters," elucidated the shortcomings in this regard. Likewise, *Screens Fade to Black* illustrates the absurdity of claims of racial transcendence within popular culture, demonstrating the ways in which race infects the textual/representational utterances, the context of audience reception, and the larger social/cultural/economic landscape. To fully understand such utterances and the problems embedded in a discourse, while constructing a new lens to comprehend the racial significance of contemporary African American film, it is important to explore the notion of colorblind or new racism as the majority of the films discussed herein are emblematic of a new cultural project.

TOWARD AN UNDERSTANDING OF THE NEW RACISM

According to Eduardo Bonilla-Silva colorblind racism became the dominant racial ideology as the mechanism and practices for keeping blacks and other minorities at the bottom of the well (2003, pp. 2–3). The nature of colorblind racism is subtle, institutional, and composed of apparently nonracial practices, yet inequality, segregation, and white privilege remain intact. For example, whereas Jim Crow segregation was enforced through overly racist signs, restrictive covenants, or violence, today's practices are defined by landlords not show units, not advertising vacant properties, denying vacancy, quoting higher prices to minority applications, and real estate agents steering people of color into certain neighborhoods. The tactics of each era is different, but the result has remained constant. Likewise, films of the 1920s and 1930s rely on extreme racist stereotypes that mocked and demonized people

of color, whereas contemporary representations rely on more subtle representations and coded demonization to naturalize difference, inequality, and
white supremacy. Bonilla-Silva describes the shift within racism as follows:

Yet this new ideology has become a formidable political tool for the maintenance of
the racial order. Much as Jim Crow racism served as the glue for defending a brutal
and overt system of racial oppression in the pre-Civil Rights era, color-blind racism
serves today as the ideological armor for a covert and institutionalized system in the
post-Civil Rights era. And the beauty of this new ideology is that it aids the maintenance of white privilege without fanfare, without naming who it subjects and those
who rewards (2003, p. 3).

As evident here, the prominence of colorblindness and the use of implicit
racial language appear to reflect the newest form of the system, with the
maintaining of white privilege and ideological/institutional justifications of
white supremacy reflecting the continuation of the old forms of racism. "This
new racism reflects the juxtaposition of old and new, in some cases a continuation of long-standing practices of racial rule and, in other cases the development of something original" (Collins 2004, pp. 54–55).

Bonilla-Silva identifies four central frames of colorblind racism, all of which
embody a new racist discourse discourses. Each are not only crucial toward
conceptualizing the newness of new racism, but crucial toward generating an
understanding the ways in which contemporary black films enact not only a
new racist politics, but the overall reception of those films. Frames "operate
as cul-de-sacs because after people filter issues through them, they explain
racial phenomena following a predicable route" (Bonilla-Silva 2003, p. 26).
Specifically, Bonilla-Silva argues that four dominant frames guide post-
Civil Rights racial discourses within the United States: abstract liberalism,
naturalization, cultural racism, and minimization of racism. The two latter
frames are particularly useful in understanding contemporary black cinema
and the approach of *Screens Fade to Black* in particular. "Cultural racism is a
frame that relies on culturally-based arguments" (Bonilla-Silva 2003, p. 28).
Instead of basing exclusion and inequality on purely biological explanations,
dominant racial discourses locate social problems in the cultural deficiencies
of people of color.[2] Rather than offering representations that reveal the biological inferiority of black men and women so commonplace in the history
of Hollywood, contemporary films (like the broader discursive field) focus
instead on the cultural and class differences within the black community,
offering narratives that both celebrate racial progress and the procurement of
the American Dream for many African Americans and demonize and blame
those who continue to live in their own nightmare because of personal failures and deficiencies.

A second frame that both dominates contemporary racial discourses
and infects our understanding of contemporary cinematic representations
of blackness is that which minimizes the continued importance of racism.

The minimization of racism frame "suggests that discrimination is no longer a central factor affecting minorities' life chances" (Bonilla-Silva 2003, p. 29). Dismissing hate crimes, police brutality, racial profiling, continued inequality, and individual prejudice, whites accuse people of color of using race as a "crutch," of being overly sensitive when it comes to racism, and of deploying the race card (Bonilla-Silva 2003, p. 29). Likewise, the reduction of race to cultural differences, especially those that are commodifiable and fetisihized, the use of comedies as a means to silence critics with claims of something being just a joke, and the overall erasure of racism and its consequences on all people of color within cinematic narratives reflects this common practice. These frames represent a powerful determining voice with Hollywood, affecting image and ideology. More important, these frames are key elements of a new racist project, whose understanding is essential in our effort to underscore the textual and contextual significance of contemporary African American film.

At the beginning of the twentieth century, W. E. B. DuBois predicted that the problem for that American century would be the color line. Specifically to DuBois, the greatest challenge facing the United States, and the entire world in fact, would be colonialism and practices of racial segregation, each of which contributed to inequality and division amongst the "races." The practice of Jim Crow established a color line throughout American cities beginning in the late nineteenth century, establishing clear racial boundaries impenetrable to people of color. The opportunities of education, jobs, health care, housing, and leisure were all affected by the existence of a color line, with violence and intimidation being as crucial to separating the races as the laws themselves.

The ascension of the Civil Rights Movement during the 1950s and 1960s resulted in an end to the formal enactment of the color line. Through protest, struggles inside the courts and in the streets, and "ceaseless agitation," the Civil Rights Movement was successful in forcing the state to formally outlaw Jim Crow segregation. The 1964 Civil Rights Act, the 1965 Voting Rights Act, and the numerous Supreme Court cases that preceded and followed these landmark cases, all of which came as the result of widespread protest, did not, however, eliminate racism or racial inequality. "The problem of the twenty-first century seems to be the absence of a color line," notes Patricia Hill Collins. "Formal Legal discrimination has been outlawed yet contemporary social practices produce virtually identical racial hierarchies as those observed by DuBois" (2004, p. 32).

Whether talking about rates of educational attainment, rates of incarceration, wealth and income disparities, infant mortality rates, AIDS or sickle cell infection rates, residential segregation or any other measure of political, residential, economic, social or cultural inequality, people of color remain clustered at the bottom of America's political, economic, and social hierarchies. The persistence of inequality is not merely the result of vestiges of the formalized color line and slavery, or the persistence of ideas of race, dominant ideologies, and social practices, all of which define racism (and facilitate similar racialized outcomes, but also new forms of racism (ideologies, practices and discourse) that contributes to contemporary racial organization. As Collins describes this exact historical moment, new racism "reflects a situation of permanence and change" (2004, p. 33). In other words, as the outcomes and realities of inequality mirror those of 1896, 1919, and 1968, the realities of racial formation, institutional organization, and contemporary racial politics embody a new form of racism. The persistence of "new racism" is dependent on the dissemination of supportive imagery, and post-9/11, colorblind offerings at the cinema are now more important than ever, as the fervent need to consume, and thus believe, that "we have overcome" is probably stronger now than at any other post-Civil Rights Moment.

The nature of new racism goes beyond its orientation toward colorblindness as shifts in both its discursive and practical manifestations go beyond its colorblindness. New racism is not merely the absence of a color line in the face of persistent white supremacy, but reflects myriad societal realities.

One of the more salient elements of new racism, especially as it relates to popular culture and political discourse, is the constancy of signs of dysfunction among communities of color that require societal control and regulation. Although neither the demonization of black bodies nor calls for societal regulation are new, the scale of the discourse of representation of dysfunctionality, the extent of commodification, and the establishment of clear class-based boundaries have rendered these old-style ideologies in its new form. Rhonda Williams describes this moment of old and new racism as living at the crossroads, where the celebration of racial progress and the visibility of black public figures do not match the persistence of violence, inequality, and representations of dysfunctionality. Today's African American college students have come of age in a political culture that regularly recycles two signs of black dysfunction: antisocial black (male) criminality and (female) sexuality are the behavioral manifestations of contemporary black cultural chaos. From "scholarly and journalist treatises" to popular music and cinema, representations and debates regarding the black "underclass anchor contemporary race talk, and speak the language that distinguishes the aberrant underclass from the striving middle class" (Williams 1998, p. 141). Throughout this book, I will discuss films that replicate such practices with representations of both the black underclass and middle class reifying common sense understandings of the black poor and the possibility of a fulfillment of the American Dream for all Americans.

Although neither the virulence nor scope of contemporary racist discourses is new, as reflected in the prominence of both adoration and condemnation of blackness within Jim Crow America, there is something new with the ubiquity of the signs of decay within contemporary popular and political culture. What specifically makes the reduction of blackness to "a problematic sign and ontological position," as well as a symbol of "cultural degeneracy" that poses a threat to dominant values and more is that it takes place at the same time as widespread and globalized commodification of a degenerative or problematic sign of blackness (Williams 1998, p. 140).

These tropes and representations—hypersexual, criminally prone, violent, and exotic—are no longer mere evidence for needed surveillance and policing, but rather represent sources of commodification. From film and television to music and virtual reality, popular culture has sought to capitalize on these representations. Although these representations are certainly an attempt by black cultural producers to convert their cultural talents into viable sources of profit, the cultural rendering of the gangsta or of a hip-hop aesthetic equally signifies the ways in which transnational capital has coveted a marketplace that sells and seeks profit from those spaces, experiences, images, and bodies that cause alarm and panic in other locations. Robin Kelley, in "Playing for Keeps," explores the powerful ways ghetto spaces and all that define an inner-city community within the dominant imagination have become sites of commodification for both media conglomerates and black youth. Although acknowledging the financial possibilities inherent in this production/consumption dyad, he warns against totalizing celebrations; he cautions about the assumptions of progress prompted by the visibility of a commodified blackness, illustrating the powerful ways in which popular culture serves a new racist project. Despite the representations of the ghetto, as evident in many of the films discussed here, as both chaotic and violent places, intervention is neither necessary nor constructive. Kelley states:

The presence of larger numbers of African-American and Latino youth together in parks, school years, subway stations, or on street corners does not necessarily mean they are conspiring to rob somebody. Nor does it mean they are leading a life of idleness.

Finally, in the struggles for survival and pleasure inside of capitalism, capitalism has become both their greatest friend and greatest foe. It has the capacity to create spaces for their entrepreneurial imaginations and their symbolic work, to turn something of a profit for some, for them to hone their skills and imagine getting paid. At the same time, it is also responsible for a shrinking labor market, the militarization of urban space, and the circulation of the very representations of race that generate terror in all of us at the sought of young black men and yet compels most of America to want to wear their shoes. (1998, p. 224)

His work and that of other scholars (Neal 2005, Collins 2004, Gray 2005, Boyd 1997) points not only to the dialectics of popular culture and new racism, and the ubiquity of a commodified and narrowly defined vision of blackness, but also to the significant ways that contemporary cinematic productions and other forms of popular culture demonize and pathologize the black working poor and black youth as a threat necessitating state and cultural policing and control. The current moment is, thus, defined by the fetishization of black urban styles and those hip-hop cultural aesthetics associated with black youth. Yet these same styles, cultural attributes, and identities prompt alarm within American discursive fields that serve as the basis for calls for control. New racism is defined by the simultaneity of commodification and demonization, of fetish and denunciation, each of which offers a narrowly defined inscription of blackness that elicits societal panic and fosters a climate justifying state violence against communities of color.

Here lies another crucial element of new racism, especially as it relates to film and popular culture: the powerful ways in which class-based codes and cultural discourses serve as the basis of projects of demonization against the black poor or black working class communities. In many of the films discussed here and evident elsewhere, representations of dysfunction are limited to the black poor, whose personal and cultural failures are marked as the basis of their inability to secure the American Dream or even integrate themselves into dominant institutions. The demonization of the black poor is especially powerful given the increased visibility of the black middle-class within American popular culture. Whether visible or off-screen (as in most of the ghettocentric films where the ghetto is marked as a space in absence of a middle class), the black middle class not only signifies the possibility of the American Dream for all, and the declining significance of race (as reflected in the existence of positive—middle class—representations and the real-life existence of a black middle class), but comes to represent a model minority within the black community. As such, new racist films and popular culture used the black middle class as the basis of naturalizing poverty, rationalizing state violence, and constructing the black underclass as behaviorally deviant and in need of monitoring, discipline, and control, all without any references to race, color, or blackness.

The problem rests with culture, class, and values; it is not about black people, but the underclass or hip-hop, both of which reflect powerful codes. Without identifying blackness as a source of blame, focusing instead on cultural attributes of the underclass, and in deploying images and representations of the black middle class as evidence of "good black folks," the possibility of the American Dream and hegemony of colorblindness, the existence of a binary between the black underclass and the black middle class is central to new racism and contemporary Hollywood cinematic representations. Thus, it is not about race any longer, should the offerings of contemporary African American film be believed, but about opportunity, self-determination, and personal choices. The institutional mechanisms of race are nonexistent and almost laughable in Hollywood's—America's—"new" racial order. Personal investment in the American Dream and embracing a bootstraps-model work ethic are key to success; these are the qualities that make "good black folks." Integral to understanding the distinctions made by new racism—between those who succeed despite their inherent pathology and those who fail or falter because of it—is a critical examination of popular culture products, especially film. It is in contemporary African American film that the greatest feat of new racism can be observed: the concurrent commodification/celebration and loathing/denunciation of hegemonic notions and aesthetics of blackness. "The electronic mass media (especially news, sport and music video) are the preeminent site where competing claims about black masculinity are waged," writes Herman Gray "Hence, in the media discourse of regulation (where fear and menace are the key touchstones of a society seen as out of control), the black male body operates symbolically to signify the erosion of morality and threats to manhood" (2005, p. 23). Although nothing new, and in fact reflecting old style racism, the simultaneity of this process within an increasingly globalized cultural landscape takes on new meaning within contemporary discourses given the hegemony of colorblindness.

The contempt that America holds for Jody (*Baby Boy*), Alonzo (*Training Day*), Devon (*Drumline*), or any number of popular cultural figures, all of which mirrors those political discourses that blame the problems of the poor on cultural deficiencies, exists alongside the celebration and commodification of the style and cultural attributes embodied by these same individuals. Hiphop and a gangsta aesthetic embody that which we fear and admire, functioning within a marketplace as a site of profiteering and ideological assaults, which in the end facilitates a continuation of white supremacy.

Although there are many defining elements of new racism, some of which reflect long-standing practices and some of which embodies a newness in racial formation, ultimately new racism embodies the persistence of racial inequality and racialized violence in the absence of a visible color line. New racism describes a contemporary situation where in spite of the visibility of people color as celebrities, political icons, or cultural representations, as well as the presumption of cultural integration, racism (white supremacy, white privilege, inequality) continues to plague the opportunities and chances of communities of color. Collins describes the realities of new racism in the following terms:

A generation of young African American men and women who were born after the struggles for civil rights, Black Power, and African nation-state independence has come of age under this new racism. Referred to as the hip-hop generation, this group has encountered, reproduced, and resisted new forms of racism that continue to rely on ideas about Black sexuality. Expecting a democratic fair society with equal opportunities, instead this group faced disappearing jobs, crumbling schools, drugs, crime, and the weakening of African American community institutions. The contradictions of the post-civil rights era affect all African Americans, yet they have been especially pronounced for Black youth. (2004, p. 35)

Taking a cue from Collins, *Screens Fade to Black* explores these contradictions in examining the rhetorical and representational devices of contemporary African American film, exploring how contemporary cinema explains away, naturalizes, justifies, or erases these contradictions and unfulfilled promises to the advancement of persistent inequality.

Given the importance of mass media, particularly cinematic representations in both making blackness into a visible/viable commodity in the name of colorblindness and profit and the erasing and individualizing of those contemporary problems associated with contemporary America, it is crucial that we examine current Hollywood representations of blackness. To understand colorblind racism and persistent racial inequality raises questions in and around popular culture: How does Hollywood embody and contribute to new racism? Are there instances of resistance? Are their counter-narratives that illustrate the persistence of institutional racism, challenging the orthodoxy of colorblind discourses? How specifically do contemporary African American films, notwithstanding the power of specific artists, contribute to the hegemony of colorblindness? How does their participation in a Hollywood project that ultimately reifies racial inequality and white privilege in itself legitimize claims of progress and colorblindness? How does the increased "blackening" of America's big screens naturalize, rationalize, and/or erase the effects of new racism? Such questions sit at the center of *Screens Fade to Black,* which at its core attempts to understand contemporary African American productions as vehicles of new racism, not only by serving as evidence of racial progress of black celebrities, but also through their ideological construction, their discursive articulation, and the overall reactionary politics of the vast majority of today's (African American) films. As revealed here, contemporary African American films as assumed do not challenge the existence of racism or the representation offered by their white cinematic brethren; rather they advance its ideological core, its discursive justifications, and its insidious representations, ultimately serving as evidence for a hegemony that denies racism through words and images of these films.

The importance of such an undertaking is much greater than challenging stereotypes or merely analyzing contemporary representations of blackness on the big screen. It lies in examining the ways in which black films contribute to racial common sense about colorblindness, racial progress, meritocracy, all the while demonizing and pathologizing those left behind by the American Dream. These films are doing the dirty work, justifying and rationalizing inequality, amid ongoing suffering. The importance resides with the 1 million black men and women incarcerated inside American prisons, with the levels of poverty inside New Orleans, or the rates of AIDS throughout the black community and how film contributes to these injustices and societal reactions.

Although an oversimplification and reflective of a binary, a good place to start our study of recent African American cinematic productions is with the idea that all films exist within the continuum of two opposing poles: containment and resistance. Whereas films of containment "maintain the values and representations that shape popular media discourses are determined by the dominant classes," those resistant in nature "have the capacity to subvert dominant ideologies and regimes of representations (Watkins 1998, p. 51). Although it is nice to think about black films as either working in the name of hegemony or in opposition to it, as either detrimental or liberating to the African American community, the films discussed here are marked by contradictions, instability, and multiple meanings. Still, this work demonstrates a pattern as the vast majority of contemporary African American films naturalize/rationalize racial inequality; erase the relevance of racism within contemporary America; celebrate the American Dream, racial progress, and the growth of the black middle class at the expense of the black poor; and ultimately minimize the importance of racial difference beyond cultural and commodifiable traits. So whereas Stuart Hall rightly describes popular culture as a "struggle for ideological dominance in absence of pure victory or pure domination" (Hall 1992, p. 24) and Craig Watkins rightly describes cinematic as a "perpetual theater of struggle in which the forces of containment remain in a constant state of negotiation" (Watkins 1998, p. 51), the films discussed within *Screens Fade to Black* ultimately give way to the interest of a white supremacist hegemony.

Although these films contain ruptures and contradictions, the vast majority of them, in spite of presumptions of colorblindness, serves the interest of perpetuating the existence of white privilege and existing formations of racial identity. Although they serve as sites of pleasure and financial gain, the films discussed herein also function as a powerful vehicle in defining, constructing, and disseminating the message of the dominant political and cultural landscapes. The importance of these productions is not limited to their reconstitution of African American voices, communities, or experiences, but in their perpetuation, rationalization, and justification of the silencing of African American voices, the violence inflicted on African American communities, and limited experiences available to African Americans. The surprise that Americans felt after Hurricane Katrina over the level and extent of poverty embodies this erasure, in that contemporary representations of black bodies and voices have systematically erased, demonized, commodified, or otherwise mocked the black underclass. In celebrating the achievement of the American Dream or the transcendence of racial obstacles amongst the black middle-class; pathologizing and blaming the black underclass for their own failures—cultural, moral, and communal—for their inability to secure the American Dream; or merely mocking those who remain locked outside the mainstream all the way to the bank, the last decade of African American cinematic productions became visible in the days after Hurricane Katrina. Given the magnitude of suffering and poverty, and the inability to deny connections between representations and societal/institutional responses to poverty, mass incarceration, high infant morality rates, persistent segregation, unemployment, state violence, and the media/political responses to this natural disaster, efforts to examine the textual representations and contextual meaning of contemporary African American cinema within *Screens Fade to Black* is significant.

According to Mark Reid, "The politics of any white or black independent or mainstream filmmaker do not easily establish a correlation to film's representational politics, regardless of whether it is progressive, centrist, conservative or fascist" (2005, p. 5). In fact, one of the central arguments of this book is that despite an increased number of "black productions," its representational politics are increasingly more reactionary and working toward the rearticulation and relegitimacy of white supremacy. It demonstrates the fallacy of new racism with its claims about the declining significance of race because of the increased visibility of people of color within the American cultural landscape. So although Stuart Hall argues that there are no guarantees in terms of author and politics, *Screens Fade to Black* makes clear that contemporary Hollywood, whether with white, black, Asian, or Latino productions or authors, offers a certain guarantee in terms of its promulgation of new racist ideologies and the rationalization of white supremacy.

NOTES

1. In eschewing muddied definitions of racism that lets whites off the hook, this project understands racism in terms of white supremacy. George Fredrickson defines white supremacy as "the attitudes, ideologies, and policies associated with the rise of blatant forms of white European dominance over 'nonwhite' populations . . . making invidious distinctions of a socially crucial kind that are based primarily if not exclusively characteristic and ancestry" (George Fredrickson, *White Supremacy: A Comparative Study in American and South African History*. New York: Oxford University Press, 1982).

2. The shift from biologically based arguments within dominant discourses (white nationalists continue to use biological notions of race) should not be understood as a major rupture in that biological and cultural theories of race represent different sides of same coin; each emerges out of an identical epistemological system.

2

THE GHETTOCENTRIC
IMAGINATION

A widely popular genre for Hollywood has been the black urban picture. Beginning in the 1970s with the era of Blaxploitation through the ghettocentric pictures of the early 1990s, and into the present, films centering on black ghettos remain popular at the box office. This chapter, while examining this history, pays particular attention to the recent incarnations of the ghettocentric genre. By specifically exploring the way that these films—*Baby Boy* (2001), *Antwone Fisher* (2002), *Training Day* (2001), and *Prison Song* (2001)—envision black urban spaces, this chapter evaluates how these films deal with questions of unemployment, housing segregation, police brutality, and individual choice. Equally prominent here are discussions of how masculinity, femininity, and family are treated, especially compared to those films of the early 1990s (*Menace II Society*, 1991; and *Boyz n the Hood*, 1991). In just 10 years, the vision, message, and representations surrounding inner-city communities has dramatically changed, even among the same filmmakers. What has remained constant, however, is America's love/hate relationship with black inner-city communities, a desire to commodify, whether in hip-hop music, film, or video games, simultaneous to a discursive and state yearning (need) to demonize and police those bodies and institutions that inhabit these same communities.

The continuity of place and processes of commodification of ghetto experiences links these various cinematic eras; yet those recent films represent a dramatic rupture in the ghettocentric imagination. No longer representing the ghetto as a product of American racism or besieged by state violence and poverty, *Training Day*, *Antwone Fisher*, and *Baby Boy* each focus on the failures of individuals and the dysfunctionality of "ghetto culture" as the explanation for persistent struggles. Beyond replicating long-standing white supremacist stereotypes that depict blackness in terms of violence, hypersexuality, laziness, anger, and cultural deprivation, these films imagine America ghettos as places where individual choices/failures, and not the state/policy/racism, has the greatest impact. That is, individuals hold the responsibility to change their own lives toward securing the American Dream. Replicating assumptions about the single black mother addicted to welfare, and the young black male addicted to crime, these films don't merely naturalize hegemonic racialized stereotypes and naturalize dominant policy that has resulted in the erosion of social services, the increased power of the criminal justice system, and the erasure of public debates regarding persistent racism and poverty; they also deny the humanity, resistance, and struggles of working people inside American ghettos. As Robin Kelley argues, popular culture fails to imagine ghetto as places of family, daily–living, or work. With the exception of *Prison Song,* none of the films discussed herein sufficiently illustrate the complexity of inner-city life. None show:

Men and women who go to work every day in foundries, hospitals, nursing homes, private homes, police stations, sanitation departments, banks, garment factories, assembly plans, pawn shops, construction sites, loading docks, storefront churches, telephone companies, grocery and department stores, public transit, restaurants, welfare offices, recreation centers; or the street venders, the cab drivers, the bus drivers, the ice cream truck drivers, the seamstresses, the numerologists and fortune tellers, the folks who protect . . . or clean . . . downtown buildings all night long. (1998, p. 196)

Whether through denying the humanity or productivity of African Americans living inside America's ghettos, or focusing on the criminality, cultural degradation, or chaos that supposedly defines a ghetto existence, the films *Baby Boy, Antwone Fisher,* and *Training Day* legitimize the dominant social order (and those discourses that both pathologize and erase the black working poor) by playing on racialized fears, moral panics, and societal yearnings for discipline and order. Stuart Hall argues that popular culture serves as a powerful device in mobilizing the masses toward maintaining white hegemony:

The themes of crime and social delinquency, articulated through the discourses of popular morality, touch the direct experience, the anxieties and uncertainties of ordinary people. This has led to a dovetailing of the "cry for discipline from below" into the call for an enforced restoration of social order "from above." The articulation forms the bridge, between the real material sources of popular discontent, and their representation through specific ideological forces and campaigns, as the general need for a "disciplined society." It has as its principal effect, the awakening of popular support for a restoration or order through imposition: the basis of a populist "law and order campaign." This, in turn, has given a wide legitimacy to the title of balance within the operations of the state towards the "coercive pole," whilst preserving its popular legitimacy. (Watkins 1998, pp. 25–26)

Yet these films, unlike their predecessors, don't merely reinscribe dominant stereotypes that play to uncertainties and fears that naturalize social decay in the name of increased state intervention within communities of color. They also offer narratives that successfully deny racism and provide legitimacy to claims of a colorblind America, all the while justifying a coercive and violent state presence within American ghettos needed to protect and contain those whose poor choices and cultural values make them a threat to all Americans. With this in mind, this chapter examines these themes, specifically looking at how these films reimagine America's ghettos, successfully commodifying spaces in absence of its residents while simultaneously erasing the poor from public discourses, demonizing and pathologizing those who live inside America's ghettos, and celebrating the possibility of the American Dream in absence of state assistance. No film is more reflective of this process than *Baby Boy*.

A return to familiar territory for director John Singleton, who in *Baby Boy*, like *Boyz n the Hood*, once again explores motherhood/fatherhood, accountability, and masculinity among young African American men. Singleton's premise: "I broke it down to this character who's 20 years old, he lives with his mother, who's 36, and he has two children by two different women. The mother's still young and good-looking, she wants to get her groove on, and gets a new boyfriend, who's a survivor and a thug in his own right, who moves in with her, and causes friction with her son, the other man of the house. [Jody's] obviously intimidated the moment Melvin [Ving Rhames] comes on the screen, with that shot of Melvin's big arm. That's the premise that I started with" (http://www.reelimagesmagazine.com/txt_features/conversations/reel_conversation_john_singleton.htm).

Baby Boy is set in the urban areas of Los Angeles and picks up the predominant themes of family, community, work, and the American Dream of Singleton's previous film. It brings viewers into the life of Jody (Tyreese Gibson), "a young, unemployed, selfish, immature black man" who refuses to move out of his mother's house or to work, even though he has two different women. Without a father and burdened by a permissive mother, Jody meanders through life, unable to figure out what it takes to be a productive part of society. The film chronicles these struggles, offering a narrative that celebrates work, patriarchal masculinity, and the necessity of black fatherhood. Furthermore, *Baby Boy* further articulates the conservative ideologies of its forbearers, in both its gender politics and its denial of institutional racism/state violence. While celebrating *Baby Boy* as breath of fresh air, a review on Amazon.com captures the films narrative when it stated that *Baby Boy* "expresses compassionate but unforgiving criticism of young, African American black men who lead reckless, irresponsible lives while blithely blaming racism for their chronic disadvantage." Not surprisingly, *Baby Boy* was successful among cultural commentators and at the box office, amassing almost $30 million in box office receipts. Reflective of the increasingly conservative turn of Hollywood and its commodification of blackness and America's ghetto in absence of racism, state violence, and poverty, *Baby Boy* continues the long-standing tradition of blaming blackness, black cultural deficiencies, black woman, and black families for the problems of the black community.

BABY BOY

Jody is a 20-year-old "baby boy," the father of two children by different women who still lives with his own mother. Jody is the definitive "baby having babies," physically primed for reproduction but mentally and psychologically immature for the consequences and responsibilities of fatherhood. The film opens with the image of Jody, as a full-grown man, nestled in his mother's womb, with Jody explaining how black men have been conditioned into perpetual childhood:

There is this psychiatrist, a lady by the name of Frances Crest Wilson; she has a theory about black men in America. She says that because of the system of racism the black man in this country has been made to think of himself as a baby, a not yet fully formed being who has not realized his full potential. To support her claim she offers the following: First off, what does a black man call his woman? Mama! Secondly, what does a black man call his closest acquaintances? His boys! And finally, what does a black man call his place of residence? The crib.

These words and fully-grown Jody inside his mother's womb are quickly juxtaposed with a grown Jody, standing outside a medical clinic aimlessly eating Lemon Heads, while his girlfriend Yvette is inside receiving an abortion. The candy and his failure to even take responsibility for helping Yvette with the abortion (he even asked his mother for the money) are indicative of his immaturity and his selfishness. More important, it reflects the film's vision of black masculinity, defined by a failure to provide emotional and loving support, or financial stability.

Jody is a baby despite his age. *Baby Boy* ostensibly tells the story of what has become the extremely difficult transition Jody takes into manhood. With his mother starting a new relationship, he immediately feels threatened by the presence of Melvin, his mother's new boyfriend who, as a fellow male, is infringing on Jody's territory. Melvin, however, serves as a major catalyst in Jody's transition; he is evidence that Juanita, Jody's mother, is finished raising her son and is ready to move on with her life. Jody resists this notion at every turn, insulting Melvin and his mother's judgment in letting a stranger into their home. He insists that Melvin will make her evict her son, who will surely die without the protection of his mother's home. The conflict between Jody and Melvin comes to a head when Melvin hits Jody, who then moves out and stays out.

In telling Jody's story—his struggles with coming to grips with his own manhood, initially unwilling to "leave the nest"—*Baby Boy* offers concrete visions of black masculinity through Jody and Melvin. Throughout the film, audiences are constantly presented with the contrasting images/characters of Melvin and Jody: Melvin is Singleton's ideal of a "man": responsible, independent, and ambitious; a small business owner who knows how to respect a woman. Jody, on the other hand, is unemployed, steals/borrows Yvette's car, and while claiming to be in love with Yvette, admits to "fucking other females." While Melvin may have flaws (temper, ex-con), he owns these mistakes, working to overcome them through hard work and self-reflection. Jody blames others for his problems, making excuses in every instance. Melvin is fearless and Jody is scared. Melvin works hard and is always in his landscaping jump suit; Jody hardly works—he barely commits himself to dealing drugs or selling stolen dresses. The establishment of such a clear binary reflects *Baby Boy's* unwavering inscription of patriarchy and narrow vision of manhood, as well as its failure to underscore the ways in which race, class, and gender impact the ways in which masculinity and femininity operate within society. If a car, house, and steady income are conditional elements for securing a true manhood, wealthy white heterosexuals will always come to embody the essence of manhood. Jody, who lives with his Mama, rides a bike, and has no steady income, is thus a boy at best.

The process of Jody coming to terms with his status as a father is another predominant theme in the film. Yvette, the mother of his son, is employed full-time and perfectly capable of supporting herself and her son. Curiously, Jody spends little time with his other "baby mama" and his daughter. Thus the idea of manhood carrying on one's legacy through a son is reinforced: Jody says so in a scene after making love to Yvette. Likewise, after his son Jojo was born, Jody said he was reconciled with the possibilities of death or prison, because a part of him would still be in the world. And Jody proclaims love for Yvette, whereas Peanut, the mother of his daughter, is apparently just another female for Jody to fuck.

Singleton's problematic gender constructions are perpetuated throughout *Baby Boy*. Jody says he loves Yvette, but acts with little respect toward her. He sleeps with other women, provides little financial support for her or their son, and expects her to cook and clean at his will. After Yvette's abortion, Jody offers little emotional support, instead leaving her at home so he can see Peanut, his other baby's Mama. During his visit with her, he spends little time with his daughter, instead demanding that Peanut fix him something to eat, after which he smokes some weed and has sex, further solidifying his immaturity and his inability to treat the woman in his life with respect.

Jody acts in similar disregard for his mother. He hates the idea of her dating, of taking her attention away from him. He has little regard for Juanita's identity as a grown woman, and her right and desire for a sex life, or a life outside the home. The gender politics of *Baby Boy* are highly problematic. Through Jody's eyes, for most of the film women are part of a man's territory: Yvette is his girl, not to be touched by another guy, and Juanita is very much the same. It seems that as Jody becomes a "man" and Juanita's relationship with Melvin progresses, she is merely changing hands, coming under new ownership. Likewise, at the close of the film when Jody moves in with Yvette, it is after Rodney, an ex-con and a threat to Jody's territory (he moves in temporarily with Yvette), is murdered by Jody and his friend Sweetpea.

Jody takes some initiative in self-sufficiency by starting his own small business, which consists of lifting women's clothing from dry cleaners and reselling them to women on the street and in salons. This is an example of how capitalism/gettin' paid plays out: Jody starts this venture after making an inspired speech to Sweetpea on the difference between buyers and sellers. In Jody's mind, the sellers are the ones moving up, the shepherds among the sheep. Jody definitely has a motive to move up: as mentioned before, his territory is being attacked from multiple sides, and he needs to prove himself a man.

Until Melvin beats up Jody (arguably the moment in the film where Jody becomes a man), he is incapable of solving his problems with Yvette or Peanut in a nonsexual way. After a screaming match with Yvette over Jody's cheating, the camera cuts to their having "make-up" sex. And later, in a more serious fight over Jody cheating, Jody slaps Yvette and attempts an apology by forcing her to perform oral sex. Thus Jody's manhood and sexuality are intertwined, one constantly informing the other. Jody's only source of reconciliation with Peanut, as with Yvette, is sex.

Jody and Yvette's lives are further complicated when Rodney, a former boyfriend of Yvette's, is released from prison and forcibly moves in with Yvette. At this point, Jody and Yvette are in the midst of a breakup, leaving Yvette vulnerable—without the protection of her man. Rodney is violent toward Yvette, nearly raping her in front of her son at one point. This is the last straw, the catalyst that leads both to Rodney's murder and Yvette and Jody getting back together "for good." Of course Singleton cannot make it through a film without killing someone off; however, Rodney's death is constructed as something "positive" that benefits Jody and Yvette. After Rodney's death, Jody has completed the transition from boy to man, finally moving out of his mother's house and in with Yvette. A seemingly "happy" ending by Hollywood standards; however, questions remain unanswered. Where are Peanut and her daughter? They have been cast out of Jody's ideal of family, a standing challenge to Jody's status as a "man." Their fate remains unaddressed, whereas Jody, Yvette, Juanita, Melvin, and Sweetpea have all found some sort of resolution or redemption. Singleton's vision of gender relations and his continued efforts to elevate the importance of black men raising black boys beyond any other parental relationship (father-daughter) is finalized with the film's ending. Jody does not live "happily ever after" with Peanut and his daughter; instead he builds his home, his nuclear family, with Yvette and Jojo, reifying those dominant discourses that cite single black mothers as the source of the black community's problems and celebrating Jody's growth and efforts to take responsibility for *his* son as the needed corrective step in the advancement of the African American community.

To fully understand the range of problems with this film, it is important to expand on several ideas discussed previously in terms of its vision of black female sexuality, black masculinity, and gender relations. Also, we need to discuss how the film's narrative reifies long-standing racist ideas about the African American family and the African American community. In doing so, it blames the problems of the African American community on single mothers, baby boys, and a series of dysfunctional culture values rather than racism, state violence, or capitalism. In a sense, *Baby Boy* does not make excuses for the problems facing America's black community; instead chastising black men and women for their own degradation and despair.

Associated with its vision of the childish black male is *Baby Boy*'s vision of black sexuality. While replicating hegemonic and long-standing visions of a black hypersexuality, *Baby Boy* inscribes hypersexuality not purely as a genetic characteristic, but both a cultural phenomena and a symbol of a failure to grow up (childlike and immediate gratification). That Jody has children with multiple women and cheats on his girlfriend is not merely on embodiment of classic representation of the hypersexual black brute, but reflects the inability to withhold pleasure, that defines children. Jody is constantly having sex, yet he is unable and unwilling to father the products (children) of his sexual activity. In this sense, the *Baby Boy* phenomenon and the dysfunctionality of the African American community is reflected in the sexual productivity of Jody and others.

Although *Baby Boy* certainly takes on alternative forms, the film's reinscription of long-standing stereotypes of hypersexual black males and females underscores its place within a wave of new racist films. Patricia Hill Collins, in *Black Sexual Politics,* argues:

In the post civil rights era, gender has emerged as a prominent feature of what some call a 'new' racism. Ironically, many African Americans deny the existence of sexism, or see it as a secondary concern that is best addressed when the more pressing problem of racism has been solved. But if racism and sexism are deeply intertwined, racism can never be solved without seeing and challenging sexism. African American men and women both are affected by racism, but in gender-specific ways. (2004, p. 5)

Throughout *Baby Boy,* the narrative and the film's camera work all inscribe hypersexuality onto its characters. The basis of every relationship, whether casual or long term, is sex. Jody's relationship with Yvette has little meaning outside of sex. Their ties that bond their relationship together stem from their sexual attraction (lust) and their children, who are a product of their sexual relationships. The film offers little insight into their relationship beyond their sexual urges for each other, locating sex as the basis of their happiness and relationship. The focus on sexuality as the basis of Jody and Yvette's relationship is not unique; every relationship within the film appears to be exclusively sexual. In one instance, as Yvette confides to her friend about her ongoing relationship problems with Jody, her friend barely listens. As Yvette seeks her advice, her friend turns her attention to her boyfriend with whom she begins to have sex while she is still on the phone.

The sight of a distraught Yvette seeking refuge and advice from her closest friend while her friend and her boyfriend have sex is a powerful commentary about *Baby Boy's* sexual politics. It reduces its black men and women to hypersexual animals, or insatiable teenagers, who cannot control themselves because of the immense pleasures and satisfaction that sex brings into their otherwise meaningless lives and relationships. Throughout *Baby Boy,* we witness an insatiable sexuality that is neither healthy nor controllable. In two particular scenes, we see the film's reduction of blackness to animalistic sexuality, which not only fulfills long-standing stereotypes about black sexuality, but also gives legitimacy to dominant discourses that demonize black sexual practices as the source of problems or dysfunctionality within the black community.

Although Melvin and Juanita's relationship is positioned as a more ideal relationship than any other in the film, its foundation seems to be sex. Almost every instance in which Melvin and Juanita are together, Melvin gropes her ass, kisses her sexually, or otherwise conveys an aura of sex. We never learn why Melvin and Juanita love one another; we learn only about their sex lives. In fact, Melvin and Juanita don't even make love; rather, they fuck like animals. For example, in one scene Melvin and Juanita engage in a position Melvin refers to as "the African Swamp Stomp," in which he dances around the room prancing like an "animal" while she wraps her legs around his waist, all while they are having sex. As they "stomp," through the room, the T.V. remains on, providing a powerful backdrop of meaning by its display of an interview with Mike Tyson. Their sexuality, combined with an image of Mike Tyson explaining the allegations of rape to Larry King, is particularly powerful, offering a clear understanding of the film's vision of a black hypersexuality.

In another instance, a sweaty Melvin, after what appears to be a lengthy sex session, cooks eggs for Juanita, naked, despite Jody's presence in the house. This scene, which combines "stereotypes of rapacious sexuality [his sweat] and criminality [his defiance of societal norms on appropriate behavior], further reveals Melvin's increasing threat to Jody, given not only his physical place within the house, but his tendency to put his body on display for the watchful eye of both Jody and audience" (Giroux 2003, p. 132). The gaze of the camera leads our eye toward his naked body bulging with muscles and perspiring from a hot session of sex. Jody's resentment of Melvin's mere presence in his (mother's) house, let alone the sight of a naked, sweaty, postcoital Melvin, is transferred to the audience through the camera's gaze, reinforcing the hegemonic perceptions of a hypersexual, imposing, threatening black manhood.

Whereas Melvin and Juanita exhibit a productive relationship through their excessive sexual appetites, there is nothing productive in the relationship between Yvette and Jody outside of their sexual magic. As Yvette searches for a "real man"—one who doesn't live with his mama, who has a job, who provides for his family, and takes responsibility—she instead finds Jody, whose only masculine quality resides within his pants. Without his penis and his sexual prowess, Jody is nothing but a boy. After a fight between Jody and Yvette, in which she professes her hatred for Jody because he "ain't nothing but a boy," the two find the only path of reconciliation available to them—in bed and through wild, passionate, sex. The scene reveals a powerful and disturbing theme within *Baby Boy* regarding black sexuality:

Yvette: I hate you.

Jody: I hate you too [Flashing inside, a naked Yvette gyrates with extreme pleasure as a direct contrast to her anger exhibited minutes before].

Yvette: I love you. I love you so much [Utilizing quick shots, the film flashes quickly to Jody, now on top, but the camera captures both of them, emphasizing the mutual pleasure of their sexual moment].

Jody: I love you too. I ain't going no where.

Through the use of close-ups and short edits, the film flashes to multiple positions to emphasize the rawness of their sexuality, and their dialogue captures the basis of their relationship and the film's vision of black sexuality.

Jody: You feelin it?

Yvette: Yeah, Yes, I'm feeling you.

Jody: You feelin me?

Yvette: I'm feeling; oh God, it's so big!

Jody: You feelin it?

Yvette: I feel Daddy's dick!

Jody: You love Daddy's dick?

Yvette: I love Daddy's dick!

Jody: Say you love Daddy's dick.

Yvette: I love Daddy's dick.

Jody: You gonna do what I say: get up in there and clean all that mess up [now spanking her to her satisfaction]?

Yvette: I'm gonna clean-up; I'm gonna clean up!

Jody: Cook them tacos?

Yvette: I am about to cum; yes, yes! I am going to make the tacos!

After sex, the couple does not snuggle or even hold a conversation. Rather, Jody reminds Yvette that, given her sexual satisfaction and his role in providing her with immense pleasure, it was time for her to get in the kitchen to cook and clean:

Yvette: I'm gonna cook; I'm gonna clean. You put it down, I'll feed you. I love you boy.
Jody: I love you too.
Yvette: Come here, bring that chocolate over here.

This scene not only plays on long-standing stereotypes of ravenous, uninhibited black sexuality, with several shots of Yvette's breasts and Jody's ass added to the wildness of their sexual entanglements. It also goes to great lengths to reduce the sex and their relationship to a simple patriarchal exchange: Jody provides Yvette with sexual satisfaction, with pleasure resulting from his powerful black penis, while Yvette provides Jody with satisfaction and pleasure through cooking and cleaning and otherwise performing her duties as a "good girlfriend."

Manhood is alluded to only after the ability to violently defend oneself or one's "property:" Melvin confesses to being a gangsta in his adolescence, part of his transition to manhood. Jody and Sweetpea are accepted as men after they assert their manhood by protecting Jody's property, Yvette, by killing Rodney. The men of *Baby Boy* are hypersexual, erratic in behavior, and irresponsible, with the possible exception of Melvin, although he is, at times, presented as a hypersexual male.

Baby Boy does not merely recycle long-standing stereotypes of black sexuality, but links hypersexuality—the excessive need for immediate pleasure and personal gratification—to its conception of baby boys. Specifically, we see the manifestation of this immaturity in Jody's cheating, Melvin's sexuality, and Rodney's (Snoop Dog) propensity toward rape. The narrative of *Baby Boy* revolves around sex and sexuality in general, leading one to conclude that the despair and destruction in the black community emanates from the black man's dick: the source of his uncontrollable sexuality and the basis of her love and obsession that drives him to be a baby boy.

This notion of black masculinity and hypersexuality is reminiscent of feminist theorist and cultural critic bell hooks's discussion of black masculinity in the chapter "It's a Dick Thing" from her book *We Real Cool: Black Men and Masculinity*. She writes, "Sex becomes the ultimate playing field, where the quest for freedom can be pursued in a would that denies black males access to other forms of liberating power" (hooks, 2004, p. 74). Furthermore, she furthers the discussion of this long-standing stereotype of sexualized black bodies when she writes, "within the neo-colonial white-supremacist capitalist patriarchy, the black male body continues to be perceived as the embodiment of bestial, violent, penis-as-weapon hyper masculine assertion" (hooks, 2004, p.79).

Despite the problems that result from excessive sexuality, that is, the black man's penis, the film also limits his desirability to his sexuality. As a baby, Jody has little to offer other than sexual gratification. He can't provide emotional, financial, intellectual, or parental support to Yvette or Peanut, but he does give them "Daddy's Dick." Even his multiple attempts to sell dresses center on his ability to appeal to female sexuality, to use his sexuality and the black male body as a source of enticement. Jody also uses his sexual prowess to keep Yvette, given his failures elsewhere.

After a fight between Yvette and Jody that resulted from her realizing that he indeed was cheating on her with many women, Jody makes it up to her by performing oral sex. Although she hits him and verbally abuses him, almost to the point that the film rationalizes his physical response, it is in fact Jody who initiates their reconciliation through sex. Immediately after Jody slaps Yvette, resulting in her falling to the ground, he picks her up and carries her into the bedroom, where he immediately removes her pants. Lying on her back, Yvette's pain quickly transforms into pleasure not only because of the sexual stimulation, but through the corresponding fantasies and thought that run through Yvette's mind: their walking together, their wedding, and a passionate lovemaking session. The film's construction of domestic violence—that is, he blackens her eye because of his childish qualities (his personal failures), and this ultimately serves as a catalyst to an improved relationship (and a huge orgasm in the meantime)—is particularly disturbing and dangerous.

We are living in a culture that condones and celebrates the sexual exploitation and violence of black women. To transform this culture we have to fully commit ourselves to eradicating and resisting patriarchy. In *Mapping the Margins: Intersectionality, Identity Politics, and Violence Against Women of Color* Kimberle Crenshaw discusses how the race and gender dimensions of violence against women of color leave women of color with virtually no support. She politicizes domestic violence and illustrates how black women are often left with no agency. She writes, "Women of color are often reluctant to call the police, a hesitancy likely due to the general unwillingness among people of color to subject their private lives to the scrutiny and control of a police force that is frequently hostile" (Crenshaw, 1991, p. 367).

In the wake of public discussions regarding the Justin Timberlake/Janet Jackson wardrobe malfunction at the 2003 Super Bowl, feminists and their allies rightly noted how the performance promoted and sanctioned sexual violence. Timberlake not only sings about how he is "gonna have her naked before the end of this song," but eventually rips her clothing off without her sanction. In effect, the performance sexualizes violence as titillating and fetish. Cindy Richards, columnist with *The Chicago Sun Times,* penned the following observation, which is instructive in thinking about *Baby Boy:*

Newsies have spent the week flapping their jaws about the impropriety of breasts on television. Yes, it was shocking to sit in the family room and see the big finale of the Justin Timberlake-Janet Jackson performance during the not-so-super halftime show last week. But a nearly bare breast was the least shocking part of it.

The real shock was that a man would rip off a woman's clothes—planned or not— and we would talk only about what was exposed in the process. It doesn't matter whether her wardrobe malfunctioned. What matters is that he was messing with her wardrobe in the first place. (Richards, 2004)

Barbara Shaw, director of the Illinois Violence Prevention Authority, saw a problem not with Jackson's breast, but with the show's promotion of sexual violence on the day in which many instances of domestic violence occur throughout the nation. In her words, "it's a very sad day for society when a bare breast is more offensive than the glorification of sexual violence. [Sexual violence] is so pervasive that we don't even know it when we see it" (Richards). The performative power of Timberlake's simulated (and actual) violence against Jackson is particularly powerful when read within the larger context of media representation of women of color and America's rape culture. Given that black women are virtually erased from popular media except as sex objects, it is no wonder that the problem of rape for women of color exists outside contemporary public discourses.

Being routinely disbelieved by those who control the definitions of violence, encountering mass media representations that depict Black women as 'bitches,' 'hoes,' and other controlling images, and/or experiencing daily assaults such as having their breasts and buttocks fondled by friends and perfect strangers in school, the workplace, families, and/or on the streets of African American communities may become so routine that African American women cannot perceive their own pain. (Collins 2004, p. 229)

The representations offered by *Baby Boy*, the Super Bowl performance, and virtual silence concerning sexual violence specific to women of color amid the racialized culture war/moral panic are particularly troubling given current statistics regarding rape and black women. Considering that a rape occurs every 18 seconds in the United States; that an estimated 3 percent of American men are guilty of battery; that American men batter more than 8,200 women and rape more than 2,345 women per day; and that in a single year, America sees 3 million cases of battery and more than 1 million incidents of rape, it is powerful to think about the ways in which popular culture naturalizes, sexualizes, and transforms a societal problem into highly sexually charged performances.

Popular culture exoticizes black women's bodies and simultaneously demonizes too much exposure as well. The naturalization of sexual violence and the reduction of black women to unrapable, hypersexual jezebels, although certainly not a casual relationship, contribute to the absence of public discussion about rape and African American women (Moorti 2002). This, in turn, certainly contributes to dismal reporting of rape among black women. That 1:6 rapes involving white women are reported and only 1:16 rapes of black women are reported cannot be understood outside cultural representations and discursive articulations of black women. "Both black men and black women are required to 'assume the position' of subordination within a new Multicultural America, and that practices of a rape culture help foster this outcome" (Collins 2004, pp. 243–244). Just as minstrel shows and Jim Crow culture rationalized and justified white-on-black sexual violence during and after slavery, representations like those inside *Baby Boy* and within much of popular culture in general contribute to a particularly racialized rape culture that denies victimhood to women of color as it elevates the dangerous position white women hold within America.

To talk about the performance through a colorblind lens ignores the historical occurrences of white sexual violence inflicted on black women. It erases slavery, Joan Little, Fannie Lou Hamer, and the hundreds of thousands of black women who have experienced sexual violence as a result of America's white supremacist society. Building on the work of Patricia Hill Collins and Sujata Moorti, I argue that the sexual violence presented in multiple forms within *Baby Boy,* as well as its representation of black female sexuality, plays on the history and discursive articulations of white supremacy, offering a mere racial shift of perpetrators.

This movement to transform our media-driven exploitive culture can progress only as men come to feminist thinking and actively challenge sexism and male violence. Manning Marable writes, "Rape, spouse abuse, sexual harassment on the job, are all essential to the perpetuation of a sexist society. For the sexist, violence is necessary and logical part of the unequal, exploitative relationship. To dominate and control, sexism requires violence. Rape and sexual harassment are therefore not accidental to the structure of gender relations within a sexist order" (1992).

In the end our conversation cannot conclude with condemnation against films such as *Baby Boy* or even the development of a literacy that understand its racist and sexist elements, but works toward the development of a framework that sees *Baby Boy* and any film within a larger historical, ideological, and discursive context. Reflecting on the tendency to demonize hip-hop as a source of societal sexism, Mark Anthony Neal reminds us, "Mr. 50 Cent isn't the only thug or pimp in the room; there are more than a few in the White House and at the Pentagon" (2005, p. 147). Equally important, we must connect our conversations to contexts of jobs, housing, health care, and education.

As *Baby Boy* demonizes Jody for his immaturity—for his inability to secure a true authentic and productive black manhood, as evident by his bike, his joblessness, his excessive sexuality, his tendency to play with model toys, and his overall laziness—it offers a clear proscription for him and the entire African American community toward greater productivity in a true black masculinity. At the center of the film's understanding of manhood is work and ironically violence. In other words, the way to overcome these unproductive elements that result in a poor and dysfunctional African American community is through personal responsibility, financial stability (hard work), taking care of one's family, and ultimately securing true manhood.

Baby Boy's vision of self-help and personal empowerment stems from its conception of masculinity and manhood. The failure of the black community and of Jody is the failure of the African American community to enact a truthful, authentic, and productive black masculinity. Specifically, that failure results in laziness and in a lack of desire to work. As such, improved family and community will come through hard work—through black men becoming real men who go to work, put food on their tables, and become sellers rather than buyers. This notion of building wealth and operating a business is captured in a conversation between Jody and Sweetpea:

Jody: How many millionaires you got on brah. I count at least three.

Sweetpea: What the fuck you talking bout?

Jody: Look around man, see what I see; I see money. Look at the man over there selling t-shirts. Look at the brother over there selling pie and paper. Cake man over there. Every body moving, making money, right? Why we standing still being broke. I figure all this shit out, all this; the whole world moves forward through transactions, commerce, Nigger. The exchange of goods and services. All the ballers, real successful folk are sellers. And all the broke ass people playin catch up are buyers. I ain't tryin to go out like that, Pee. I'm gonna be a seller.

In another instance, Melvin lectures Jody and Sweetpea about the differences between "Guns" and "Butter," and about the problems facing the black community being the result of its obsession with "butter," those things—diamonds, cars, clothes—that don't appreciate in value yet give immediate gratification. Communal improvement will thus come once black men focus on "guns"—stocks, bonds, real estate—not only as a source of financial stability, but as means toward enacting real manhood. Reflecting on academic and popular discourses "concerned" with black masculinity, bell hooks offers a thoughtful piece of analysis concerning the vision of masculinity (and femininity) constructed within *Baby Boy:*

The portraits of black masculinity that emerges in this work perpetually construct black men as "failures," who are psychologically "fucked up," dangerous, violent sex maniacs whose insanity is informed by their inability to fulfill their phallocentric masculine destiny in a racist context.

It does not interrogate the conventional construction of patriarchal masculinity or question the extent to which black men have historically internalized the norm. It never assumes the existence of black men whose creative agency has enabled them to subvert norms and develop ways of thinking about masculinity that challenge patriarchy. (1992, p. 89)

Denying racism and demonizing black men, while erasing the heterogeneity of black masculinity, *Baby Boy* legitimizes and justifies state violence in all its forms.

The power of *Baby Boy* lies not just with its inscription of white supremacist stereotypes of black sexuality or even its place within a history of racist imagery, but with its connection to contemporary discourse and social/political/economic articulations. Its troubling power resonates with both the historical continuity of image and its ideological function in the contemporary moment. *Baby Boy* legitimizes hegemonic discourses of colorblindness, as race and racism bear little influence on the life chances of Jody, Sweetpea, and a generation of baby boys. In the erasing of state violence, job discrimination, and twenty-first century apartheid, *Baby Boy* supports conservative arguments about poverty and the persistence of America's ghetto being a result of personal failures and destructive cultural values. The failures of Jody or his perpetual boy status is not a public or communal problem but one of his own doing that can ultimately be rectified through responsibility, true manhood, self-help, and violence.

Specifically, the film connects manhood to violence, simultaneously locating the *Baby Boy* phenomenon and then enactment of a true, useful black masculinity, within displays of violence. Unable to act like a man in other ways—protecting and supporting his family—Jody proves himself to be a man through beating up Yvette and the neighborhood kids.

Yet Jody initially remains stuck in a phase of childhood, because he can't even find his manhood through violence. He becomes almost paralyzed at certain moments because of his fear of dying. He is ambivalent toward street violence. After a group of neighborhood kids steal his bike, Jody, along with Sweetpea, confronts them at the park. Unsure of how to proceed, Jody is coaxed into punching the youth. Unable to match their skills and intensity, Jody eventually gives up, allowing Sweatpea the honor of teaching the youth "some manners." The film locates the pathology of Jody (black men) within a culture violence, but it also denotes his baby boy status through his ambivalence toward violence; he is scared and incapable of being a man because he won't or can't kick ass. As such, Jody fulfills his manhood through a series of violent acts.

Although Melvin's violent confrontation with Jody results in Jody being thrown out of the house, this fight represents Jody's first step toward securing an authentic black manhood. Melvin is not the only source of redemption for Jody. Sweetpea offers Jody a lesson in violence and authority when they "discipline" a group of neighborhood kids. Finally, Jody finds his manhood in the shooting of Rodney. Although he is reluctant, leaving the final shot to Sweetpea, Jody fulfills his duty as a man in procuring the murder of Rodney, protecting his woman, Yvette, whom Rodney attempted to rape. The film pathologizes, but it ultimately concludes that manhood and success come through violence. After Rodney's murder, Jody finds solace in the arms of Melvin, symbolically marking his transformation into manhood. Whether getting his ass kicked by Melvin or enacting violence on another, Jody grows from narcissistic boy to responsible adult through acts of aggression.

Just as the film defines manhood through violence, *Baby Boy* links desire and manhood to sex and patriarchy. As with *Boyz n the Hood*, *Baby Boy* inscribes the emasculation of black men as a result of the predominance of the single-mother home. hooks challenges our gaze of the single mother home as a space where the emasculation of black men takes place and further interrogates the notions of manhood, sex, and patriarchy in an essay entitled "Plantation Patriarchy":

Transplanted African men, even those coming from communities where sex roles shaped the division of labor, where the status of men was different and most times higher than that of women, had to be taught to equate their status as men with the right to dominate women, they had to be taught patriarchal masculinity. They had to be taught that it was acceptable to use violence to establish patriarchal power. The gender politics of slavery and white-supremacist domination of free black men was the school where black men from different African tribes, with different languages and value systems, learned in the 'new world' patriarchal masculinity. (hooks 2004, p. 3)

Thus, the reintroduction of patriarchy, as hooks describes it, shifts the guiding light of family organization from a problem of single mother homes to a result of white supremacist capitalist patriarchy. If this approach were understood, one might see a reversal of the baby boy phenomenon. *Baby Boy* concludes that black women wouldn't drive black men to pathological, irresponsible, and innate behavior. Yvette's constant nagging pushes Jody to promiscuity; his mother leaves him without the maturity or need to leave the nest, get a job, or even a car, all symbols of manhood. *Baby Boy* even blames black women for high rates of homicide and death. As mothers ill-prepare their children for the real world, they set them up for failure. After Jody's mother throws him out of the house, Jody tells her, "If I get killed it's on you." The ambiguous inscription of patriarchy through an ambivalent mother reflects the ideological project of film. The women of *Baby Boy* exist for little more than the pleasure and service of their men. They fuck them, feed them, and serve them. We know little about these women except that they offer pain and pleasure to the men. "All of the main characters in this film are defined largely as props for men's pleasures and as integral to maintaining some semblance of family values, and all their actions are devoid of contextualization" (Giroux 2003, p. 144).

Rather than contextualizing or problematizing domestic violence or abuse, *Baby Boy* represents Yvette as responding to misogyny through sex and other acts of pleasure. After several arguments and Jody's abuse of Yvette, Yvette responds not by fighting back or leaving Jody; she offers to make him dinner or give him her body sexually. The nature of their relationship and the patriarchal message of the film are no more evident than when Yvette and Jody have sex. As he lies on top of her giving her the one pleasure he is capable of providing through his penis, she promises to give him her femininity by making him dinner and cleaning house. In the end, their relationship lacks any meaning beyond functionality, and the absence of love, compassion, or even friendship serves as both the evidence of a failed black family and persistent failures within the community. All the while racism and state violence are pushed further away from the popular imagination.

The wave of early 1990s ghettocentric films, although never progressive, effectively challenged the role of the state in the production of the "ghetto." *Menace II Society* and *Boyz n the Hood* each prescribed an impact of racial segregation and police brutality on young black men. *Straight Out of Brooklyn* and *Set It Off* successfully elucidate the historical context of the 1980s with massive job cuts and deindustrialization. These films, to varying degrees, constructed the "problems" of "black life" in the ghetto, not as individual problems but as products of deindustrialization, police brutality, decreased investment in social programs, and racism. *Baby Boy*, on the other hand, erases these contextual elements, instead focusing on the failures of black men to "leave the nest," a phenomenon induced by the failures of black fathers to uphold their parental responsibilities and the inability of black mothers to raise productive black men. Yet *Baby Boy* approaches these questions in a very different manner than the Moynihan Report or past efforts that demonize black men and women as the source of communal problems, erasing race and racism from the discussion.

In the absence of a systematic critique of American apartheid, state violence, or post-Civil Rights racism, *Baby Boy* reinscribes dominant discourses locating the problems of the African American community in the cultural, psychological, or communal realms. Following in the tradition of Richard Herrnstein, Dinesh D'Souza, and David Horowitz, *Baby Boy* "psychologizes the problems of races "as issues" of character individual pathology or genetic inferiorities" (Giroux 2003, p. 123). "*Baby Boy* echoes the conservative call for black males to stop complaining, pick themselves and the larger society up by exercising some self criticism aimed at the infinite and irresponsible lives they lead" (Giroux 2003, p. 136). In other words, the problems of poverty, crime, and family disorganization, all of which are central to the story of *Baby Boy*, are a result of the shortcomings of the black community; Jody is merely a symptom of a larger problem, as his disease is his immaturity, irresponsibility, and persistent childlike status. His problems (and those of the black community) are a product of his being a baby boy.

In *Black Skin/White Masks*, Frantz Fanon notes that within the white (colonial) imagination: "The Negro is just a child" (Fanon 1967, p. 27) incapable of self-governing or personal responsibility. As "social problems become personal problems and systematic issues are reduced to private solutions," solutions are limited to personal transformation. *Baby Boy* is thus a call for private and personal growth. Improved life chances will not result from increasing social programs, government intervention, or even social movement. They will result from self-help, individual responsibility, personal growth and a willingness to get a job, take care of family, and become productive members of the community.

Yet this notion of self-help and individual responsibility becomes challenging, when one deals emotionally with alternative notions of what family is. Nowhere is this more prevalent than in *Antwone Fisher*, in which self-help and personal responsibility take center stage in one man's quest for inner peace and family. Here, as in *Baby Boy*, social mechanisms of oppression take a back seat to the American Dream, as Antwone seeks to resolve his inner demons by finding his family. Although *Antwone Fisher* is visually displaced from the "ghetto," the ghettocentric imagination is manifest in *Antwone Fisher's* dedication to self-help in the face of societal inequality.

ANTWONE FISHER

Antwone Fisher may seem to be a strange fit in a chapter on the ghettocentric imagination, but it offers a powerful commentary on America's ghetto by its very absence. A majority of the film takes place in San Diego, on a navy ship, far from America's inner cities, but it also provides a brief glimpse into the violent and abusive nature of 1980s Cleveland, with all of the trappings of poverty, drugs, violence, and criminality. Even more important, it illustrates the supposed effects of the pathology and destruction that defines "ghetto life." In chronicling America's black ghettos in their visual absence, *Antwone Fisher* plays on hegemonic (common sense) ideas of the ghettocentric imagination, providing an instructive, yet reactionary, commentary on race, black manhood, and America in the twenty-first century.

Antwone Fisher marks the directorial debut of Denzel Washington, who agreed to take up the project of directing this film in 1997, but was delayed until 2001 because of his own acting gigs. Written by Antwone Quenton Fisher originally as a screenplay and then published in 2001 as a memoir (*Finding Fish*), *Antwone Fisher* chronicles Fisher's life, from his birth in a women's prison to being beaten by his foster mother, to joining the U.S. Navy. Producer Todd Black first heard the story more than 12 years ago, when Fisher was working as a security guard at Sony Pictures Studios. Director Denzel Washington said of *Antwone Fisher*: "It's a triumph of spirit. I'm inspired by Antwone. When you look at all he's gone through and survived and can still be a gentle soul . . . hopefully it will touch all who see it . . . hopefully we'll reach out to those who are dealing with difficult times and thinking that they can't make it. They'll see this young man's life and say, 'Hey, you know, I can make it'" (http://www2.foxsearchlight. com/antwonefisher/main.php).

The audience first meets Antwone as a child, in a dream sequence. Antwone is standing in a wheat field, gazing at an old barn. After a female voice calls him in, he runs to the barn doors, and as they open, an awesome sight greets him—his family, going back generations (various eras are represented through costume), surrounds a long dinner table where no one has yet to be seated. The seat at the head of the table is reserved for Antwone, a visual representation of what he has longed for most of his conscious life: a close, loving family, and a place in the world. As he takes his seat at the head of the table and his family moves to serve him, Antwone wakes up and is snapped back to reality—he is 25 years old, for all practical purposes an orphan, and an enlisted man in the U.S. Navy. The dream, as we are soon to discover, is far from reality.

Antwone likes to fight. His terrible childhood, revealed in periodic flashbacks, has left him with a lot of anger and no coping mechanisms. In the early moments of the film, Antwone (Derek Luke) strikes a white NCO (noncommissioned officer) because the officer used a racial epithet to address Antwone. As a result of the assault, the ship's commanding officer orders Antwone to three sessions with the navy's resident psychologist, Jerome Davenport (Denzel Washington). Antwone refuses to talk to Jerome and goes through the first and second sessions silent. Antwone finally opens up in his third session with Jerome, telling him about his abusive foster mother, Mrs. Tate. Responding to questions about his parentage, Antwone had previously told Jerome that he came "from under a rock." Antwone divulges many gruesome details about his childhood in this session, not just the fact of his abusive foster parents but that he was born in a prison and his father was murdered before he was born. Antwone was not alone in the abuse he received from Mrs. Tate—he had two foster brothers who endured the same treatment.

Not all is gloomy in Antwone's life, however. He has a few buddies on ship and is romantically interested in Cheryl (Joy Bryant), a fellow navy enlistee, but his pursuit of her is fumbling and awkward at best. Cheryl is stationed on land near where Antwone's ship is docked, and Antwone goes out of his way to go ashore and see her at the Navy Exchange, where she works. After some coaching/encouragement from Jerome, Antwone finally gets up the courage to ask Cheryl out, and their romance blooms. This is Antwone's first serious romantic relationship.

At the end of the third session with Jerome, the good doctor gives Antwone a book called *The Slave Community* (1979) to help him try to understand the mentality of the Tates. After catching heat from his friends for reading the book on deck, Antwone throws it away and shows up, angry and confrontational, at Jerome's office. After a loud display of his frustrations in the office waiting room, Jerome agreed to meet with Antwone without official sanction. Throughout their sessions, more disturbing elements of Antwone's childhood are revealed, and one of the more profound revelations occurs in a navy jail cell, after Antwone, while docked somewhere in Mexico, gets in a fight with a fellow sailor in a club and is flown back to base. Antwone reveals that in addition to being abused by Mrs. Tate, he was also molested by Mrs. Tate's cousin, Nadine, when he was 11 years old.

The sessions with Jerome continue, and after a session at Jerome's home, Antwone receives and accepts an invitation to the Davenports for Thanksgiving. After dinner, Antwone gives Jerome a poem, titled "Who Will Cry for the Little Boy?" as an expression of gratitude for Jerome's support and guidance.

Soon after, Jerome tells Antwone that it is time for their sessions to end and for Antwone to move on and find his real family. Antwone becomes distraught, thinking that, once again, those whom he loves are abandoning him. This moment leads to another flashback, where we hear the story of Jesse, his best friend from childhood. Jesse was killed while attempting to rob a convenience store when the boys were teenagers. Jerome reassures Antwone that this is not abandonment, but a step that will help Antwone finally find peace with his past.

Antwone takes Jerome's advice and books a flight to Cleveland to find his family, with Cheryl by his side. His first stop is the Tate's, where he stands up to Mrs. Tate and Nadine, proclaiming that he is still standing, despite what they did to him. From this confrontation, Antwone gets his father's full name. He then visits Social Services and gets his birth record from the state. His search commences via phone calls to everyone in the area with the same surname as his father, and late that first night in Cleveland, Antwone hits pay dirt: he finds an aunt.

The next day he and Cheryl visit Aunt Annette (sister of his deceased father), and she and two other family members decide that Antwone is truly their relative, and that one of his uncles knows who Antwone's mother is, and where she lives. Antwone and the uncle proceed to visit Eva, who has done little with her life. She lives alone in a housing project, and on meeting her son, cannot find anything to say to him. Nonetheless, he assures her that he has no children, does not deal drugs, and has forgiven her for her past transgressions, that is, not coming to claim him after she got out of prison. Antwone returns to Annette's, and is greeted by what he has been dreaming of his whole life: a family. Aunts, uncles, cousins, grandparents have all gathered to give Antwone an official welcome home.

Antwone returns to the base and relays his findings to Jerome. Jerome, in turn, tells Antwone that the redemptive and resolute aspects of their relationship have been dialectical—that Jerome has become a better man and husband because of Antwone. They salute each other, and they walk off into the proverbial sunset together.

Following in the traditions of its ghettocentric brethren, from *Boyz n the Hood* to *Menace* and *Baby Boy, Antwone Fisher* chronicles a lone individual struggling to make it out of the ghetto. Antwone, unlike Doughboy or Jody, ultimately makes positive decisions, choices that allow him to overcome the obstacles (particularly cultural and communal) preventing his movement outside a ghetto life. Todd Black, one of the film's producers, summarizes the film's focus on individuality, choice, and the potential of the "human spirit" within one of the DVD extras: "It is one thing to say you suffer through pain, from injustices, as an adult and hopefully lift yourself up. But as a child, as you go through things you did, that he did and still lifted himself up without guidance, without any helping hand, it is pretty amazing."

The film's focus on Antwone's choices, his ability to overcome so much toward eventually securing the American Dream, ultimately lays the success and/or failure of America's poor in their own laps. Despite facing years of abuse and the absence of opportunity, Antwone makes it out of the ghetto because of his own actions and the help of the U.S. military. The emphasis on individuality and bootstraps ideology reflects a dominant racial discourse that erases the contemporary effects of racism and state violence.

The power of the narrative rests not just with its conclusion, as we all know the outcome before entering the theater, but in the narrative style and approach. The film's ending, which through camera angles and narrative juxtaposes a successful Fisher dressed in his naval uniform with his estranged mother, is indicative of this message. She has dark skin, nappy hair, and chapped lips that are slightly white, all of which makes us wonder if she is sick or a mere crack head. Her clothes and house are a mess, a stark contrast to the order and sterility of Antwone's military lifestyle.

Through this particular scene, the camera works to further alienate us from his mother, Eva Mae, the embodiment of an undesirable and pathological blackness, by emphasizing the impoverished state of her life. More important, we are left to wonder what choices he made, and what qualities of his character, allowed him to become something other than his mother, to avoid the mistakes of his friends (Jesse), and the confines of the ghetto. What about Antwone resulted in the formation of productive black identity? Encapsulating the film's emphasis on the American Dream and bootstrapism, Antwone tells his mother his life story, with the camera adding to the drama, foregrounding his body and his words as it denies her equal footing.

I have taken care of myself. I have. I have never been in trouble with the law. I have read hundreds of books, written poems, painted pictures and I have traveled the world. I have served my country. I speak two languages and I am working on a third. I never fathered any children. I have never done drugs or even smoked a cigarette.

The film makes clear that Antwone is a model minority, securing the American Dream in spite of physical and sexual abuse, extreme poverty, and a culture of violence. This depiction is usually reserved for Asian Americans and certain other immigrant communities. Even more, we understand the power of the narrative with our knowledge of his true-life story, with Antwone overcoming the obstacles of Hollywood, eventually becoming a published author and credited screenwriter.

Although the film certainly focuses on Antwone's personal strength, spirit, and perseverance, his growth and success come from his relationship the United States Navy and specifically with Davenport. Despite telling the story of this young black man, *Antwone Fisher* comes across as an advertisement for the U.S. Navy. Within the special features of the DVD, the real-life Fisher, Todd Black, and others all celebrate the navy as his source of redemption, as his savior. Black notes that the "Navy taught him about discipline and focus." Fisher agrees, thereby erasing the history of racism and racial conflict within the U.S. military. Fisher tells the DVD audience: "The Navy can help you."

Both this commentary and the film itself celebrate the navy (the military) as a space of integration, opportunity, and colorblindness.

Through the film, references to racial conflict are laughable or invented, as when Fisher fabricates an accusation of a racial slur after a fight with a white sailor. His references to race and racism are used as signs of his irrational, erratic, and self-destructive behavior. After the fight, the ship's captain sends Fisher to the "nut house," a historical practice that often put soldiers of color under surveillance. Yet in the film, this step is presented as the first instance of intervention toward Antwone's redemption. While the Captain and Davenport are clearly invested in helping him, Fisher resists:

Why something gotta be bothering me? Why cause, I jumped on a white boy? Something gotta be wrong with me? Send him to the psychiatrist. Nigger tried to kill his master. He must be crazy.

As the audience just witnessed, Fisher attacked his white shipmate without provocation. We are left to believe that he is indeed crazy—his desire to deploy the race card, to use race as his "get out of jail free card," not only signifies his internal demons, but also thereby reaffirms the colorblind position of the U.S. Navy. In these early moments, the film not only erases the racial significance of the narrative, the persistent meaning of blackness, but also links his erratic/irrational/destructive behavior to both his propensity toward violence and his unethical willingness to play the race card.

Beyond fulfilling hegemonic visions of blackness—as violent, angry—the film also replicates dominant views of the military as a raceless place, a model for American integration, as the source of opportunity for all Americans. As Fisher is irrational, angry, and hotheaded, the navy, and specifically Davenport, serves as his father, his source of growth and maturation.

As the only father figure in his life, Fisher learns numerous lessons from Davenport. Davenport teaches him discipline, accountability, focus, and how to be a man. He provides him with books on African American history to understand the persistent effects of slavery on the black psyche; he teaches him about love, dating, and romance. Yet his most important lesson may have been his message about anger management, about Antwone Fisher finding ways to be less confrontational, aggressive, and "ghetto-like." Davenport successfully breaks the cycle, instilling a new (military-based) culture and set of values. During one session, Davenport compassionately forces Antwone to overcome his accustomed culture of poverty:

Davenport: I understand you like to fight.
Fisher: Only way some people learn.
Davenport: But you pay the price for teaching.

It is ironic that the military, through its black representative, curtails Fisher's violence. Moreover, the film constructs the military as a ticket out of the ghetto, as an opportunity to not only move up America's class ladder, but toward the acquisition of new values and morals. Antwone, who doesn't know what a frappuccino is, and avoids vegetables, not only matures, but secures a new class status that includes blended coffees, vegetables, books, and controlled anger. He secures this class status because of the opportunities afforded by the military, because Davenport helps Antwone find a productive manhood.

In positioning a patriarchal navy and Davenport as Antwone's source of redemption—those who teach him how to be a man—*Antwone Fisher* reifies dominant ideologies of black manhood and womanhood. Not only in absence of a black father figure, but because of the abuse of several dark-skinned black women (Eva, Mrs. Tate, Nadine), Antwone is unable to successfully assimilate into society. The film thus legitimizes dominant ideologies regarding the black family and those of black women, and pathological values, and not racism, remain the entrenched obstacles to communal success. The problems of gender and sexuality, evident in the capitulation of long-standing discourses that have demonized black women (mothers) from the Moynihan report, and widespread debates concerning welfare to panics surrounding crack babies and single-mothered homes, is nothing new to Hollywood or the ghettocentric genre. In fact, *Boyz n the Hood, Menace II Society*, and several films that moved this genre forward in the early 1990s were rightly criticized by scholars and African American leaders for the tendency of those films to legitimize dominant white claims about black mothers. Specifically, *Boyz*, and to a lesser degree *Menace*, articulate dominant ideology that "boys need fathers" and more specifically that black male children require the fatherly presence of black men; and without their presence and their effort to teach black boys how to be productive black men, problems will continue to beset the black community.

S. Craig Watkins, in *Representing: Hip-Hop Culture and the Production of Black Cinema*, criticizes these films for their celebration of black patriarchy and denunciation of black women, all the while denying the intersectional importance of poverty and state violence. "Rather than develop a representational politic that reverses the pathology paradigm, the creations of the ghetto action cycle tend to construct filmic worlds that reinforce this popular interpretation of black familiar life," argues Watkins. "The gender politics of the ghetto action film cycle also reveal how deep the stream of conservative commonsense racial ideology flows. Moreover, the failure to challenge the rising tide of conservative is not insignificant, insofar as" those commodified black filmmakers within Hollywood "are often celebrated for 'their authentic' representations of postindustrial ghetto life" (1998, pp. 225–226). Just as with *Boyz* and *Menace*, the new generation of ghetto action dramas remains fixated on the familial pathology and the absence of responsible black fathers as a source of communal problems, further advancing a conservative agenda that denies the existence of racism, structural violence, and in turn ignores the persistent effects of segregation, poverty, and structural adjustment pro-grams on communities of color across the country.

Even more transparent, this new wave of films places increasing emphasis on individual, communal and cultural problems as the basis of understand-ing persistent inequality. *Antwone Fisher* and *Baby Boy* not only demonize black women, blaming them for the problems of poverty, violence, drug abuse, etc. (Jody is Jody because of the enabling women in his life—he finds his manhood with the help of Melvin; Antwone was Antwone because of his mother and father, finding redemption from Davenport) but provides a conservative and reactionary message that lets society off the hook for prob-lems and solutions. As poverty is not the result of an exodus of jobs or of violence, not the result of the war on drugs, but rather the failures of fathers, then the solution must be better fathers. The argument that racism does not matter, failures of capitalism do not matter, state violence does not matter, and so on because problems are the result of bad single mothers is troubling. The idea that the "American Dream" can be secured through proper guid-ance and leadership and is available only through fathers is equally troubling and simplistic as well.

Antwone Fisher centers on a discourse of bootstrap redemption that is facilitated by one's own will and determination, as well as the lessons and val-ues instilled by the U.S. Navy. It also chronicles the redemption of Colonel Davenport. Despite having faced poverty, having been subjected to violence, and having been virtually abandoned by all, Antwone teaches Davenport as much as he learns about life, family, and manhood, redeeming his character along the way. In the early moments of their relationship, Davenport appears distant, as someone struggling with his own demons. During Antwone's initial meeting of Davenport's wife, Bertha (Salli Richardson) and during Thanksgiving dinner, the film emphasizes the physical and emotional dis-tance reeking havoc on the Davenport family. It is a sterile home, one with-out life, as Bertha struggles with their inability to have children.

Although the film is a different take on the classic interracial buddy film, *Antwone Fisher* deploys the long-standing trope of the "Huck Finn fixation" to illustrate how each man grows, overcomes struggle, and is ultimately redeemed with the assistance of the other. A theme related to the buddy formula that Hollywood has embraced over the last 10 years has been that of redemption. Filmmakers tell stories of interracial friendships resulting in the redemption or growth of the white protagonists. Whereas in the past, films revealed the maturation in black characters through their contact with whites, a role reversal has taken place within Hollywood. The bulk of films elucidate the ways that black-white friendships improve the life experiences of whites, without any attention to what blacks gain from such relationships. The career of Cuba Gooding Jr. reflects this trend, with films like *Jerry Maguire* (1996) *Men of Honor* (2000), and *Radio* (2003). In *Men of Honor*, Billy Sunday, the racist master diver played by Robert De Niro, evolves as a husband and a man because of his interactions with Carl Brasheer (Gooding). Witnessing honor, dignity, and dedication in Brasheer, Sunday is forced to interrogate his own racism, anger, and alcoholism, becoming a new man in the process.

Tomas Bogle, borrowing from Mark Twain's classic *Huckleberry Finn*, describes this type of relationship as a "Huck Finn fixation," in which "the white hero grows in stature from his association with the dusty black" (Bogle 2001, p. 140). Reflecting a liberal humanist positivity and the desire to counter both identity politics and the deleterious incidences of 1990s racism, the idea of redemption through friendship and integration infects a spectrum of films. The examples are endless as the wave of films using the "Huck Finn fixation" increase each year. Films like the *Die Hard* and *Lethal Weapon* series, *The Shawshank Redemption* (1994), *The Green Mile* (1999), *Hardball* (2001), *and Monster's Ball* (2002) all tell stories of honorable black men (children in *Hardball* and Halle Berry in *Monster's Ball*) teaching disreputable white men.

Although not interracial, *Antwone Fisher* embraces this common trope to illustrate the redemptive qualities of the two men's relationship, additionally demonstrating the power of coming from undesirable circumstances. The son (Fisher) makes the father (Davenport) into a better man, husband, and doctor. Antwone allows him to open up in a way he could not with his wife, to address his own problems, his pain at not having a child: "You put me to shame. Because of you, I am a better doctor, man, and learning to be a better husband. You don't owe me anything. I owe you. You are the champ, son. You have beaten everyone, who has beaten you—I salute you." As with *Training Day*, *Antwone Fisher* elevates the theme of redemption beyond the classic version seen in *Shawshank Redemption* or *Green Mile*. The emphasis on boostrapism, rising out of the ghetto, and the mutuality of redemption between two black men reflects the power of the narrative. In focusing on redemption (and bootstraps), *Antwone Fisher* recasts the struggles and history that define Antwone Fisher's life (a black history of sorts) as a cultural and psychological asset. Antwone is able to overcome his own problems, albeit with some assistance, and redeem others *because* of the violence, poverty, despair, and abuse. The almost fetishization of a productive ghettocentric set of values defines *Antwone Fisher*, which in turn lets America and the state off-the-hook because the problems inducted by twenty-first century capitalism and persistent racism (or in the film abusive black women) are also the source of growth, redemption, liberation, and strength.

Although the cinematic story of *Antwone Fisher* recasts the state as a savior, *Finding Fish*, Antwone's own autobiography, demonstrates how the social welfare system failed him. Given the history of the social welfare system and its relationship to black families (so powerfully recounted by Malcolm X, James Baldwin, and the film *Claudine*, 1974), *Finding Fish* offers, unlike the film version of his life, a powerful commentary on racism and the child (social) welfare system. The film erases this critique, instead casting the Tate family as the villain, and the state (the Navy) as both sources of safety and liberation.

Antwone Fisher is ostensibly a story of several evil black women, rather than a narrative of a failing nation with inadequate resources geared toward children of color. It is a story of four black women: one who killed Antwone's father, who the film memorializes as a saint; one who abandoned him, his mother who chooses drugs over her responsibility; one who abuses him, Mrs. Tate, who psychological tortures and beats young Antwone; and one (Nadine) who sexually assaults him. It is important to briefly reflect on these last instances as emblematic of how *Antwone Fisher* simultaneously demonizes (dark-skinned) black women for the inhumanity experienced by Antwone (and Dwight and Keith) and exonerates/elevates America and its most patriotic institutions.

After the murder of his father and the abandonment by his mother, the state, which is not visible at this point in the film, places Antwone with the Tate family. From moment one, Mrs. Tate abuses Antwone and the other boys in the house, ridiculing them when not physically assaulting them; she uses belts, shoes and fire to threaten and control the boys. Mrs. Tate is not just a bad foster parent, but the embodiment of evil, a person who uses fear and intimidation to control these already scared children.

Although *Antwone Fisher* makes mention of the abuse inflicted on the children by Reverend Tate, the visual power of Mrs. Tate beating the children, threatening to burn Antwone, and otherwise terrorizing her foster children, puts the emphasis on her failures. If not physically abusing the boys, Mrs. Tate constantly calls the boys "nigger," instilling a negative sense of self-worth that limits and controls Antwone. He eventually finds redemption in the navy.

Mrs. Tate is not the film's only villain. Nadine, Mrs. Tate's niece, sexually abused Antwone beginning at the age of six. She is callous, cold, and sexually aggressive. Without character development, Nadine exists as a stock character that reflects long-standing stereotypes of black female sexuality. But history reveals that the unmasking and oversexualizing of black bodies is long-standing and central to American popular culture. As Jacqueline Bobo states, in *Black Women as Cultural Readers,* "Representations of black women in mainstream media constitute a venerable tradition of distorted and limited imagery" (1995, p. 33). Rather than constituting black women as the victims of the lust of white assailants, dominant representations have posited black women as sexually deviant, aggressive, domineering or wretched victims—as mammies or jezebels. According to Bobo, Nelly Nkweto Simmons, Jacquie Jones, and others, the most resilient image has been that of the jezebel, the "sexual siren." From Nina Mae McKinney in *Hallelujah* (1929), and Dorothy Dandridge in *Carmen Jones* (1954), to Tracy Camilla Johns in *She's Gotta Have It* (1986) and any number of women discussed in this book, black women's sexuality has been demonized, pathologized, policed, and ultimately consumed. As hooks reminds us: "The sexuality of black female signifiers beginning in the 18th century became an icon for deviant sexuality" (hooks 1992, p. 62). This history has had a tremendous effect in the way U.S. society today sees black sexuality, including the way(s) it reacts to "displays" of black sexuality and its identification of black female sexuality as the source of degradation for black man and the larger black community.

In one instance, Mrs. Tate, Dwight, and Keith leave Antwone and Nadine alone. Before the door was shut, Nadine makes her way down the stairs slapping him across the face before ordering him to go to the basement "and drop them." Although *Antwone Fisher* elucidates the horrors of this abuse as an explanation for Antwone's attitude and troubles (including those regarding intimacy and dating), it does not tell the story of these women. Rather the film references slavery as an explanation for their violent and abusive behavior. It equally reduces violence and life opportunities to choice, as Antwone chooses to overcome the legacy of slavery and to rise above the abuse of Mrs. Tate, whereas his mother, Nadine, and Mrs. Tate all succumb to the problematic legacies of slavery and cultures of poverty. In telling this narrative, *Antwone Fisher* exonerates the state (which placed him with the Tate family, which ignored signs of abuse, which created economic and political conditions of 1980s ghettos), placing blame on individuals, dysfunctional family values, and bad choices. Whether they are bad people or the cultural manifestation of a "slave community," it is ultimately about choice, about individual responsibility, illustrated by the success garnered through the positive decisions of Antwone Fisher.

Although not necessarily an overt explanation as to the sinister, uncaring, and pathological existence of Mrs. Tate, Nadine, and his mother, the film casts these women with dark-skinned, and unattractive (or they appear to be so in the film) actresses. In playing on white supremacist notions of color, *Antwone Fisher* uses their blackness, their dark skin, as a signifier of their evilness. The fact that each of the evil women is dark skinned is especially powerful given that the film's other women (Berta; Cheryl), who are nice, are light skinned and presumably mixed-race. Those who harm Antwone are clearly black, marked and limited by their dark skin, whereas his beautiful girlfriend and Davenport's wife are both light skinned and positive influences on their men's lives. The skin color politics articulated in the film changes the gaze to the actual people who hurt Antwone Fisher rather than the systemic institutional powers that divide light- and dark-skinned people. Furthermore, this demonizes blackness and forces Antwone to turn away everything that is black.

I have ended two semesters of African American film with screenings of *Antwone Fisher*. Hoping to finish each term with a provocative conversation that brings together the ongoing themes of race, visions of blackness, and contemporary Hollywood, I was not prepared for what occurred during both class meetings.

During the first meeting, several students questioned whether *Antwone Fisher* was indeed African American cinema. Although a majority had identified black film as one written, directed, and starring African Americans, many did not see this film as fulfilling this definition. So, while *Antwone Fisher* was written, directed, and starred African Americans, this film, in their estimation, did not give voice to a black experience. Citing the lack of attention to racism and its narrative location being a military setting, several wondered how it contributed to an understanding of contemporary black life. The conversation certainly raised issues as to the politics of the film, and the meaning of blackness within contemporary America, questioning whether a film that erases racism and focuses on a black experience outside the ghettocentric imagination represented an authentic black experience.

The second experience proved to be more contentious, while mirroring similar issues. It concluded with crying, swearing, and a near classroom fight. Several white students in the class celebrated the film, how it, unlike so many other black films, made them feel good at its conclusion; it had a happy ending worth celebrating. Several echoed this sentiment, prompting a tense debate, where several students of color questioned why the pleasure of white customers should be so important: "It's not always about you," one student stated. Others agreed, noting how giving voice to problems of American racism and the failures of society is rarely pleasurable. This conversation again gave voice to the issues raised within this chapter as several students of color questioned its erasure of state violence, racism, and societal inequality in the place of telling a story of triumph, fortitude, perseverance, and that of a young black male pulling himself up by his bootstraps.

Yet the same issues that prompted outrage from students of color also elicited praise from several white students. Antwone's confrontation with Mrs. Tate illustrates this fact—searching for his mother, he returns home and reluctantly seeks out the help of Mrs. Tate. She is initially uncooperative, but Antwone blasts her: "This is my time. It don't matter what you tried to do, you couldn't destroy me. I'm still standing. I'm still strong. And I always will be." As I looked around the classroom, the racial divide was clear. Several white students cried at the sight of resiliency; others silently clapped as proud parents might. Students of color were less festive, voicing their contempt for its overly simplistic narrative, one that lets America off the hook while expressing resentment for the celebration of Antowne's success, as if it exonerated America.

These conversations do more than give voice to issues concerning the film's narrative, audience reception, and its ideological pronouncements regarding race, privilege, and the American Dream. The clear ways that *Antwone Fisher* does not unsettle hegemonic notions of blackness, nation, the state, or contemporary American race relations confirm more than challenge the often harsh conditions of black urban communities. *Antwone Fisher* tells viewers resources and programs in black urban communities across the globe do not need to be institutionalized or supported; rather each member of that society has a choice to make their situation better. Thus, all accountability is taken off social programs and placed solely on the individual.

TRAINING DAY

Set in the urban center of L.A., *Training Day* is writer David Ayer and director Antoine Fuqua's vision of the (seemingly) never-ending street conflicts between cops and criminals. Ayer hails from South Central Los Angeles and Fuqua from Pittsburgh; thus the representations in this film exist under the auspices of authenticity. In writing this film, Ayer essentially set out to answer one particular question: do we want more effective police or police who follow the letter of the law? Ayer and Fuqua set the stage for answering this question with the oppositional characters of Officer Jake Hoyt and Detective Sergeant Alonzo Harris: the first a rookie naïve to the ways of the street, the second a seasoned, if corrupt, veteran of the street wars. "I wanted to capture the rough and raw reality of the law enforcement mind-set in inner cities and look at where it comes from and also where it can lead. I wanted to ask the question: 'When a cop goes bad, what does it do not only to the man but to the community?'" says Ayer (On Yahoo.com).

"I know how lucky I am," says Officer Jake Hoyt (Ethan Hawk) to his wife in the opening scene of *Training Day*. Hoyt is referring to his impending trial, his training day, with Detective Sergeant Alonzo Harris (Denzel Washington), the commanding officer of one of the LAPD's most aggressive narcotics units. Hoyt first meets with Alonzo at a coffee shop, where he is introduced not only to Alonzo the cop, but Alonzo the homophobe—already, Alonzo bears the marks of dominant notions of black masculinity—crude, sexually aggressive (Alonzo offers to sleep with Jake's wife for the sake of giving her a son; "I'll hook your old lady up . . . I can't miss"), and homophobic. The two men proceed to Alonzo's car ("the office") where Jake professes that he will do anything Alonzo wants him to.

In the car, Alonzo and Jake make their way to a corner on which an associate/informant of Alonzo's waits to make a deal. After this dealer makes a sale to a couple of college students, Alonzo and Jake run down the kids and confiscate the weed they just purchased. In a ploy to make Jake prove his loyalty to the cause, Alonzo forces Jake to smoke the marijuana they just confiscated, because "an effective narcotics officer should know, and love, narcotics." Jake tentatively obliges, and the two men move onto the home of another Alonzo associate, Roger (an LA kingpin played by Scott Glenn), where Alonzo's looming conflict with the Russian mafia is first introduced. Apparently, Alonzo overextended himself in Las Vegas over the weekend and is in it deep with said Russians.

After their visit, they return to the "office" where, in a drug-induced stupor, Jake sees two men attacking a teenage girl in an alley. Jake makes Alonzo stop the car, and Jake flies to the girl's rescue, beating the men into submission as Alonzo watches quietly until the men are subdued. Alonzo enters the scene, calming the girl down by telling her to get her cousins to "get her back," and sends her on her way. Alonzo begins his interrogation/punishment of the attackers, pistol-whipping one of the men. Jake, in silent dismay, watches Alonzo in action. The conflict ends with Jake picking up the girl's wallet and getting back into the car with Alonzo. In the car, Alonzo passes along some gems of wisdom in law enforcement—let the animals take care of the animals, let street justice prevail. Alonzo envisions himself as a wolf out to catch other wolves in order to protect the sheep. "Let the garbage men take care of the garbage; we're professional anglers, we go after the big fish," says Alonzo.

Back in the office it's back to fishing. Alonzo and Jake roll up to a street corner where they attempt to bait a dealer in a wheelchair played by Snoop Dog. A pursuit ensues, ending in another Alonzo-style interrogation culminating in naming Snoop's supplier, enigmatically referred to as "The Sandman." Jake and Alonzo track the true identity of the Sandman and proceed to his house. Alonzo serves a fake warrant to the Sandman's significant other (Macy Gray) to gain entry into her house. Charged with suspect control, Jake catches a glimpse of Alonzo pocketing something in the bedroom. The men leave, Alonzo claiming that they had made a mistake. At the urging of Macy Gray, Alonzo gives her the warrant (a take-out Chinese menu) and leaves. Alonzo gets into a shoot-out with some random gang-bangers outside of the house, and the men flee in a hail of gunfire.

Out of harm's way, the men move onto another neighborhood known as the Jungle, a place where Jake is not to go without Alonzo by his side. This neighborhood is not only the home of Alonzo's mistress and son, but a place where Alonzo reins as alpha wolf due to his coercion of the black and Latino male population; he boasts that he'll jail any who cross the line. After this interlude, it's back to the office and off to a meeting with the Wise Men— a three-member collective of LAPD superiors and DAs. Alonzo and the Wise Men confer on how to handle the situation with the Russians.

Back in the office, Alonzo phones his team to tell them it's time to cash in an account—the ill-gained retirement fund of Roger. Alonzo's team greet Jake with hostility. Nevertheless, they suit up in their SWAT gear and serve the search warrant to Roger. Alonzo explains that Roger is being taxed by the Wise Men, and the team proceeds to unearth and confiscate Roger's fortune. Covering the true motivations behind the cash confiscation, Alonzo executes Roger, but later reports, with his team's support, that Jake killed Roger upon entry to the house. This marks Jake's break with Alonzo, as Alonzo reveals that he had planned this set-up of Jake all week. "It's not what you know, it's what you can prove," says Alonzo. And it is now the word of Alonzo and his men against that of Jake. "I didn't sign up for this," says Jake. Indeed, it seems that street justice and the life of a wolf is not the life for Jake.

After the raid at Roger's, Jake and Alonzo move to the house of another informant of Alonzo's. This visit masquerades as philanthropy, as Alonzo claims he is dropping off goods for the family of an incarcerated informant. The family is Latino, the men marked by their toughness and gang affiliations—that is, their criminality. Alonzo disappears and Jake is left with the Latino men, who refuse to let Jake leave. Jake slowly begins to realize that this is another setup, and he is the intended victim. Jake attempts an escape from the house and is beaten, cuffed, and dragged into the bathtub, where he is to be executed. One of the men finds the wallet of the girl in Jake's pocket; the girl happens to be the cousin of Smiley, one of the gangstas. Jake's act of duty earlier in the day now pays off, and Jake's life is spared.

Alonzo, all the while, is back at the home of his mistress and preparing for his meeting with the Russians. Jake tracks Alonzo down, intending to keep him from his meeting and bring some justice to the corrupt day. A fight ensues, which includes a gun battle that endangers Alonzo's mistress and his son. Jake triumphs in the fight, but his success depended on the interference of the neighborhood gang members, who, tired of Alonzo's corruption, align themselves with Jake and allow him to leave the 'hood with Alonzo's money. Alonzo swears vindication against those who have wronged him, proclaiming "King Kong ain't got shit on me!" Despite his bravado and threats of prosecution, Alonzo's colleagues turn their collective back as Alonzo proceeds to his meeting without his payoff cash, which causes the Russians to surround his car and execute him. Jake goes home with the cash while a voiceover news broadcast explains that Alonzo died while serving a high-risk warrant, which is a reference to a threat made by Alonzo against Jake after raiding Roger's house.

Despite the warped yet hegemonic relationship between Hoyt and Harris (virtuous white protagonist, corrupt black antagonist), *Training Day* deploys the classic buddy formula. However, the film deviates from both the long-standing formula that paints the white buddy as a source of salvation for the otherwise uncivilized black male. In this newer version, there is no possibility for Alonzo's redemption; Jake and Alonzo function as an alternative twosome. *Training Day* thus tells the classic story of good and evil, of criminal and law-abiding, of Jake Hoyt, one of LAPD's finest triumphing over the corrupt and dangerous Alonzo Harris.

From our initial introduction to Alonzo Harris, strutting across the street without regard for cars or rule of law, his leather jacket, gold chain and skull cap, and his arrogance, we quickly realize that he is not a typical cop. His car is "sexy," a black Monte Carlo, decked out with phat chrome, hydraulics, and a bangin system. Just as his guns are not department issued, Alonzo Harris is clearly more criminal than cop.

Hoyt's initial introduction is quite different, with the focus being on his family. Unlike Harris, who has four children, Jake Hoyt embodies the traditional American family, the identity of a real police officer. He has a wife, a child, a suburban house, and is actively pursuing the American Dream. He fantasizes about a big house and a career as a detective. He merely wants what others have already achieved in terms of financial and professional success. The source of redemption for the LAPD and the state within *Training Day* emanates from the actions of Jake Hoyt. Unlike Alonzo, who embodies all that is corrupt within the police, Hoyt represents that which is good, not only within the police but within humanity. As Alonzo spends much of his day scheming and engaging in criminal activities, Jake Hoyt is dedicated to protecting and serving the community, particularly its women and children. Nowhere is this more evident than when Jake recklessly and selflessly saves the young, light-skinned Chicana, Letty, a Catholic schoolgirl, from two would-be-rapists. Able to overcome his PCP high (induced because of pressure from Alonzo) and a lack of concern for protecting the streets from his partner, Jake witnesses the attempted rape from the car, instinctually jumping out of the car to save this young woman. As Alonzo slowly walks to the aid of his partner, the two would-be rapists beat Hoyt, who places himself in harm's way because it is his job, because of his yearning to protect and serve. Whereas Harris takes this moment to abuse, intimidate, and beat up the black suspect, who initially tells him to "suck his dick," Hoyt ignores the more benign and less sexualized taunts from the white suspect, who repeatedly calls him a "pig" and a "pussy," instead picking up the young girl's wallet as he returns to his job of securing justice within and for the community. Unhappy with how Harris handled the situation, Hoyt passively contradicts him for letting the suspects go:

Harris: You want to run and gun stay in patrol. This is investigation, alright. Let the garbage men handle the garbage. We're professional anglers; we go after big fish. Going after that monkey-strong crack head motherfuckers, anyways. You know they would have killed you without hesitating.

Hoyt: That is why they belong in prison.

Harris: For what; they got beat down. They lost their rock; they lost their money. Those eses from the Eastside are probably gonna smoke 'em. What else do you want?

Hoyt: I want justice.

Harris: Is that not justice?

Hoyt: That's street justice.

Harris: What's wrong with street justice?

Hoyt: Oh, just let the animals wipe themselves out.

Harris: God willing Fuck 'em and everybody who look likes them. . . . To protect the sheep you gotta catch the wolf. It takes a wolf to catch a wolf.

Hoyt: What?

Harris: I said, you protect the sheep by killing the motherfuckin' wolf.

The film's attempt to give voice to police abuse and to the ways "street justice" falls short because of the racial text of the film. In individualizing criminally minded police through the black body of Harris vis-à-vis the law-abiding white body of Hoyt, the problem becomes not the police or even the state but the infiltration of these institutions by criminals. In other words, according to *Training Day,* abuse does not reflect a systemic problem but rather the presence of wolves within the sheep's den. Alonzo, as a wolf, a criminal, is the source of abuse rather than the institutions of policing. Just as criminals are constructed within the film and throughout American culture, Harris is shown to have little respect for life or the rights of others, telling Hoyt, "we're the police, we gonna do whatever we want." Throughout the film, however, Hoyt embodies a benevolent and proper vision of policing, eschewing Harris's attempts to corrupt him, eventually telling him that "I became a police officer to put away the drug dealer, the criminals, not to become one." Given the varied meanings of race, the film thus replicates the widespread belief in blackness as deviant and criminal, regardless of whether they are in prison or are responsible for enforcing laws, whereas whiteness (and therefore the police, the state) signifies protection, heroism, and kindness.

The film's redemption of the badge through Hoyt and his embodiment of a protecting white masculinity is not limited by instincts to save Letty, or even his actions compared to those of Alonzo. Alonzo takes the opportunity to terrorize these "monkey-strong crack heads," who he refers to as his maggots and garbage as he taunts them with sexual threats, promises of death, and challenges to their masculinity. Rather redemption comes through Hoyt's decision to restrain his power. Compelled by Alonzo to terrorize the men, Hoyt opts to take the high road, refusing to succumb to the criminality of the assaults. The scene is especially instructive because while it appears to be a normalized struggle between good (cops) and evil (assailants) in the name of an innocent Chicana, it reifies dominant notions of blackness as the embodiment of evil. Both Alonzo and the black assailant signify the degeneracy, criminality, and hypersexuality often associated with black masculinity. Just as Alonzo terrorizes the assailants through sexual threats ("suck my dick," or his threat to send him to "booty house"), the black attacker insults Hoyt with equally sexualized language ("I'm gonna fuck you too cop," "Suck my dick, bitch"), reducing goodness to whiteness while blackness is equated to criminality/hypersexuality. Beyond replicating long-standing stereotypes, this scene, as representative of the larger narrative structure, reduces state violence to the criminality of a black cop, not only deinstitutionalizing the state's involvement with the degradation of ghetto life, but denying the effects of racism on contemporary life since a black man is the source of suffering for black and brown residents of South Central Los Angeles. In other words, Hoyt's selfless decision to save Letty reflects the larger argument of the film that crime, poverty, and the struggles of

America's ghetto reflects a criminalized (and sexualized) culture that guides those who police and live within the jungle. Jake, who nobly chooses protecting a young Chicana woman over his own safety, is ultimately saved because of his choice.

The deployment of racialized and sexualized stereotypes of blackness is not limited to this scene, just as a reconstitution of whiteness and the police (state) as sources of salvation and redemption through Hoyt transcend this particular scene. In one scene, as Detective Harris terrorizes a woman (played by Macy Gray) and her son as he searches to steal some drug money, Hoyt sits with the young boy, hoping to put his nerves at ease. The juxtaposing shots of Hoyt and the young man, alongside the chaos of Harris pillaging their house as a thief, embodies another theme of this film and another recent inscription of the Hollywood ghettocentric imagination: the sources of danger are those criminals, not the system.

In another scene, Hoyt sits with Hector, Alonzo's son, who gets little attention from his father. Stopping by the house for some lunch and sex, Harris fulfills dominant visions of black masculinity as absentee father guided by his sexual needs, whereas Hoyt is compassionate and concerned, ultimately falling asleep with the boy in his arms. The varied visions of protector and father-figure guides much of the film: Harris is a failure as a father of his own children and those he has been empowered to protect, and Hoyt sacrifices everything for his wife, child, and community. The goodness that Jake provides to this otherwise ignored community of blacks and Latinos is reflected not just in his compassion and care for Hector (he and not Alonzo hugs and protects this child) but in his acceptance of the nuclear family. It is Jake who is monogamous with one child, while Alonzo not only has a mistress, but at least one "illegitimate" child. Thus the film uses their relationship to family/women as key toward understanding their approaches to policing, which, as with other films, erases state violence and persistence of institutional racism for explanations focusing on the individual (and cultural) failures of people of color.

Although one might read *Training Day,* with its narrative focus on police corruption, as a voice of opposition, it ultimately validates the role of the state, and in turn discounts the prevalence of racialized state violence through Hoyt, who gives the street back to the people. Given dominant stigmas of black criminality, Alonzo functions as a rogue cop who cannot escape his blackness; it becomes the ultimate sign (or the only explanation) of his behavior. The problem is not the state or the occupation of America's "jungles" with police, but with those criminals who run the streets, whether they have a badge or a gang affiliation. Jared Sexton poignantly argues:

Alonzo's adventurism surely serves as a stage for the film's extended meditation on proper police conduct (its immediate inspiration is the notorious Ramparts Division scandal), yet the frightening image of unchecked cops-turned-criminal is overshadowed by a discourse of *a priori* black criminality. Hence, the supposed scandal of the black "rogue cop"—which might otherwise provoke incisive reappraisal about the reach of law—cannot avoid contamination by an extant culture of criminalization that takes blackness as its master sign. (Sexton 2003)

In other words, *Training Day* does more than redefines state violence through Alonzo and his embodiment of blackness. His threat and danger emanate not only from his criminal predilections and his abuse of power but from his threats to the dominant visions of Christian morality—his hypersexuality, his multiple children ("I got four sons"—five in fact), and his propensity for vice. Like those he's empowered to arrest, Alonzo is the true threat to prosperity and safety within South Central Los Angeles, until Hoyt (as the true representative of the state) can purge his presence from the ghetto.

Alonzo is more than a corrupt cop who inflicts violence on communities of color, or someone who joins forces with the Three Wise Men or the Russian mob to fill his own pockets. He demonstrates evil through his propensity toward vice (drug use, drinking on job) and violence, his sexual appetite, and his lack of concern for women and children (his ignoring the raping of the Chicano girl; his use of his son as a shield). By contrast, Jake represents all that is good—he is loyal, trustworthy, family-minded, honest, and compassionate. His moral and righteous qualities motivate his interactions at home and his desire to be a police officer, as well as his efforts in the streets. Unlike Alonzo who loses the trust and respect of the people through his criminality, his abuse of power, and his contempt for the people, Jake garners their support through his actions. Throughout the film, Hoyt shows himself to be worthy, to be a servant of the people, whose actions, although not intended to be a source of salvation, ultimately spares his life and leads to his acceptance within the community. While Alonzo doesn't "believe in nada," Jake gains acceptance through his actions, especially in comparison to the evil perpetrated by Alonzo. Jared Sexton offers the following assessment of *Training Day,* in terms of its understanding of policing inside the black community:

Winning hearts and minds, then, is in leading by example. The community's specific hatred of this black cop overrides their general (I would think healthy) skepticism and hostility toward all cops and even goes so far as to encourage their active backing of a white cop who will likely return, as per his job description, to violate many among their ranks. Imagine the target of an assassination helping the shooter to clean the rifle and adjust the sights. Something more than self-incrimination. (Sexton 2003)

Communal disdain for the police and state violence is erased through the film's inscription of community support for Hoyt, and "good policing." Rather than revolt or rise up against the state and its domestic army, the residents of the jungle (and even the Chicanos empowered to kill Hoyt) collaborate with Hoyt to eject the black cop, rather than the LAPD, from the jungle.

Hoping to meet his deadline, which requires Harris to pay $1 million to the Russian mob or face death following an altercation resulting in the death of a Russian mobster, Harris concludes that he must disarm Hoyt, the protector of the law. Leaving him at the house of a group of Latino *vatos,* contracted by Harris to kill Hoyt, young Jake narrowly escapes this death sentence. Unknowingly, he had saved Smiley's (one of his would-be assassins) cousin, Letty, demonstrating that he was down, that he was invested in "protecting and serving" the community. His efforts to be "real cop" not only resulted in his life being spared, but garnered the support of Smiley and his homeboys, who were willing to kill him not just for the money but because he "was a pig," "for being a cop," and "for being a buster."

With his life spared, Hoyt does not return home, but rather enters the "jungle," a place Harris had told him never to enter without him, as he (the white cop) was not safe without the assistance and legitimacy of a black male (cop). After Hoyt's successful repossession of the drug money Harris had stolen in an effort to save his own life with the Russian mob, and a shootout that results in Hoyt risking his own life to protector Hector (Alonzo's son) and Harris using that same child as part of his escape and efforts to kill Jake, the two partners meet in the midst of the "jungle," with its residents venturing out of their houses as to witness the final battle between good and evil. Unable to subdue Hoyt, Alonzo Harris calls on his black brethren to kill Hoyt, leading only one individual to place a gun on the ground, telling him "you gotta put your own work in around here." Not surprised, Jake reminds Alonzo, "they are not like you. I'm not like you." Realizing he was not on his own, Hoyt exhibits force and violence for the first time in the film when Alonzo attempts to retrieve his gun; Hoyt shoots Harris in the ass. Refusing to kill this unarmed man, Hoyt once again demonstrates his righteousness, disarming him physically and disempowering him emotionally in snatching his badge from his neck: "You don't deserve this." Representing the film's most dramatic moments, Jake's act of righteousness and justice resonates with the residents of the jungle, prompting the same man who had provided Alonzo with a gun to retrieve that same weapon, raising it in the direction of Harris—"Jake, go ahead and bounce, homey. Get up out of here. We got your back." With these words, Jake safely leaves the "jungle," subjected only to the angry words of Harris:

I'm putting cases on all you bitches. You think you can do this to me. . . . Jake . . . You think you can do this to me. You motherfuckers will be playin basketball in Pelican Bay [one of California's most notorious prisons] when I get finished with you. Show program. Nigger, 23-hour lockdown. I am the man up in this peace. You'll never see the light of day. Who the fuck you think you fucking with. I am the police. I run shit here. You just live here. . . . King Kong ain't got shit on me. . . . You can shoot me, but you can't kill me.

In fact, Alonzo Harris did find death, not at the hands of the law, but because of his temper and deviant behavior, and because he long turned his back on the community. The film ends with the Russian mob executing him, as he appears to be on his way to the airport. As the camera centers on Harris, arms spread, back to the car, as if he were Jesus, as if he were sacrificed, cruci- fied gangsta style, for the return of good and order. While Harris is left on the street, where the film implies he deserves to rest, the film ends with Hoyt returning home to his wife, his child, his suburban home, and the persistent dream of American success.

Offering a powerful commentary, *Training Day* imagines the goodness of the state (rather than criminals like Harris) controlling places like the jungle. The film rightly constitutes most individuals inside the "jungle" as law-abiding and intolerant of street terrorism, but it positions the state as an institution of protection. Given scholarship surrounding contemporary American police, and even popular culture inscriptions evident in *Prison Song* or the artistry of Jay-Z, Talib Kwali, and NWA, the celluloid residents of *Training Day's* jungle are likely to experience harassment, surveillance, and systematic arrest in the real-life version of this community. *Training Day,* like *Baby Boy* and *Antoine Fisher,* however, erases the inherent violence of an increasingly powerful police state, focusing instead on the inherent crimi- nality of blackness, which is incapable of participating in the goodness of humanity or the righteous actions of officers like Jake Hoyt.

In reconstituting police abuse and brutality through the criminalized body of Alonzo Harris, *Training Day* erases the racial context and history of Amer- ican policing. In other words, the abuse and corruption that Harris inflicts on his own people are disconnected from Rodney King, the Rampart scandal, or any number of incidences of police brutality, abuse and corruption, all of which have been particularly harmful to communities of color. Rather he is connected to the "blackcriminalman," to those communities often associated with violence and criminality on the other side of the law. "Detective Alonzo Harris, veritably embodied the dark side of law enforcement, cast as a unscru- pulous 'rogue cop' whose singular ferociousness and ultimately incompetent scheming seemed to absorb the corruption of the entire LAPD, highlight- ing and absolving a racist city power structure in one breathtaking gesture," argues Jared Sexton. In other words, *Training Day* chronicles the "living nightmare of unchecked (white) police power and purging the (racial) ter- ror that such impunity necessarily produces through his spectacularly violent death." Before discussing the ultimate slaying of King-King, it is important to reflect on his initial purging from the jungle, to what amounted to be a most heroic and redemptive act employed by Hoyt.

Although it is easy to see the connection between *Training Day* and the history of ghettocentric films, ranging from *Superfly* to *Baby Boy,* in terms of their mutual concern with the "ghetto condition," *Training Day* is particu- larly powerful because of its inscription of post-Civil Rights racial condition. Unlike other films that are defined by their inscription of an unmarked rac- ism, deployment of cultural theories of poverty, or their imagination of the

"Man" as the source of problems, *Training Day* imagines the ghetto through a narrative where blacks are in power. Read along side the visible presence of Condoleezza Rice, Colin Powell, and police chiefs, mayors and others in "officialdom," Alonzo represents a powerful public discourse of post-Civil Rights America: one where blacks are in power and therefore persistent problems must be considered outside of racial contexts. In essence, Alonzo, as a cop, as someone in connection with the "Three Wise Men," not only signifies power as a controlling force inside the "jungle," but because of his criminality, his willingness to violate laws, holds the ultimate power within communities of color. In chronicling corruption and state violence through this black male body, *Training Day* not only plays off long-standing stereotypes of blackness and reconstitutes state violence through a criminalized body, but reifies dominant narratives that imagine the last 30 years as one of progress, one that resulted in the ascendance of Powell, Rice, and Alonzo Harris.

Jadakiss once asked the question: "Why did Denzel have to be crooked before he took it?" The *it* refers to the Oscar he received for his performance as Alonzo Harris in *Training Day*. Perhaps Alonzo was more than crooked, but the reincarnation of King-Kong at the closing of the twentieth century, ushering in the twenty-first century of African American cinema. Like King Kong, Alonzo Harris embodied a threat to the community, to order, mandating his extermination at the hands of Jake Hoyt, a white police officer who represents the possibility of good policing. Deviating from past ghettocentric imaginations, such as *Menace II Society* and *Boyz n the Hood Trainging Day,* reimagines the police as savior, as protector and benevolent white father that rightly works to disempower the criminalized, culturally-polluted, and dangerous black masculinity evident in varying ways in the bodies of Jody, Antwone and Alonzo. Whether through mimicking white masculinity, joining the military or the intervention of the police, all three films erase racism through historic lenses, instead painting redemption of black masculinity and the entire community through white intervention.

PRISON SONG

Before a single line is delivered or even a visual introduction of the film's main character, *Prison Song* establishes a clear tone, ideology, and progressive politics with its opening sequence. Following in the tradition of *Boyz n the Hood,* albeit with greater progressive focus, *Prison Song* begins with a powerful set of statistics, immediately followed by a visual juxtaposition of prisons with schools, establishing a clear narrative and political trajectory in its initial five minutes.

- Seven million children have a parent who is currently in prison or jail or has been recently released on probation or parole.
- Black children are 46 times more likely than whites to be sentenced to juvenile prison.

- A total of 4.6 million black men out of a voting population of 10.4 million have lost their right to vote due to felony convictions
- Newborn black males have greater than a one in four chance of going to prison during their lifetimes.

These jarring statistics are immediately followed by a crucial opening scene, which not only establishes the politics of the film but also sets the foundation for its narrative. Immediately thereafter, the film cuts to a close-up, revealing a school bus that now serves as a vehicle used to transport youth to a juvenile justice center. As several young black and Latino youth wearing orange jump-suits get on the bus, the film jumps to a shot of several black and Latino youth quickly walking to school; they are surrounded by fences, graffiti, and the despair of their community. Entering school, they are frisked and must past through metal detectors, yet they arrive at school on a yellow bus, rather than the blue prison buses that pass by and transport their classmates each and every day. This powerful opening scenes sets the tone for this impor-tant counternarrative that reveals the greater odds (and societal emphasis) of black and brown youth spending time in prison than within educational insti-tutions, as well as the widespread effects of the prison industrial complex on black and brown youth. Compared to previously discussed films, *Prison Song* begins with a clear commentary on race and America's institutions, painting a picture of a failed racist system, rather than one about individual failures unable to capitalize on the fulfillment of King's dream. *Prison Song* makes clear from the get-go that racism, greed, and the system have over the last 20 years pushed black and Latino youth onto blue rather than yellow buses, resulting in societal problem that demands action. In this light, *Prison Song* is successful in challenging the dominant ghettocentric imagination.

Prison Song, originally intended to be a full-fledged musical (this concept tested poorly with audiences) is a drama about a young black boy growing up in urban America. Produced by Robert DeNiro's Tribecca films and written and directed by Darnell Martin (Q-Tip also holds a writing credit), *Prison Song* is comprised of a cast of various hip-hop artists from Q-Tip to Fat Joe. Specifically, *Prison Song* chronicles the trials and tribulations of Elijah (Q-Tip), who loses his father, mother, best friend, and mentor to the criminal justice system. Finding solace and opposition in art, he secures a brighter future with a scholarship to college, only to lose it because of limited scholarship avail-ability, and eventually joining his family and friends inside one of America's private prisons. While chronicling this sad tale and giving voice to Elijah's own resistance through art, the film's narrative is merely a vehicle of critique for the prison industrial complex and its effect on the black community.

This film illustrates how hip-hop culture holds the potential to offer a critical social and political commentary of what goes on in urban areas across the United States. It goes beyond a tale of an individual, elucidating how state violence and massive levels of incarceration within the black community impact families and communities. The main character, Elijah, is surrounded by his mother (Mary J. Blige), his father figure Uncle Steve (Harold Perrineau Jr.), and his neighborhood best friend. The film offers a critical commentary about the prison industrial complex, juvenile court system, children of color in foster care, mental illness, and artistic resistance to economic and racial exploitation.

Prison Song, while not a perfect film, represents a response to the ghetto-centric imagination that focuses on personal failures, constructing America's black communities as sites of degradation, pathology, and self-failure. Whether blaming black mothers for the criminal actions of black males, citing culture of poverty theories, or merely erasing the realities of racism, the hegemonic vision of the ghetto that emanates from both white and black Hollywood reaffirms dominant ideologies and depictions of America's black inner cities. *Prison Song* offers an alternative vision to dominant Hollywood with a film that documents simultaneously the realities of racism, focusing on the role of the state as a force of oppression, and the ways in which African Americans resist subjugation at various levels.

Prison Song tells the story of Elijah and his family, of their struggles with and against state violence, racial profiling, incarceration, and poverty; but it also chronicles the nature, effects, and complexities of the prison industrial complex.

In the 1970s, Angela Davis coined the idea of the prison industrial complex to describe the growth of the prison industry. According to the Website for Critical Resistance, a national abolitionist group, "The prison industrial complex (PIC) is a complicated system situated at the intersection of governmental and private interests that uses prisons as a solution to social, political, and economic problems. The PIC depends upon the oppressive systems of racism, classism, sexism, and homophobia. It includes human rights violations, the death penalty, industry and labor issues, policing, courts, media, community powerlessness, the imprisonment of political prisoners, and the elimination of dissent." Beginning in the wake of the 1960s economic downturns and 1960s radicalism, the decade saw a drastic reallocation of funds toward imprisonment over social programs as a means to deal with protests and economic instability. And this was only the beginning, as each decade ushered in greater spending on prisons and less focus on social programs, resulting in a continuous increase in America's prison population.

Specifically, *Prison Song* elucidates the effects of deindustrialization on black America. Whereas so many films within the ghettocentric genre document the impact of deindustrialization in Los Angeles, *Prison Song* illuminates its effects in New York City. Set in Harlem, we see a city without businesses, without a manufacturing base, and lacking communal foundation.

Beginning in the 1970s and continuing through the 1990s, America's multinational corporations moved manufacturing plants overseas and into less populated suburbs. The movement of jobs from already depressed black communities left many black families in dire straights. A 1982 report authored by the California legislature concluded that South Central Los Angeles neighborhoods experienced a 50 percent rise in unemployment and a significant drop in purchasing power in the wake of deindustrialization (Kelley 1996, p. 192). In a mere three years, the median income for black families had dropped by $2,500 to about $5,900 dollars yearly (Kelley 1996, p. 192). Similar developments were visible in black communities throughout the United States, and in many cases situations were growing worse, rather than improving through the 1980s and 1990s. In 1985, midwestern cities experienced unemployment rates of 50 to 70 percent for black teenagers (Kelley 1998, p. 198). Increased profits, the ease of relocation, and the examples set by other U.S. companies, left inner city blacks, especially youth, without many options. We see this reality with Uncle Steve, Elijah, his mother, and so many others struggling to find economic solvency.

To understand the prison industrial complex in the real world, as well as its presence in the world of Elijah, it is crucial to comprehend the context of deindustrialization. Without jobs, opportunities, or investment in social services for people like Uncle Steve, Elijah, and Thomas, prisons exist as a place of control and confinement. In the wake of the systematic exportation of jobs overseas and the continued gutting of social services, those from urban communities of color increasingly represent a surplus population within capitalist America. A series of structural adjustments that sought to stave off the economic downturns of the late 1960s and 1970s, left huge segments of America's population without an economic future. The most disadvantaged, predominantly people of color, were sacrificed to revitalize the profit margins of the richest few. Such structural changes not only resulted in plant closures, a gutting of social programs, an increased number of part-time jobs, and horrible working conditions, but also facilitated a heightened level of state violence and control. Christian Parenti, in *Lockdown America*, argues that an inherent contradiction exists within all capitalist systems, whereby the poor are both needed and feared. In dealing with such inherent conflicts and contradictions, the state uses various forms of state violence to minimize potential conflict. Parenti states:

Capitalism needs the poor and creates poverty, intentionally through policy and organically through crisis. Yet capitalism is also directly and indirectly threatened by the poor. Capitalism always creates surplus populations, needs surplus populations, yet faces the threat of political, aesthetic, or cultural disruption from those populations. Prison and criminal justice are about managing these irreconcilable contradictions. (Parenti 2000, pp. 238–239)

Beginning in the 1970s and continuing today, there has been a dramatic increase in both state support of the criminal justice system and the number of black youth spending part or all of their life in jail.

Prison Song also shows the business side of private prisons. As with the defense industry, the prison industrial complex represents big business for both the public and private sectors. In fact, owning or running a prison, or working in concert with its maintenance, "no longer constitutes a marginal area of the larger economy" (Davis 2003, p. 88). Leading the prison privatization movement is Corrections Corporation of America (CCA). Early in the Reagan presidency, the Immigration and Naturalization Services (INS) ran an experiment, housing detainees in Houston and Laredo, Texas. Building on its success and the financial support of Kentucky Fried Chicken, Doctor Crants and Tom Beasley, two Tennessee entrepreneurs, set up CCA as the nation's first private prison company. Fifteen years later, CCA controls over half the private prisons in the United States, having amassed 63,000 prison beds. Globally, CCA runs almost 80 prisons in 25 states, Puerto Rico, Australia, and the United Kingdom. Financially, CCA has proven to be a stable and successful company. In 1995, CCA went public at $8 per share. By the end of that year, its stocks soared 462.5 percent to $37 per share. In 1996–1997, CCA's profits increased by 58 percent, from $293 million to $462 million.

With his sentence of 15 years to life, the judge does not send Elijah to Attica or another New York state prison, but to United Prisons Corporation. Although it was uncommon to house murderers at United Prison Corporation, Elijah finds himself there because he is a valuable dollar sign to the prison owners. "State pays $25,000 for that bunk right there," Thomas reminds Elijah and the audience. "It does whatever to make sure it is filled." Beyond maintaining full capacity, the warden increases profits through cutting programs, such as school and recreation, and by withholding basic human necessities like food and water. Elijah's prison experience is very telling concerning private prisons, which usually provide terrible conditions. With limited state oversight and an emphasis on profit over the living conditions of prisoners (seen as animals within larger public undeserving of human rights), abuses are commonplace within private prisons. The power of *Prison Song* lies with its ability to give voice to this problem, all within the narrative. For example, on Elijah's first day in prison, the warden warns him and others of the inhumanity of their private prison: "The privileges you had in state, you don't have here." The U.S. Prisons Corporation is profit business, so cutting back on non-necessities like school or water, and increasing prison populations, are all good for business.

Prison Song offers further insight into private prisons with a powerfully subtle scene that juxtaposes the pristine and massive prison complex with the warden escorting its stockholders around the prison ground. The buildings are modern, resembling an office building or a postmodern industrial park that exudes power and financial growth. The visual glimpse at the prison is startling, especially in comparison to Elijah's school. It is clear that more money was put into this upscale prison than his elementary or high schools. In the background, the warden talks about finances, including plans for prison expansion. It is clear that owning and operating prisons is not just big business, but big profit.

Prison Song also documents the phenomenon of prison labor. As early as the 1970s, Supreme Court Justice Warren Burger called on the state to turn prisons into "factories with fences" (Parenti 2000, p. 230). In recent years, Senator Phil Gramm announced that he wants "to turn every federal prison into a mini industrial park" (Parenti 2000, p. 230). Prison labor is nothing new, dating back to the days of indentured servants, slavery, and chain gangs, but the advance of the prison industrial complex has ushered in an era of greater reliance on and profitability in the exploitation of prison labor. Although sometimes superficial, the narrative gives voice to the often-ignored reality of prison labor, a story erased in both popular culture and other public discourses. As Linda Evans and Eve Goldberg note, prisons are big business:

For private businesses, prison labor is like a pot of gold. No strikes. No union organizing. No health benefits, unemployment insurance, or workers' compensation to pay. No language barriers, as in foreign countries. New leviathan prisons are being built on thousands of eerie acres of factories inside the walls. Prisoners do data entry for Chevron, make telephone reservations for TWA, raise hogs, shovel manure, and make circuit boards, limousines, waterbeds, and lingerie for Victoria's Secret, all at a fraction of the cost of 'free labor.' (Goldberg and Evans 1998)

Other companies using prison labor or reaping prison profits include Boeing, IBM, American Express, Compaq, Honeywell, Motorola, Revlon, Pierre Cardin, GE, and NIKE. Extrark offers a sizable cheap labor source, providing prisoners to Microsoft, Starbucks, JanSport, and U.S. West for packaging and "literature assembly." Eddie Bauer and Victoria's Secret, who pay prisoners 23 cents an hour, use prisoner labor for packaging and manufacturing. "Given all this hard work going on in the big house it would appear that America's 1.8 prisoners are becoming a Third World within, a cheap and bountiful labor reservoir already being tapped by big business and Uncle Sam alike" (Parenti 2000, p. 231). The allure of prison labor is tremendous, given the scant wages paid to prisoners and headaches associated with free labor sources, including strikes, unions, job searches, and insurance.

The biggest employer of prison labor is UNICOR, or the Federal Correctional Industries, which "employs" 18,000 prisoners, offering different products to state agencies. It provides everything from safety goggles, to university furniture, to body armor for the Border Patrol and road signs for the Park Service. In 1998, UNICOR produced $512 million in goods and services by paying its prison workers $40/month for a 40-hour workweek. Some might identify the lack of direct information on the prison industrial complex in this film as a weakness, in that it works from the assumption that the previously noted information is a known reality, but by constructing a narrative that works from a broader context, *Prison Song* gives hope that this history will increasingly enter into public discourses.

To increase profits for stockholders of United Prison Corporations, the warden arranges for prisoners to help destroy a deserted warehouse. As Elijah and his peers are paid only $1.10/hour, this job generates significant profits for both the stockholders and warehouse owners. With an ample amount of cheap labor, the warden and shareholders are able to secure lucrative contracts, while businesses on the outside take advantage of the cheap labor source as well. Even the prisoners desperately tried to secure placement at the warehouse. Although the wages were "worse than those of illegal aliens" and working conditions put them at risk for asbestos poisoning, the little amounts of money give Elijah the ability to buy painting supplies and others the ability to send money to families. Without any money to purchase goods on the inside or send money to families on the outside, Elijah desperately seeks this job without concern for his death. This is but one example of the film's engagement with realities of prison labor.

As United Prison Corporation builds its fortunes off the backs of prisoners (of color), its existence also injures the economic livelihood of its employees. For example, during one scene two guards complain how the arrival of prison resulted in loss of $20/hour job in construction, forcing the guard to accept a poor-paying, unsatisfying, job at the prison. As a system, the prison industrial complex generates huge profits at the expense of prisoners of color and the working-class on the outside. Offering keen analysis on class dynamics, as well as American racism, *Prison Song* stands alone in its progressive reading of the prison industrial complex.

A final issue concerns the conditions of the prisons like those illustrated through *Prison Song*. Despite the hegemonic image generated by *OZ* and Hollywood of prisons being "not so bad," prisons are neither pleasant nor safe. *Prison Song* illustrates the inhumanity of confinement. Regardless of the fact that prisons provide "three hots and a cot," *Prison Song* reveals the pain and difficulty associated with being locked-up—violence, harassment from correctional officers, and the lack of power/agency inherent in a prisoner's life. Numerous wide-angle shots of the inside of cells, or close-ups of barbed wire fences, all the while illustrating the mental anguish resulted from being told when to eat, sleep, and go to bathroom, reflect a powerful counternarrative and image to the dominant story about prisons.

What is crucial to the development of *Prison Song* is the espoused relationship between private prisons, the conditions of those prisons, and agency. Private prisons, as previously mentioned, tend to be more oppressive because of the lack of oversight and accountability. Elijah sets fire to the warehouse as a protest against the dangerous and exploitative "working" conditions. With America's prisons, as evident in *Prison Song*, protest always meets with violent state repression. In this case, Elijah's attempt to regain power and agency elicits a strong response in which the warden orders all water to be cut off for several months; he also removes weights and closes school.

In the midst of a second protest led by Thomas, as a statement in solidity with Elijah, the warden unleashes the guards with an arsenal of mace. Spraying indiscriminately, leaving the prisoners without water to flush out their eyes, these prison guards treated Thomas and his allies as nothing more than animals. Faced with threats of a complaint to the justice department or a lawsuit, a correctional officer reminded Thomas that he was housed at a private prison: "Send all the letters you want. This ain't state; we make out own rules." The unregulated management of the private prison—the social and physical distance between the incarcerated and their means of justice—challenges discourses of "paying one's debt to society" that run rampant through American popular, social, and penal culture. Indeed, "serving time" is the result of policing, the patrolling of racial, class—and economic—borders.

A key element to understanding both the prison industrial complex/state violence and *Prison Song* is policing. Ostensibly, the film documents the ways in which police exist as an occupying army within communities. While engaging in surveillance and constantly harassing youth of color, the police usher or push black men into the prison. Three specific examples from *Prison Song* illustrate this powerful point.

"You got any priors?" Trying to make a living by selling pictures on the streets of New York, Uncle Steve heard these words as the police approached to see if he had the proper permits. Without needed state approval, Uncle Steve was not only subjected to a potential ticket, but in the absence of power, he faced a barrage of disrespect and disempowering police action. Telling him to get his shit out of the area as quickly as possible, the officer continuously asserted his dominance. Uncle Steve, not wanting any trouble, submits to leaving, yet asks the officer not to use profanity in front of Elijah. "This convict is trying to tell me not to swear," the officer tells his partner, throwing the photo display onto the ground. Angered by this repeated disrespect, Uncle Steve intervenes, demonstrating his own agency through a demonstration of his own masculinity. He spits in the direction of the officer, prompting the officer to assert state power by writing Steve a ticket. As the cop shoves the ticket into Steve's pocket, the cop once again reminds Steve of his power as a white male cop: "Take your monkey son home," he says, almost goading Steve into a confrontation. Taking the bait, Steve punches the officer, promoting his swift arrest and incarceration, forever changing his own life, and that of Elijah and his mother. In this case, as in others, the police were wrong. As Uncle Steve warned, in America when a black man gets angry because "they" are wrong, it is the black man who becomes yet another person of color locked up behind bars.

The impact of the police is not limited to a single instance. As a child, Elijah experiences constant surveillance from police, whether at school or in neighborhoods. Without after-school programs, safe parks, or any sort of social programs, as a result of widespread economic cutbacks (structural adjustment programs) during the 1970s and 1980s, Elijah and Thomas find themselves flashing a laser pen at the police. Assuming (probably because they are in a black neighborhood) that they are under attack, the police shoot at the boys. In an attempt to protect themselves, the police then arrest the boys, turning them over to child welfare. Angered by the mistreatment, Elijah's mother attempts to free him, only to be arrested for stabbing one of the prison guards. Her anger, her frustration with the system, and her attempt to assert her own agency result in her incarceration as well.

As Elijah and his girlfriend walk through the neighborhood, the camera focuses on an inconspicuous truck. Two men sit inside, listening and watching for possible criminal activities. Within the black community, the police are constantly watching for, and assuming the existence of, crime, a virtual guarantee of a prison population of more than 1 million African Americans.

The power and progressive orientation of *Prison Song* do not lie solely with its documenting of the extent and effects of the prison industrial complex, but also in its chronicling of related social institutions. It does not simply reveal the pernicious nature of America's prison system, but also the relationship between the prison system, education, mental health professionals, and the police. In revealing how vanishing funds for America's schools relates to growing prison populations or the links between policing (the war on drugs) and incarceration, all within the context of twenty-first century racism, *Prison Song* tells a powerful story while delivering a progressive definition of the prison industrial complex.

From its initial moments, with its visual juxtaposition of prison and schools, *Prison Song* makes clear that the absence of educational opportunities for youth of color is systematically funneling them into America's prisons. Whether because of increased spending for prisons at the expense of schools or because schools function as a transition into prisons, these American institutions are inextricably linked. The simultaneity in the rise of prison populations of color and the systematic dismantling of public schools is not a coincidence. In New York, the richest school district spent $38,572 per student in 1992; that's seven times what the poorest district spent—$5,423. In *Prison Song,* Elijah and Thomas attend a school that looks like a prison rather than a place of learning. No play yards, jungle gyms, or books. Instead, these 12-year-olds pass through medal detectors to enter school. Kenneth Saltman, in the introduction to *Education as Enforcement,* warns about the transformation of American public schools—those that predominantly house students of color—into places increasingly resembling prisons and military installations:

Military generations running schools, students in uniforms, metal detectors, police presence, high-tech ID card dog tags, real time Internet-based surveillance cameras, mobile hidden surveillance cameras, security consultants, chainlink fences, surprise searches—as U.S. public schools invest in record level of school security apparatus they increasingly resemble the military and prisons. (2004, p. 1)

Throughout the country and visible within *Prison Song,* youth of color face constant surveillance from security guards rather than encouragement from teachers. The environment in which Elijah, Thomas, and their black and Latino friends are required to learn is no more encouraging to their future. An early scene captures this sentiment, as Elijah eagerly sits in the front of the class awaiting that day's lesson. The camera pans between his beaming anticipation and evidence of the lack of interest of his classmates. Elijah, unlike his peers, who are too busy throwing paper airplanes, fighting, or otherwise participating in the class-sanctioned chaos to notice the arrival of teachers, shows an eagerness and determination. He is alone, without even a teacher to help him fulfill his goals and dreams. His white teacher enters the dilapidated classroom, as the camera flashes to a moldy ceiling with water dripping at a steady pace onto the teacher's desk. The obviously despondent and defeated teacher sits down, throwing his paycheck of $315 dollars onto the desk, resolved not to teach as his kids run around the room. This initial scene makes clear the existence of two Americas: an America with passionate teachers, pristine classrooms, and opportunity, and an America with frustrated, paralyzed teachers, dirty classrooms, and despair. Frantz Fanon, in *Wretched of the Earth,* brilliantly reflects on the geographic and physical differences between those communities of color and those of the white majority.

The zone where the natives live is not complementary to the zone inhabited by the settlers. The two zones are opposed, but not in the service of a higher unity. Obedient to the rule of Aristotelian logic, they both follow the principle of reciprocal exclusivity. No conciliation is possible, for of the two terms, one is superfluous. The settlers' town is a strongly built town, all made of stone and steel. It is a brightly lit town; the streets are covered with asphalt, and the garbage cans swallow all the leavings, unseen, unknown and hardly thought about. The settler's feet are never visible, except perhaps in the sea; but there you're never close enough to see them. His feet are protected by strong shoes although the streets of his town are clean and even, with no holes and stones. The settler's town is a well-fed town, an easygoing town; its belly is always full of good things. The settlers' town is a town of white people, of foreigners.

The town belonging to the colonized people, or at least the native town, the Negro village, the medina, the reservation, is a place of ill fame, peopled by men of evil repute. They are born there, it matters little where or how; they die there, it matters not where, nor how. It is a world without spaciousness; men live there on top of the other. The native town is a hungry town, starved of bread, of meat, of shoes, of coal, of light. The native town is a crouching village, a town on its knees, a town wallowing in the mire. (1965, pp. 38–39)

Just as in colonial Africa, people of color remain confined to America's ghetto, inside its worst schools. *Prison Song* provides representation of this reality, illustrating the effects of these conditions beyond high dropout rates and low rates of college attendance. As the foundation for a story on prisons, the film's initial engagement with America's schools encapsulates its argument that education (and its failures) exists as a foundation for incarceration as much as it does for opportunity. The path into prison, made clear by these powerful juxtapositions, begins with inept teachers and dreadful schools that prepare youth of color to sing a prison song rather than a university fight song.

Prison Song, however, does not tell a predetermined story, as if Elijah's ticket into prison was punched as a one-way trip to lockdown America. Elijah resists, and to a certain degree overcomes, the obstacles of state violence and white supremacy. Whether in the face of poor schools, police harassment, the arrest of "Uncle Steve," or the institutionalization of his mother, Elijah finds a way to make it. Without support or guidance, especially while living in a group home, Elijah still secures admission into college. He plays the "game" by their rules and gets into art school, challenging dominant stereotypes (of media; Hollywood, white supremacist discourses) and too-often traveled paths into prison. Unfortunately, the promise of state financial assistance is put into question by budget cuts, leaving him with $4,000 less support. Without needed tuition dollars, Elijah turns to Big Ski, the neighborhood drug dealer for a little bit of work. Without the possibility of a job, support from state, or parental contributions (his father was killed, his mother institutionalized, his father figure incarcerated, and jobs shipped to the Sun Belt or overseas), Big Ski offered him the best option to secure the money needed to attend school.

Not everyone agreed with Elijah's plan despite its appearance of rationality. On hearing about Elijah's new job, Uncle Steve confronts Elijah during his regular visit in prison.

Steve: Why you fucking with Big Ski?

Elijah: I need the money.

Steve: Since when you all concerned with the money.

Elijah: Let me show you something [camera cuts to letter]. They cut the state and the fed. Aight. They cut the state and the fed.

Steve: What you talking bout?

Elijah: $4,000 dollars. I gotta come with $4,000 dollars in 2 months, man.

Steve: How they gonna soup you up, tell you can get into the school and not give you money to go to school. Does that make any sense to you?

Elijah: That's how it is! Aight! Thy do their things so I gotta do my mother-fuckin thing. You feel me?

Steve: I feel you. You have the right to be mad. They wrong! You right; they wrong! They have you the scholarship, they have you the money and they took it away. They wrong! They gave you opportunity. You have a right to be mad—I hear you! But let me tell you something, E, when a black man gets mad he winds up in here. And I don't want to see you here. You feel me?

This powerful cinematic moment of foreshadowing offers a scathing critique of the state for its failure to offer educational opportunities to black youth. The emphasis on policing over learning, on prison construction over new schools, on stipends for prisoners over scholarships, leaves Elijah without the possibility of fulfilling his dream. He does have the right to be mad: his obedience to their rules did not generate the promised outcome.

In the end, Elijah tears up his papers for art school, leaving himself with little hope or promise. His frustrations manifest in an argument with his girlfriend, who chides him for leaving her for college. Big Pete (Fat Joe) then challenges Elijah, who he thinks is a stuck-up college boy. This altercation, his anger, mirrors Uncle Steve's worst nightmare, as his anger and his frustrations with the system result in his incarceration.

Another key dimension of the ghettocentric genre is providing voice and vision to daily resistance. In varying degrees, this genre of film not only elucidates the effects/realities of racism, violence, and poverty inside America's ghettos, but also the ways that African Americans resist through daily struggle. When O-Dog and Doughboy sell drugs as an alternative to traditional capitalism, or Furious Styles starts his own business as a challenge to gentrification, the ghettocentric genre challenges discourses of passivity and contentment. In the face of state violence, poverty, and police surveillance, communities of color find ways to resist. Robin Kelley describes this phenomenon as part of a hidden transcript or infrapolitics, whereupon disempowered folks wage struggle daily "outside the visible end of the spectrum." The hidden transcript captures daily efforts to resist subject positions whether through "daily confrontations, evasive actions, and stifled thoughts" (Kelley 1996, p. 8–9). These daily actions not only embody sites of agency but constitute a challenge and disruption of power relations. Although less common within contemporary popular culture, partially because of the hegemony of colorblind discourses and the ubiquity of projects of commodification, the inclusion of sites and practices of resistance within popular culture, especially film, is crucial to oppositional cinematic texts.

Prison Song successfully elucidates the hidden transcript in providing depth and complexity to the daily struggles with American oppression. Neither Elijah nor Thomas, Uncle Steve, or his mother submit to the prison industrial complex or structural adjustment programs in this neighborhood, finding ways to redefine themselves and their place within an American community.

Despite having to work multiple jobs and take care of her children, Elijah's mother studies to become a lawyer. Even as one of the managing partners at a lawyer firm where she seeks an internship discourages her from pursuing a career in the law, she remains determined to improve her family's life. She refuses to let the school place Elijah in special education and otherwise confronts the realities of American racism as a mere obstacle.

Uncle Steve follows suit, working hard even though New York law restricts employment for ex-cons. In New York, laws ban criminalized citizens from more than 40 jobs, including plumbing and barbering. In some states, those "who paid their debt to society" cannot even visit public housing. Federal law prevents felons from receiving student loans, welfare, food stamps, or a job in education. Such laws erect "invisible barriers to a productive future," which don't exist as an "effective deterrent, but rather an invitation to a continued life of crime." Nonetheless, Uncle Steve works hard to provide financially for the family as he parents Elijah, although he is not blood related. (again, a challenge to hegemonic Hollywood of the absentee black father). Even in the face of a life of confinement, Uncle Steve still guides and parents Elijah to deal with his anger.

Other examples play through *Prison Song* from protests inside and outside of prison to daily workings of Elijah. For Elijah, his art is resistance, as part of his hidden transcript. On the outside he takes pictures of his world, using the sometimes oppressive gaze of the camera as a source of liberation. Rather than allowing the state or others to put him under surveillance, he uses his camera not only as a device to watch them, but also as a tool to transcend his spatial confinement. While in prison, he uses paints and canvas as a point of opposition to confinement and denied agency. Accepting Thomas's suggestion that he "do the time," and not let the "time do you," Elijah documents the lives and struggles of those on the inside. Similar to Diego Rivera, who Elijah mentions in the film, he uses his art to explain his own exploitation within the context of the prison industrial complex. When Elijah's teacher asks him how his art connected to their course materials, Elijah reminded the teacher that his documentation of life inside the prison system resembled the stories told through the work of Rivera, except that his paintings showed prisoners working without compensation, whereas Rivera chronicled the exploitation of Mexican workers.

As Elijah finds his own identity as an artist, as a man in control of his daily destiny within the context of prison life, he gives his peers their own agency, subjectivity, and identity. Even as prisons attempt to perform "the magic trick of making people disappear," Elijah resists through his art, eventually showing others on the outside the humanity of America's prisoners and the inhumanity of the prison industrial complex. Here lies another example of the hidden transcript and another source of strength of *Prison Song*.

Notwithstanding the strengths of this film, *Prison Song* has its own problems. Its tendency toward critique and progressive politics is sometimes undercut by elements of conventionality. In fact, the casting of so many hip-hop artists and the strategic insertions of songs embody its place within a larger context of Hollywood moneymaking. The inclusion of so many hip artists is an attempt to draw in viewers through the popularity of artists like Q-Tip, Fat Joe, Mary J. Blige, and Snow. At a certain level, the strategy of using hip-hop star power to propel a film that likely would be dismissed because of its political message and oppositional ideology was smart, guaranteeing its release on BET. Similar to the inclusion of several sex scenes in *Sweetback,* an overtly political 1970s film, the packaging of this scathing critique of state violence and racism through hip-hop represents a necessary choice in the context of today's entertainment industry.

The decision to use hip-hop artists and the use of song in a way that makes *Prison Song* a pseudo-musical also limit the power and potential of the film. Throughout the film, characters randomly break into song to express their struggle.. Beyond being hokey, the timing of song within the narrative disarms the power of the message, politics, and story. With rare exception, song follows a moment of conflict, whether the incarceration of Uncle Steve or depicting Elijah's struggle. Although attempting to highlight the struggle, this cinematic technique has the opposite effect, turning serious filmmaking into silly musical.

Notwithstanding the progressive orientation and oppositional time, *Prison Song* unfortunately inscribes the hegemonic images and ideologies so often found within Hollywood films. As with *Baby Boy* and other films already discussed, *Prison Song* cannot completely avoid dominant constructions of blackness, American race relations, or ghetto life.

While ultimately falling short, the story of Elijah legitimizes the possibility of the American dream. Beyond Elijah's initial success in school as the source of despair in his ultimate incarceration, the film tends to inscribe others to illustrate Elijah's power and goodness. Compared to Thomas, Elijah is good. The film juxtaposes the studious Elijah with Thomas, almost suggesting that Elijah does not deserve to be in prison but Thomas does. Elijah, despite American racism and obstacles, almost makes it, thereby illustrating the possibility of fulfilling the American Dream.

Moreover, the film constructs Elijah as an anomaly. He is different from his grade school peers because he wants to learn. He his distinct from his peers at the group home because he has ambition. He does not fulfill the assessment of his girlfriend when she describes the fellow residents of group home as lazy: "All you do is sleep and lounge." Elijah works hard and attempts to make his life better. Additionally, the film shows these others (all of color) as violent, hypersexual, and otherwise dysfunctional. Elijah, however, is focused, determined, and pays more attention on his art than on his sex life. These other youth merely serve as a foil for the goodness and strength of Elijah, an anomaly who simultaneously legitimizes both the possibility of making it and arguments that society's failure are those of individuals.

The film's finale encapsulates both the power and limitations of *Prison Song.* After a failed prison escape, Elijah he finds himself trapped inside the final security gate, tasting freedom, yet still confined inside the prison. In a panic, Elijah takes a guard hostage, hoping he can trade this man's life for his own freedom. Recognizing that the guard was not the true enemy (the film argues that both guards and prisoners suffer because of the prison industrial complex), Elijah lets him go, running toward the exit enclosed by a barbed wire fence and protected by a guard holding a machine gun. Despite the permanence of his confinement, the mere sight of this "caged animal" attempting to flee provokes the guard, who shoots him several times in the chest. Illustrating the violence and repression of state authority, this scene solidifies the painful and sour message of *Prison Song*.

This oppositional message is disarmed with a feeling of hope and the fulfillment of Elijah's dream in the subsequent scene. The film does not leave the audience with the image of his bullet-riddled body, with the sight of the unfulfilled promise of America, but rather with Elijah's paintings.

In the days after the Elijah is murdered, the lone white prisoner (Danny Hoch) calls his mother, a museum curator. Together, they fulfill Elijah's dreams by putting on an exhibit that gives voice to his experience and that of America's prisons. Once again, someone on the outside controls Elijah's future, ultimately profiting off his labor, his creativity, and his identity. While *Prison Song* leaves its audience with a joyous ending, there is little to celebrate concerning the prison industrial complex, rendering this film as a rare find: a contemporary film that both speaks to social injustice and reflects on methods of resistance on and off the screen. More important, rather than denying or commodifying race, and erasing racism, *Prison Song* tells a story of the ways in which race and racism continue to impact African American life experiences, something not done in the other films discussed in this chapter.

CONCLUSION

The rise of neoliberalism and the hegemony of colorblind rhetoric have increasingly infiltrated the genre of African American film, rendering analysis of the state and white supremacy as obsolete. Whereas the era of Blaxploitation produced films like *Sweetback, Superfly,* and *Shaft,* all of which offered analysis and critiques against capitalism, police brutality, and American racial violence, and the early 1990s produced *Boyz n the Hood, Menace II Society,* and *New Jack City,* all of which brought attention to persistent problems facing American inner-city communities, emphasizing state failures, those recent Hollywood inscriptions of the ghetto instead focus on individual and cultural failures. Replicating hegemonic discourses that deny racism and celebrate colorblind ideologies, all the while celebrating racial progress and the availability of the American Dream, this new wave of films erase history and structural contexts, rendering Hollywood current commodification project as inherently problematic and reactionary at its core.

Unfortunately, *Baby Boy, Antwone Fisher,* and *Training Day* do not sufficiently acknowledge the state's implication in racial violence and social disintegration, thereby refusing or denying the responsibility of the state in preventing the effects of violence and poverty within America's ghettos. Moreover, these films leave intact the myth regarding individual motivation and cultural pathology as a sources of unemployment, mass levels of incarceration, welfare dependency, bad housing, inadequate schools, and crumbling infrastructures. Whereas past films, despite their failures, and even *Prison Song*, argue the persistent significance of racism, whether in state violence, or limited economic opportunities, the films discussed in this chapter tell stories of dysfunctionality and cultural depravation. For example, in *Baby Boy*, Jody fails as a "man," as a boyfriend, and as a father not because of the unavailability of jobs or the effects of widespread policing within his community, but because he is socially and culturally dysfunctional. He is the failure and so is his inscription of masculinity, rather than a product of a failing system. With *Antwone Fisher*, it is black women and the black family that fails Antwone. Yet his own determination and the help of the military brings about hope and opportunity. Denying institutional racism also defines *Training Day*, which explores police brutality and corruption not at a systemic level, but in the failures and shortcomings of Alonzo Harris. Each of these films bemoans the failures of African American men and women, yet each erases the role of the state or even structures within this process. These films not only fail to assess the impact of "prevailing social conditions" or existing resources but deem those factors as insignificant and irrelevant.

Imagine how different all three films (in the mold of *Prison Song*) would be if they addressed racism, whether discrimination in the workplace or school, the dismantling of social programs (Head Start, drug treatment), destruction of infrastructure (parks), the destruction of social welfare programs (or their criminalization), or militarization of the police. This observation is not a call for the production of alternative films, but it illustrates how narrative and representative choices not only affect cinematic meaning and ideology but the place of the recent wave of ghettocentric films within a larger discursive field, given the erasure of racial context and its refusal to interrogate the impact of state violence. The commodification of gangsta narratives and the deployment of sights, sounds, and voices of hip-hop serve as a vehicle or a cover for the deployment of reactionary cinematic projects that legitimize the status quo as white supremacy. In telling stories about individual choices, individual failures, pathology, personal choice, and even a benevolent state (whiteness does not signify racism or even conflict in all three films compared to *Prison Song*), the films reflect the conservative ideology that defines today's Hollywood. The widespread characterization of black men and women in these films as violent, hypersexual, lazy, angry, and culturally deficient signifies a larger trend within and beyond Hollywood: a turn to "reactionary throwbacks" that embody a "national epidemic that deforms discourse of race: denial" (Giroux 2003, p. 142). The problem isn't the state of racism, but Jody, Alonzo, Mrs. Tate, and blackness in general. These films, unlike even *Prison Song*, *Boyz n the Hood*, or *Menace II Society*, legitimize the hegemony of the current racial state and the persistence of state violence, mass incarceration, unemployment, poverty, rates of infant mortality, and limited educational opportunities. Contemporary Hollywood, as evident in these films, like the military and the economic power structures contributes to maintenance of the power structure. David Theo Goldberg argues that the state uses:

Physical force, violence, coercion, manipulation, deceit, cajoling, incentives, laws(s), taxes, penalties, surveillance, military force, representative apparatus, ideological mechanism and media—in short, all the mean's at the state's disposal—ultimately to the ends of racial rule. Which is to say, to the ends of reproducing the racial order and so representing for the most part the interest of the racial ruling class. (Goldberg 2001, p. 112)

Unfortunately, the films discussed through most of this chapter fail to reflect on the role of the state and its effects on communities of color. Whereas *Prison Song* and *Boyz n the Hood* successfully bring state violence (in many of its forms) to life, reflecting on the deleterious impact of state violence, laws, media representations, and surveillance on the black community, those other films discussed in this chapter, as well as the bulk of today's productions, not only erase these state spectacles and emphasize the pathology and cultural deficiencies of communities of color, but simultaneously deny the continued importance of race and racism

Whether talking about an expanding prison system, a declining social welfare system, increased levels of poverty, declining job opportunities, or the persistence of state and structural violence, the recent wave of films fails to provide narratives or representations that offer understanding of contemporary racial problems. Rather, these films advance those racial projects that demonize and pathologize black youth, providing legitimacy to discourses and policies of mass incarceration, America's "war on crime," and other programs that deny reasonable opportunities for communities of color. In a sense, these films not only deny the despair and the violence that have besieged communities such as New Orleans, Los Angeles, Oakland, Chicago, Harlem, East Palo Alto, and others, but give voice to reactionary, individualized, and privatized explanations that both deny state culpability and responsibility and place blame for problems and solutions onto bodies of color.

Prison Song points to the promise and possibility of using film to raise consciousness, to force conversation regarding contemporary racial problems, and to disrupt the status quo, but the bulk of today's urban films "reinforce rather than rupture those racially oppressive trends in American Society that disfigure possibility of racial justice, democratic politics and responsible citizenship" (Giroux 2003, p. 142). Rather than challenging, they naturalize and sanction dominant discourses and images, erasing and/or demonizing those who have been left behind by America's turn away from the Civil Rights Movement, by America's turn to the right, by America's turn to criminalization over welfare.

3

---•◦•---

IS THIS REALLY AFRICAN AMERICAN CINEMA? BLACK MIDDLE-CLASS DRAMAS AND HOLLYWOOD

In the wake of the numerous ghettocentric films of the 1990s, Hollywood produced a series of more positive dramatic films centering on the black middle class. Unlike films in the past, which tended to reduce black middle-class situations to universal struggles, films like *Soul Food* (1997), *Love & Basketball, Drumline,* and *Brown Sugar* all take the audience into a "black world," in terms of themes, concepts, and community. Each interjects a historical cultural reality (soul food, black athletics, black colleges, and hip-hop) into the film narrative. Nonetheless, these films have provoked significant amounts of debate from both audiences and critics, as to whether they are absurd fantasy or reflective reality. This chapter enters into this debate, examining these films in terms of their vision of the black community, culture, gender relations, and race relations. It also asks why these films have been so popular in that each defies, at some level, Hollywood's logic of universal themes and integrated settings.

In the early 1980s, *The Cosby Show* entered the American cultural marketplace as a counter-narrative to those of the blaxploitation era and those dominant representations that reduced blackness to a demonized and stereotyped urban identity. *The Cosby Show,* through its representation of a black family and its narrative of a doctor (Bill Cosby) and a lawyer (Phylicia Rashad), confirmed America's value for individual success and mobility, so often erased as a black experience. According to Patricia Hill Collins, whose *Black Sexual Politics* examines contemporary manifestations of new racism within popular culture, *The Cosby Show* provided a powerful template for contemporary black masculinity, which was a safe, unassuming and nonthreatening black identity defined by neither sexual prowess nor violence (2004, p. 167). *The Cosby*

Show and the increasing visibility of Oprah Winfrey, Michael Jordan and other celebrities indicating black economic and cultural integration, did not merely signify the possibilities of Reverend King's dream, but its success in securing a colorblind society. The representations of the black middle class beginning with *The Cosby Show* through those discussed herein, thus, present African Americans as friendly and as facing the same problems of the white middle class. According to popular culture, "What 'black people should be like' is being physically Black so that racial integration can be seen, but not culturally Black, for example, display any of the behaviors of an assumed authentic Blackness" (Collins 2004, p 168). As evident with Cosby, or Danny Glover in *Grand Canyon* (1991), Hollywood offered a clear celebration of a post-Civil Rights America, yet rendered blackness insignificant beyond a marker of colorblindness and integration. In other words, blackness within popular culture merely marked difference to confirm that America no longer saw race.

The recent wave of films (and television shows) recreating the narratives of the black middle class does not attempt to erase the blackness (aesthetic, experience, or culture) of the black middle class. Films such as *The Wood, Love Jones, Love & Basketball, Drumline,* or *Brown Sugar* center around a black cultural experience, commodifying cultural difference, but by using narratives of the black middle class these films present hip-hop, basketball, or spoken word as safe and -nonthreatening. Whereas *The Cosby Show* rendered blackness insignificant given integration, these recent films make clear that blackness, in all its cultural forms, still matters despite the rise of the black middle-class. Yet because of class status the commodification and performative processes are far more desirable and palatable to white audiences. Despite such differences, both eras of black middle class cultural productions share a common erasure of state violence and the persistent effects of American racism, which is not surprising given the mutual celebration of positivity and the American Dream.

The Cosby Show sought to challenge the "negative" stereotypes and overall negativity that defined cinematic and T.V. representations of blackness. Like so many other shows of its period, it not only brought to life the experiences of the black middle class, but did so through emphasizing the importance of individual choice, individual values, discipline, and work ethic. In this way, it offered not only a positive challenge to America's representation of black poor, but also a means to emphasize the normalcy of the Americaness of these blacks folks. Herman Gray, in "Television, Black Americans and the American Dream," describes the power of these middle-class utopian television shows in the following way:

In the genre of situation comedy, programs like the *Cosby Show, 227, Frank's Place,* and *Amen,* all show successful middle-class black Americans who have effectively negotiated their way through benign social institutions and environments. Their family-centered lives take place in attractive homes and offices. Rarely if ever do these character venture into settings or interact with people like those in the CBS documentary [a documentary about the black underclass]. As doctors, lawyers, restauranteurs, ministers, contractors, and housewives, these are representations of black Americans who have surely realized the American dream. . . . Although black, their class position (signified by their occupations, tastes, language, and setting) distances them from the codes of crime, drugs, and social problems activated by the urban underclass. . . . The characters are never presented in situations where their racial identity matters. The representations of racial encounters further appeals to the utopian desires in blacks and whites for racial oneness and equality while displacing the persistent reality of racism and racial inequality or the kinds of social struggles and cooperation required to eliminate them. (1995, p. 435)

In an effort to challenge the stereotypes and denunciation that emanated from societal representations of the black urban class, or America's ghettos, shows like *The Cosby Show* were constructive as an alternative representation that provided a glimpse into the experiences of the black middle class. Moreover, they did so in such a manner that was palpable by white America. The simultaneity of its efforts to deny racism and the persistent meaning of racial identity and the construct of the success of the black middle class as being the result of hard work, values, and ethics legitimized dominant understandings of post-Civil Rights America and underscored the popularity of these shows throughout the nation.

Despite the popularity of *The Cosby Show*, its representation of the black middle class in the absence of any references to racism, and the overall demonization of the black underclass through popular culture, prompted much debate within black cultural circles as to both the legitimacy and usefulness of these representations. Specifically, critics wondered whether *The Cosby Show* challenged or reinforced stereotypes because of the show's emphasis on success being rooted in hard work, its erasure of racial identity/racism, and its implicit message that black folks like Bill and Claire Huxtable were "positive" because they were not like Superfly, John Shaft, or the man on the corner. Amid these conversations, widespread debates about how these cultural productions further contributed to America's abandonment of urban black America and a shifting marketplace, television, and Hollywood turned once again from these middle-class utopias to the ghettocentric imagination.

Beginning with *New Jack City*, and gaining popularity with *Boyz n the Hood, Menace II Society*, and even Fox's *South Central*, dominant representations eschewed the black middle-class experience, returning instead to those stories of black gangstas and those inhabiting America's ghettos. Bringing the stories and experiences of the America's black underclass into America's psyche, whether through chronicling the spatial realities of America's inner cities, or providing in depth treatment of a generation of "America's worst nightmare: young, black and don't give a fuck," these films embody a spectrum of responses. While the discourse offered a myriad of perspectives, much of it focused on whether the narratives of Pino Brown, Doughboy, and O-Dog fueled white racism, legitimized increased levels of state violence (police brutality, the prison industrial complex, police surveillance within public schools). Critics demanded more positive representations that not only recognized the contributions of the black middle class, but celebrated the best, rather than the worst, of black America. Although reflective of societal projects to demonize America's youth of color, to emphasize their cultural failures, and the limited possibility of teaching "the truly disadvantaged," the public discourse in the wake of the turn to the ghettocentric film reflected a desired challenge to the representation of African American culture in monolithic terms and the long-standing practice that "only one form of popular representation may be available at any given time" (Boyd 1997, p. 23).

Notwithstanding these desires, widespread protests against these films through the early 1990s, and shifts in cultural, political, and social landscapes, Hollywood replaced its ghettocentric imagination with that of a bourgeoisie imagination, where films inscribed blackness as "just black enough not to offend and middle class enough to comfort" (in Boyd 1997, p. 22). While maintaining clear signifiers of blackness through commodification of hip-hop, sporting cultures, and other ghettocentric aesthetics, this wave of films brought to life the stories and experiences (or at least an element of them) of the black middle class. Although still behind the white middle class, in terms of numbers, financial compensation, and access to power and opportunity, the post-civil rights era has seen the movement of blacks into professional, managerial, and technological fields in record numbers. In 1964, only 8.5 percent of the black employed held jobs in these sectors compared to 16.7 percent in 1983. According to these same reports from the U.S. Bureau of Labor Statistics, there has been a 57 percent increase in the numbers of black professionals since 1973. Between 1973 and 2000, residential segregation for African Americans declined significantly, although rates were still higher than for any other group, revealing the increasing likelihood of black economic success translating into residential mobility. The movement into once predominantly white communities during this period (although many communities eventually became resegregated) further enhanced economic, political, and educational opportunities for the growing black middle-class. These changes in residential patterns provided access to better housing, schools, and facilities for African American children. Entry into once blocked professions, the limited success of affirmative action and antidiscrimination laws have facilitated growth in the black middle –class and residential mobility, which has in turn provided access to improved schools, health care, and communal institutions, which of course has enhanced the opportunities afforded to the black middle class.

Equally important, during the last three decades there has also been a dramatic increase in the number of African Americans attending American colleges and universities, as well as moving into once predominantly white neighborhoods. U.S. Census figures indicate that as of 2006, 11 percent of blacks age 25 and over have completed college, compared to 4.5 percent in 1970. Equally revealing, from 1960, when 2.8 million African Americans lived within America's suburbs to 1980, when the number was 6.2 million, there has been a dramatic change in the geographic orientation of the black community (http://www.aliciapatterson.org/APF0903/Lane/Lane.html). Although there has been growth in the black middle class and the movement of African Americans into leadership positions within Fortune 500 companies and within the power structure, the bulk of African Americans have been left behind in terms of opportunity/life outcomes and the institutional power available to the black working class and black underclass, as well as in their visibility within America's cultural venues.

The rise of the black middle class, although undercut by deindustrialization, the policies of Reagan, Clinton, and both Bushes, as well as the dismantling of affirmative action, welfare, and other social programs, , remained out of focus for most of America through the late 1980s and early 1990s. By the mid-1990s, first with *Love Jones,* and then with films like *The Wood, The Best Man,* and *The Brothers,* Hollywood brought to life the black middle-class experience, albeit in a sanitized way that replicated the tropes and ideologies of *The Cosby Show* of years past: one that denied racial identity and the importance of racism and erased the black underclass, all the while emphasizing hard work, "traditional" family values, morality, and cultural choice.

The wave of middle-class oriented black films sought to reinsert a middle-class black experience into the American cultural imagination, while capitalizing on consumer demand for more positive and "bougie" narratives. It was also an attempt to commodify difference through safe bodies and spaces. The onslaught of films that constructed a colorblind narrative centering on "positive" imagery of the black middle class, all the while commodifying a new black aesthetic that centered hip-hop and other markers of difference, sought to challenge concurrent trends of films that glorified and commodified a ghettocentric imagination. Simultaneously, such films challenged those past projects that imagined blackness as little more than a marker of integration and colorblindness, making clear that members of the black middle class still "act black," even if the structural constraints of racism and state violence have a limited effect on these communities. As will be discussed, these films still serve to reinforce hegemonic notions of blackness, this time through a lens of colorblind American bootstrapism. Additionally, their celebration of black cultural aesthetics and individual mobility fulfill dominant claims about equality in post-Civil Rights America, in that not only have African Americans made it, but that one can assimilate and succeed without abandoning the black community or one's blackness. In constructing a black middle-class world within a safe and sanitized understanding of blackness—one that marks cultural difference in commodifiable terms—these films reify dominant projects of colorblindness, equality, and "culture" as the only difference, which in the end celebrates America at the expense of those left behind, at the expense of those who don't embody blackness in terms and ways acceptable to America.

In 1999, Hollywood released *The Wood* (Rick Famuyiwa), which dramatically altered the cinematic landscape of blackness. Following in the footsteps of *Love Jones* (Theodore Witcher, 1997), which chronicles the relationship struggles of upwardly mobile yet clearly black (evidenced by involvement in Chicago spoken word scene), this film sought to challenge the cinematic and popular imagination regarding America's ghettos. Beyond repelling the tendency of imagining black ghettos as repositories of drugs, violence, hypersexuality, welfare, hip-hop, gangstas and of course the underclass, *The Wood* recreates the black community, Inglewood, as the home of the black middle class. In other words, it successfully challenges the dominant discourses that imagine the black middle class as living within white neighborhoods and reduce black inner-city communities to dangerous ghettos. It attempts to redefine the black community in terms of its heterogeneity. In chronicling the stories of black men on the verge of marriage, each of these films depicts the way black men—friends, brothers, peers—nurture a so-called positive and productive black masculinity (heterosexual, patriarchal, middle class). Specifically, *The Wood* chronicles the friendship of Mike, Slim, and Roland, who have been best friends since junior high. Hours before Roland's wedding, Slim and Mike are at work, helping him to overcome his anxiety and nervousness. Their friendship here is nothing new, as the film documents a lifetime of connection, revealing how the three boys became men in each other's eyes, and through their own friendships. Notwithstanding societal claims about a dysfunctional black masculinity being a product of a culture of poverty and single-mothered households, *The Wood* offers an alternative narrative of black boys and men teaching each other what it means to be a black man in contemporary America, ultimately arguing that the success of the community—through securing family and middle-class status (patriarchy)—comes through the support of family and friends.

Shortly after the release of *The Wood, The Best Man* (Malcolm Lee, 1999) and *The Brothers* (Gary Hardwick, 2001) appeared in theaters across America. Both films played on the theme of wedding/relationship jitters established by *The Wood*, contributing to widespread discourse regarding a heterosexual, patriarchal family, black men's relationship with black women, traditional Christian values, and middle-class status. Equally important, these films centered the black middle-class experience, telling stories of "successful" African Americans, and the range of professional experiences that define today's African American community. Replicating the representational world of *The Cosby Show*, these two films envision blackness to hold little significance beyond the fact that the blackness of the cast/characters demonstrates the progress of America and Hollywood. Likewise, these films follow the Cosby tradition in further reducing heterosexual black families/success to the middle class, reifying dominant discourses that treat the black family as inherently middle class, whereas the black poor are by definition composed of single mothers and absentee fathers. Although offering a slight deviation from those middle-class orientated films and shows of the 1980s, where these late 1990s films attempt to tell stories of black communities and periodically include markers of a black culture experience, each replicates the tendency of those films past as well as those discussed within this chapter; each offers narratives of happy people with happy problems. Such a trope does not merely signify the films' attempt at universality; rather, they offer patrons a "positive" cinematic experience that not only celebrates the black middle-class experience (so often erased and ignored), but praises American racial progress. In other words, positivity comes from the erasure of racism and racial identity. Lloyd Chelsey's review of *The Wood* is emblematic of the popularity and narrative orientation of these films, as it makes clear that neither race nor racism matter in these films.

Although the cast is African American, there's no color bar to the themes or entertainment the movie offers, providing a salient lesson to network TV producers under attack by the NAACP for their inability to include characters of color in TV shows. Instead of stereotyping the characters by placing them in "the hood," where gang members and tragedy rule, this life-affirming comedy depicts the lives of members of "the wood," which refers to Inglewood, a middle-class suburb of L.A. that general audiences will find easy to relate to. (at Amazon.com)

Although this reviewer demonstrates an inability to distinguish between narratives revealing racism and those that perpetuate racism (he also sees films about the black middle class as inherently positive), his comments encapsulate the short-sidedness and importance of the middle class-oriented black narrative: the erasure of racism and race, even in moments where blackness is commodified as a source of pleasurable difference. This works in concert with those others films discussed herein in both celebrating colorblindness and progress while demonizing and pathologizing those left behind in post-Civil Rights America.

In this tradition, this chapter looks at four recent films—*Drumline, Love & Basketball, Brown Sugar,* and *Good Fences,* all of which continue the tradition set by *The Cosby Show, Love Jones, The Wood,* and others. Each tells stories of the black middle class (and sometimes elite), bringing into question the dilemmas of integration, assimilation and progress. Each offers insight as to the place and identity of the black middle class, and offers commentary, often in tones of demonization and ridicule, of the black underclass, reifying hegemonic notions of the American Dream and bootstrapism. More important, except for *Good Fences,* each of these films continue long-standing traditions of popular cultural imaginings of the black middle class in ways that mark their blackness as much as needed to capitalize on popular fetishes/trends, while presenting it in a way that is safe and palpable to mainstream white audiences. In other words, this chapter looks at the ways in which *Drumline,*

Brown Sugar, and *Love & Basketball* all offer cinematic narratives that commodify particular elements of blackness, yet confine them to middle-class spaces and stories so as to deliver the most desirable narrative.

The safety in these films emanates as much from their orientation to middle-class stories as their tendency to erase racism, to reduce blackness to aesthetics, and to celebrate America's racial present. These films reduce a black middle-class experience to one of happy people with happy problems because of their values, choices, and cultural attributes, in turn both denying the burdens and obstacles faced by the black middle class as well as the structural realities that define their working, underemployed, and unemployed brothers' and sisters' experiences.

Finally, we use this chapter to look at the ways in which these films, especially *Good Fences,* challenge the dominant representations of the black middle class, one which transcends Hollywood, through their unsettling of ideas of racial transcendence, the availability of the American Dream, and its desirability. These challenges to representation remain limited in their scope, however, because simultaneous to these moves are the reinforcement of a colorblind ideology that positions contemporary racism as the acts of individuals, unsymptomatic of institutionalized, societal-level inequality. In other words, the struggles of the black middle class in these films come from individualized slights against the characters, suggesting that the American Dream remains not entirely out of reach. The failure to offer narratives of the black middle class that speak to the specificity of experience, whether cultural or enduring problems with racism, is not merely a problem because of its misrepresentation of America's racial reality. Read in conjunction with those films that imagine America's ghettos as a product of individual failures, cultures, and pathologies, the middle-class films, despite the appearance of something else, provide little ideological departure, instead fulfilling dominant understandings of race, racism, and the universality of the American Dream. In no film is this more evident than *Drumline*.

DRUMLINE

Drumline (Charles Stone III, 2002) was filmed in Atlanta, Georgia, and set at fictitious Atlanta A & T, a historically black college just down the street from Morris Brown College. Nick Cannon (Devon Miles) spent four to six hours a day learning how to play drums before filming began. Director Charles Stone wanted to make a movie with the same competitive spirit and intensity as sports films, focusing on discipline and teamwork. In an interview with Cynthia Fuchs he states: "I wanted to get that kind of power on screen, that discipline, that allegiance to the teamwork . . . There are a lot of scene in it that are stereotypical of sports movies, but for me that was important to have that because it's not a football or basketball team, so those generic moments twist what you expect. As long as the spirit was true, I wasn't worried about clichéd shots. And I think the story of an underdog appeals to every-one, despite the cultural specificity" *(www.reelimagesmagazine.com)*.

Devon Miles travels far from home—Harlem—to go to a black college, Atlanta A & T, in Atlanta, Georgia, on a band scholarship. Devon, raised by a single mother, reflects the positivity of her influence. On graduation day, he tells her that he would have never made it without her. Once at school, Devon comes into almost immediate conflict with both leading drum major Sean (Leonard Roberts) and the band's director Dr. Lee (Orlando Jones). Devon has issues with discipline, taking orders, and following the rules of the boot-camp style marching band program. On his first day on campus, Devon meets Laila (Zoe Saldana), his love interest in the film. Laila is an upperclassman, a philosophy major by her parents' choice, whose real passion is in dance. Their relationship lasts till the end of the film, but it has its share of conflict.

Devon is part of a rag-tag group of freshmen recruits which includes Jayson (GQ), a white boy/local of Atlanta who has chosen Atlanta A&T for sen-timental reasons; Ernest (Jason Weaver), who acts strangely through most of the film, as he is going through secret rushing and initiation into a band fraternity; and Diedre (Candice Carey), the only female drummer in Devon's inner circle of friends, whose presence challenges the men's notions of mas-culinity and femininity.

Through the course of the film, Devon comes into increasing, and more intense, conflicts with Sean, which ultimately results in Sean exposing Devon's musical illiteracy, which results in Devon's expulsion from the drumline. This is one example of the clash between Devon's style of learning and playing music, which is learning by listening and repeating, and Sean and Dr. Lee's more "classic" or "disciplined" approach, which is reading a piece while playing. This is not Devon's only conflict along social/class/education lines: during homecoming weekend, Laila refuses to introduce Devon to her parents because they called him a hoodlum during an altercation with another band.

After the altercation and resistance to learning to read music gets Devon both kicked off the drumline and out of the band, he retreats into himself and writes his own beats. Eventually, with the help of Sean, the band uses a cadence written by Devon at the BET Big Southern Classic, an annual competition between college marching bands. Devon's cadence helps the band reach a two-way tie with Morris Brown College, at which point Devon is allowed to suit up and "give them a taste of what they'll get next year." Atlanta A&T wins the showdown, and the film closes with the band celebrating.

Drumline is ostensibly a "coming of age" story. Although Devon is an intelligent, promising youth when he graduates high school, he matures and changes in college. Laila teaches him how to approach women, as Devon claims that "they always come at him," not the other way around. Deidre proves to Devon and the rest of the men in the group that a woman can be physically as strong, or stronger, than they, and still be attractive/desirable. By the end of the film, Diedre and Ernest have "hooked up." Devon also comes to deal with male authority in the forms of Sean and Dr. Lee, as they have seemingly become default father figures for Devon. And Devon is not the only one who matures through the film. Laila manages to defy her parents and change her major to dance; Sean's perception of Devon changes from threat or competition to teammate; and Dr. Lee learns that there is, after all, musicianship in hip-hop, that the beats of a Harlem-born-and-bred youth can work well with more 'classic' forms of music.

One of the prominent themes in films attentive to a middle-class experience within the black community is generational conflict. As with *Brown Sugar* and *Love & Basketball* (as well as *Good Fences*), generational conflict acts a stand-in for class conflict and communal anxiety regarding assimilation. In other words, the cultural and communal battles between older and young generations (pre- and post-Civil Rights) offer a narrative to discuss and think through questions of assimilation, progress, and the existence and meaning of the black community within contemporary America. In *Drumline,* this trope functions within and through the relationship between Devon and Dr. Lee and their struggles over the musical direction of the band. The film establishes this important theme in its initial moments. As the camera pans down to a group of seated students dressed to the nines in caps and gowns, awaiting their graduation from high school into a world of dreams and opportunities, a bored and disinterested Devon Miles sits in opposition. As the principal introduces the school's award-winning band, he reminds them that "no matter what obstacles confront you, you can always fly," Devon mockingly repeats the already heard and dismissed cliché. To further emphasize his protest of the irrelevance of the upwardly mobile older generation and their vision of the world, Devon orchestrates his own rendition of "I Believe I Can Fly," with a phat drum beat and an up-tempo beat straight out of the D.J. booth.

Similar to *Brown Sugar, Drumline* uses music as a theme of interrogation for generational and class conflict, with older folks identifying with R&B, Motown, and other classics not appealing to the hip-hop generation. For example, shortly after arriving to the start of A & T's band season, Dr. Lee welcomes the band to a new year and to music, as if none of them had experienced music before this day—Jay-Z, Kanye West, or even the Roots are not music in this sense. With "When the Saints Go Marching In" serving as his background music, Dr. Lee tells his future musicians:

The next two weeks will be your introduction into a great marching band legacy. If you are here it is because you believe in musicianship. If you are here it is because you believe in Coltrane, Miles Davis, Stevie Wonder, and the elements known as Earth, Wind and Fire. If you are here it is because you have fervent unequivocal belief in teamwork.

In another instance, Dr. Lee announces the week's music selection as Earth, Wind and Fire, only to experience opposition, disgust, and frustration from the band, his hip-hopped children. "What y'all complaining about? Oh, y'all think you are a band. Earth, Wind and Fire was a band. So what you all wanna play, Angie Stone?" As the band excitedly grumbles at this selection, Dr. Lee proceeds, asking them if they would rather play LL Cool J or Snoop Doggy Dog. Unphased by their nods and calls of approval, Dr. Lee reminds the band of history: "All these artists sample from this group, OK? That's what we gonna play." Despite the applause and excitement from the band, Dr. Lee proceeds with the original selection, once again emphasizing the importance of change from the hip-hop generation, a change that requires their understanding of history, forming respect for black culture (in his definition), and most important garnering discipline. Only at that time will the older generation and dominant culture adjust and/or incorporate the best elements of the hip-hop generation.

The film attempts to construct this conflict in the absence of value judgment (a point often emphasized by its director, Charles Stone III, in interviews) by imagining a cultural fusion that bridges generation and class. Its tendency to embrace dominant discourses that demonize hip-hop and its practitioners leaves the film not as a call for generations and cultures coming together, but rather the imperative of discipline, middle-class values, and change from the aesthetic of black youth.

Although generational (class and culture) conflict is a prominent theme within *Drumline*, at its core is a message about discipline. It is a film that chronicles Devon's growth as a black male and an artist. In telling his story, the film equally documents the ways in which school, discipline, and the military-like training of the Atlanta A & T marching band served as the source of his maturation. Devon arrives on campus with all the trappings of a stereotypical young, black, urban male athlete. Although a drummer, he has the swagger and arrogance that the media too often associate with contemporary black athletes. Dr. Lee recruited him and offered him a full scholarship, transporting him from the streets of New York to the pristine campus of Atlanta A & T (although in the big city of Atlanta, A & T is represented as a quiet, out-of-the-way college campus). It is clear that he feels entitled and above the rules, defying college mores by flirting with Laila, a junior, and defying his coach's first demand of a curfew by taking his boys to a hip-hop club all during his first day on campus. His defiance, visible disrespect for his elders, and lack of discipline quickly come into question by both Dr. Lee and Sean, both of whom embody the desired values of middle-class respectability.

Much of the early portion of the film focuses on the disciplinary power of the marching band. Band members are required to wear white T-shirts to practice, which Devon violates with a black T –shirt; obey curfew, and show respect to band leaders and coaches, which Devon consistently violates by referring to Shawn and Dr. Lee as "Dawg." The tryouts are reminiscent of a military boot camp. With drill sergeants screaming, the crabs (those try-ing out for the squad) are put through a regiment of exercises, including running, sit-ups and push-ups; the A & T marching band is as much about team and discipline as it is about music. *Drumline* even offers the clichéd military/sport film moment, with the members of the drum line forced to lean against the wall in the rain as part of a challenge to maintain balance, strength, and cadence. The drumline crabs are backed against a wall by drill sergeant Shawn, made to squat down and suspend their arms in front of them, while verbalizing ("tat, tat, boom, tat") their beats. This scene, along with those of the band running the stadium stairs, doing pushups, and rising at dawn for calisthenics, emphasizes Dr. Lee and Shawn's belief in "mind over matter" in the drumline. That mental discipline (concentration, submis-sion to direction, dedication to repetitious practice) is as important, if not more so, than physical ability and talent.

Yet through the effort to create "one band, one sound" through military-style training, Devon resists each step, remaining true to self and his hip-hop generation. During one practice, in which Shawn attempts to teach the crabs on the drumline to drum while looking up (rather than at the drum), the film shows Devon to be selfish and cocky, unwilling to embrace the team mental-ity needed to be successful on and off the field. After the failed attempt of others to stay with Shawn while keeping eye contact, Devon happily steps up to Shawn's drum. With little hesitancy and looking Shawn straight in the eye as if to confirm his own masculinity, Devon drums with little effort, effort-lessly copying Shawn's every movement, while never breaking eye contact. With Shawn eventually losing control of one of his sticks, succumbing to the ultimate sin of the band, Devon is left basking in glory. As to confirm his sta-tus as the top dog, Devon arrogantly grins in Shawn's direction, reminding him who indeed rules the drumline. Yet in reality Dr. Lee rules the drumline, seizing this opportunity to teach Devon something about respect, authority, and leadership: "That was impressive. What I liked most was instead of mak-ing Shawn look like a jackass, you made yourself look like a jackass." Sure that Devon had not found the needed discipline to succeed on or off the field, Dr. Lee sees his opportunity to teach Devon a lesson in team humility and respect, none of which was visible with this episode of trash-talking and arrogance. Replacing Shawn at the drum, Dr. Lee asks Devon to not simply copy his drum beat with his eyes up, but to do so while moving. Unable to complete the task, Dr. Lee reminds Devon, "You have to learn how to fol-low before you can lead." To succeed on the field and in life, Devon needed to become not just respectful (of others, of team, of music) but disciplined through eschewing his hip-hop approaches to life.

The battle between an undisciplined (hip-hopped) Devon and the forces of discipline and teamwork, Shawn and Dr. Lee, eventually come to a head dur-ing the final day of tryouts. Beaming in anticipation of the last day of tryouts and the parties that would invariably take place that night, the crabs once again needed a reminder of the importance of discipline and preparedness. Shawn takes this moment to quiz them on, of all things, the rulebook. After Devon gives a couple of successful answers, Shawn asks him to name the final rule in the team's rulebook, but Devon did not know. Almost expecting (and wanting) Devon to provide the wrong answer, Shawn reminds the line that they have a responsibility to show "boyz in the hood" the final rule.

As the line surrounds a seated Devon, he thumbs through the rulebook. Clearly having not even cracked open the book, Devon eventually finds the last rule, reading aloud, "If you do not read this rule book, your head will be shaved." The significance of this scene within the larger scope of the film is tremendous. Its importance lies not just with Shawn's reference to Devon as "Boyz n the Hood," as the ultimate marker of his supposedly unproductive ghetto/hip-hop mentality, or even the emphasis placed on discipline with the band's extensive rule book as a means toward success in the fulfillment of the American Dream. Rather it lies with the film's deployment of a narrative that positions the removal of Devon's corn-rows (a la the military and prison systems) as a method of punishing him for his failure to read the rule book and an instrument of enforced discipline. Shawn's efforts to police Devon, to control black male bodies, and even threaten him with expulsion from the team if he didn't cut his hair replicates long-standing histories of white supremacy. As noted by John Fiske, hegemony works "to control the leisure and pleasures of the subordinate" (1989, p. 70) through the "construction and enforcement of repressive legislation and the 'taming' of uncontrolled leisure pursuits into 'respectable' and disciplined forms" (Fiske 1989, p. 70). Devon's cornrows, as the sign of his status as an outsider, as a thug or gang-ster among thousands of college students, necessitated control in an effort to rid the drumline/band/community of this potential pollutant. As noted by King and Springwood, such efforts must be understood within a larger context:

Euro-American understandings of African Americans being excessive and transgres-sive have always fostered, if not demanded, disciplinarity, the application of regimes of control, regulation, and management: the bondage, beatings, surveillance, and dehumanization of slavery; and later, the lynchings, terror, spatial constraints, and segregation of Jim Crow. Although much kinder and gentler veiled as in the rhetoric of opportunity, equality, and education, intercollegiate athletic spectacles construe African Americans as deviants in need of refinement, correction, training and supervi-sion. (King and Springwood 2005, p. 197)

Read against widespread demonizing and policing of hair within the black (hip-hop) community, the film powerfully (and problematically) invokes dominant discourses that link assimilation, success, and fulfilling the American Dream, through the forced removal of Devon's cornrows, to cultural choices that pit hip-hop (and black culture) against mainstream cultural values. Threatened with being kicked off the team, Devon, who initially resists the shaving of his head and identity, eventually succumbs to the rule by allowing his teammates to shave his head. Devon's acquiescence, or forced accommodation and acceptance of the team's rules (i.e., his being disciplined) proves to be short-lived and specific to this one incidence, as Devon continues to resist rules and buck the system during the early moments of the band's season. Unfazed by Dr. Lee's efforts to discipline him, Devon spends the first half of the film playing by his own rules, all to the dismay of both Shawn and Dr. Lee. To them, his talent is being wasted because of his lack of discipline, respect, and willingness to become part of the team. He is part of the hip-hop generation, and according to the film that means he marches to his own beat regardless of societal/communal norms or the demands of others. For example, during his audition Devon doesn't play the required piece as written, instead "adding a little something, something on the end." Rather than construct his improvisation as reflective of his own genius or tradition through the history of black music, his failure to follow the assigned music reflects a larger issue of his not respecting authority or tradition.

His effort to be different—to challenge rules and authority—does not end at the audition or even in practice, but carries onto the field. After Devon disses Shawn's solo as the team prepares for Devon's first halftime performance, Shawn takes this opportunity to teach Devon some respect by giving him the solo in hopes that he would "freeze up like any other freshman." Despite Shawn's prediction to a teammate, Devon meets the challenge. After some initial reluctance on the field, momentarily freezing at the sight of thousands of cheering fans, Devon takes the step out from the line, seizing the opportunity to floss (show-off) and showboat his talents. Despite the applause and praise, Dr. Lee is none too happy about Devon's lack of discipline, ego, and inability to understand the concept of team. In the film's effort to position Dr. Lee as the authority figure, as the embodiment of middle-class respectability and in opposition to Devon's me-first showboating, the film heaps praise onto a more refined bourgeoisie black middle-class masculinity, while demonizing hip-hop culture. It imagines the path to a middle-class existence—to the American Dream—as one that travels through college as a place that provides discipline and an education, toward the undoing of the cultural values of the hip-hop generation.

To further reinforce Devon's lack of discipline as evidence of his dysfunction and faulty values, Shawn eventually outs Devon as a musical illiterate, as unable to read music, and as a fraud in violation to the most important rule for all band members.

Dr. Lee: You lied on your application; you lied at your audition when you played the required piece and you lied to me.

Devon: I didn't think it was a big deal.

Dr. Lee [Tossing sheet music in his direction]: Play that! That's the music for next week's game and you can't read it. And as far as I am concerned that's a big deal. I'm enrolling you in the applied percussions course.

Devon: That gives me five classes.

Dr. Lee: Damm right! It ought to be ten, especially if you plan on getting on line soon.

Devon: What you mean getting back on the line.

Dr. Lee: I mean now you are a p-4 [as opposed to a p-1]. If you cannot read music, you cannot be on my field.

Devon: You can't take me off the line. I'm the best drummer you got. Ain't no class gonna teach me how to do me.

Dr. Lee: Excuse me?

Devon: Doin me is what got me down here in the first place.

Dr. Lee: No, lying is what got you down here. And if you don't have the honor and the discipline to learn your craft then, quite frankly you don't deserve to be here.

The message that Dr. Lee offers to Devon mirrors that of the film: talent and "doing you" is not enough to succeed in this world; but coupled with honor, discipline, knowledge of history, and respect the potential is unlimited.

Despite Dr. Lee's effort to teach (or break down) Devon to read music and to be a respectable man, Devon continues to resist Dr. Lee's fatherly interventions, all the while finding his way back onto the field (to the university his talent is all that matters, leading to pressure for Dr. Lee to use tactics other than suspension from the team to teach him discipline). After a demand from the university president, who throughout the film shows himself to be more concerned with wins and losses, as well as alumni happiness and willingness to make financial contributions to his university, Devon is put back on the line, learning the opposite lesson. His talent, "doing me," and his importance to the institution do indeed take precedence over respect, honor, and discipline, leading to a dire situation.

During the homecoming performance, A & T's opponent offers a direct challenge to the drumline by not only drumming powder in their direction and by directly calling out A & T with a point and demand that they come closer. As the line hangs back, Devon cannot resist the direct challenge, getting so close to their line that he begins using their drum, resulting in a massive brawl between both teams.

That next day, only after Laila refused to introduce Devon to her parents, who thought he was a "thug," the team held a secret meeting to discuss Devon's attitude problem. Hoping Dr. Lee could once again save him, he turned to him for help, only to realize that Dr. Lee had already thrown him off the team, seeing that as the only method of discipline that would work for Devon.

And with that, Devon's tenure as a member of the A & T Marching Band appeared to be over. He is finally forced to deal with a system of accountability because of his hip-hop way of doing things. Devon's methodology of problem solving clearly did not mesh with Dr. Lee's philosophy of discipline and musicianship. Devon, positioned as representative of the ghetto, or the ghettocentric ideal of black male youth, repeatedly challenges what he sees as musical elitism in Dr. Lee through "outbursts" like the one that got him kicked off the line. Devon, who brings the "ghetto" to the otherwise middle-class, refined Atlanta A & T campus and band, challenges typical narratives of the black middle class in film. In challenging Hollywood's tendency to construct black youth culture only through a ghettocentric imagination by telling the stories of the black middle class at a historically black college, *Drumline* challenges the wave of middle-class films that construct the world of the black middle class as a world without the ghetto, the black underclass or whites.

From moment one, Devon is constructed as an outsider to Atlanta A & T, to the black middle class. Not only is he hip-hop, but he comes from a single parent home. Yet the film does not demonize Devon for coming from a single parent home. Even though one has to question whether the film's efforts to demonize hip-hop and construct him as undisciplined replicates long-standing ideologies regarding black mothers and a culture of poverty, the film superficially portrays his mother as the source of Devon's focus and discipline. Rather than constructing her as the basis or cause of problems, *Drumline* celebrates her efforts in facilitating his entry into the black middle class. After receiving his diploma, Devon tells his mom, "I would never have made it without you. I would not have made it." Throughout the film, it is Mom who reminds Devon to study and to take care of business. Whereas the other films in this chapter construct a black middle-class world as devoid of struggle or serious problems, and ghettocentrism gives legitimacy to those who blame single black mothers for poverty, crime and other social problems, *Drumline* identifies his mother as a source of his values, discipline, and focus. Devon is able to overcome the absence of his father, the difficulties associated with growing up in New York City, and the supposedly negative influences of hip-hop to make it to a four-year university on a full scholarship. The film's depiction of his father is not so celebratory, as it portrays him as another absentee parent that added to Devon's struggles. His father is depicted as the reason for Devon's inability to fulfill his potential, to respect authority, and to understand the histories of the black community and its musical traditions.

Immediately after thanking his mother at graduation, Devon proceeds to find his father, a New York City subway operator, to alert him of his graduation, to this milestone, and his ascendancy to the black middle class. Devon angrily tells his father of his success, in spite of the difficult path created by his father's failures:

I got my diploma. I ain't never been arrested. I ain't got a whole lot of kids running around. Unlike yourself, I am doing something with my music. I got a full scholarship to Atlanta A & T playing drums. I wanna say I hope you're proud because I made it without you.

Walking away, Devon doesn't just turn his back on his father, but to an inner-city (what we are led to believe is a gangsta/ghetto life) existence.

While Devon stands inside a subway station, the trains pass him by, moving quicker and quicker as it becomes the serene picture of a college lifestyle, of the middle class, with trees, blue skies, and all that defines the possibilities of the American Dream. It takes Devon time to catch up to the train. Although his body is at college, among the future leaders of the black community, his identity and approach remain entrenched in a hip-hop, me-first, mentality due to his lack of discipline and values. Only through the efforts of Dr. Lee, his mother, Shawn, Laila, and others does Devon truly leave the ghetto behind him.

The film's effort to disrupt those narratives that imagine the black middle-class experience as not one of happy people with happy problems, as one isolated from social reality, results in its inclusion of Jayson, the lone white character and member of the band known as "affirmative action," in order to give voice to issues of race and race relations. Rather than illustrating the realities of white privilege, intergroup racial tensions, the complex issues at work with white students attending historically black colleges, or even the nature of contemporary racism, the film positions Jayson as the true minority. Jayson chooses to attend Atlanta A & T, rather than the University of Georgia, where he would have been a star, because of his love for A & T and its marching band. At one point, Devon and Ernest mock Jayson because of his difficulty in learning the styles and moves of the A & T Marching Band. Jayson does not budge, emphasizing his skills and his life of black musical styles: "Don't even try that white men can't jump bullshit. I got skills. . . . I could have been P-1 at Georgia Tech or UGA in a minute. . . . I love this band. . . . A & T [is] the reason I picked up the drum in the first place." In constructing his motivation as one of love, rather than fascination with blackness, *Drumline* disarms possible assumptions that Jayson is yet another "wigger" obsessed with being black. Jayson is likable, adding more power to the film's positioning of him as a minority. At one instance in the film, his roommate challenges him to a battle on the field, presumably because of his whiteness, to see who will perform during that Saturday's game, because others assume that he lacks what it takes to get on the field. Only after Devon teaches him some rhythm and moves does Jayson make it back onto the field, demonstrating how the film replicates long-standing stereotypes regarding race with the musically talented Devon teaching the rhythmless Jayson how to march, how to move, and how to integrate and succeed in an all-black marching band.

Equally troubling here is the film's message about race relations in that it defines race relations as situational and based on numbers, where whites can exist and suffer as a minority in certain spaces or situations. Moreover, Jayson works hard to integrate himself and garner acceptance as to further illustrate that from the film's point of view, when minorities follow a path of hard work, accommodation, discipline, and respectability, acceptance and assimilation will likely follow. In this sense, the film imagines Jayson as a model minority, erasing his whiteness, which provides privileges regardless of the location.

The film's oversimplification of racism and its erasure of power within its narrative on the possibilities of education in securing a middle-class status are not just a prominent theme here, but through much of the genre, which tends to focus on values, work ethic, and perseverance as a means to securing the American Dream regardless of race. Ultimately, *Drumline* is a story of the American Dream, of a post-Civil Rights black America, of acceptance and success. Like *Brown Sugar* and *Love & Basketball*, its narrative of success is not limited to the clichéd stories of the middle-class, educational attainment and the acquisition of material possessions, but the ability to bridge the gap between generations through the fusion of cultural attributes.

Of equal importance here, *Drumline* positions the advancement of the black community through the successful integration of the hip-hop generation. This can happen only through its ability to become disciplined, learn respect, and follow in the footsteps of previous generations. Although Dr. Lee and Shawn (who also needs to learn his own lessons) spend ample time teaching Devon these lessons and providing him with tools needed for success, he remains resistant, choosing self over community. During their homecoming performance, Devon and the A & T band are challenged to a battle in which members of the opposing team stand face-to-face with A & T, almost daring them to out duel them. Unwilling to accept this affront to his own vision of black masculinity and this public "dis'," Devon responds hip-hop style, beating the other team's drum, sparking a massive brawl. Without discipline, Devon succumbs to his "hoodlum identity," resulting in his being excused from the team. With the culmination of his dysfunctional ways, the film positions the fight and his dismissal from the team as his rock-bottom moment where Devon learns about accountability and consequence. For Devon, this moment taught him what could be lost—scholarship, music, friends, and respect—because of a lack of discipline, as a result of his "doing me."

This incidence is not the only source of change for Devon, who also finds inspiration from his dad, who sends him a box full of "music you know and some you don't." With tapes of Art Tatum, Max Roach, and Ray Miles (his father), Devon finds inspiration in these artists of past years. He begins drumming in his room to the rhythm of these old sounds, even as the camera gazes at the posters of several hip-hop artists. In this instance Devon becomes the old and the new, Tatum and Snoop, Roach and The Roots. The father who had given him so little eventually helps him see the path toward fulfilling his dream by bridging cultural and generational gaps and by recapturing his love of music.

Devon is not alone in his maturation, as Shawn, who appears to have figured it out, also needs discipline and to put his ego aside for the good of the team. Although he sees himself as better than Devon because of his middle-class identity, Dr. Lee chastises him for his own failures. Like Devon, Shawn had put his own sound/identity ahead of that of the line, working hard not to teach Devon to sabotage his presence on the team. In a powerful scene, Devon, wearing a sweatsuit and beanie, and Shawn, donning jeans and a sweater, finally square off in a battle for the band and the black community. Their confrontation is ostensibly one of hip-hop and middle-class identities battling inside the band's music studio.

Devon: Look, man, I got some stuff I got to put down. So, hurry up with your little rudimentary shit.

Shawn: I had it with your no-talent wanna-a-be gangster ass. You wanna prove once and for all that I am better than you. Strap up.

Devon: Bring it on, big brother tin man.

[While both drumming in an effort to prove their power of their own masculinity]

Shawn: Fake thug, wanna-a-be, little drummer boy.

Devon: Whatever [flipping stick in the air]. You big bald headed bourgie my first drum having. . . .

Shawn: I ain't trying to hear you.

Devon: You ain't heard me since I stepped on campus.

Shawn: Cause I know what you about.

Devon: You don't know shit about me.

While the two boys initially point sticks at each other's faces, the camera and music capture the anger and tension in the room. Recognizing that he was failing his responsibility of teaching Devon the needed discipline, Shawn quickly puts his stick down, prompting Devon to claim victory.

Through insults and vocalizing their own prejudices, Devon and Shawn come together to make their own collective sound. They teach each other about the fallacy of their own stereotypes and the possibilities of working together as a team. This seems to be the central message of the film in that while discipline remains paramount to the success of the hip-hop generation, the film's effort to challenge the assumptions, divisions, and tensions between generations, classes, and approaches to the advancement of the black community offers its vision for a black community to work as one, as "one band, one sound." Their confrontation and eventual learning of lessons taught by Dr. Lee allow Shawn and Devon to create their own music, dreaming a new path with their own cadence of both old and new sounds, all as the film sings a song of immense possibility.

Through *Drumline*, audiences see a vision of the American Dream bound up in black youth finding discipline and respect of team, history, and community. Collaborating musically, Shawn and Devon produce the cadence and musical arrangements for the BET Big Southern Classic (the Super Bowl of band competitions), leading A & T not only to victory, which had proved to

be illusive, but to the defeat of Morris Brown, whose musical style emphasized contemporary sounds in the absence of any recognition of black artists
of previous generations. More important, in producing a sound that paid
tribute to the past and present while imagining a new future, Devon and
Shawn found a way to teach their teacher, providing Dr. Lee with a lesson on
the needed direction of the band and the black community. Inspired by their
song, selflessness, and teamwork, Dr. Lee proclaims that their performance at
the Classic embodies the new direction of the band, "honoring the past and
present at the same time;" playing classic sounds and getting crunked. So, in
the end, the film not only tells a story of discipline, growth, and redemption,
of both segments of the hip-hop generation (gangsta and middle-class), but
also sees the success of the black community through changes and adjustment of the older generation. Dr. Lee, initially resistant to anything hip-hop,
so much so that he describes hip-hop as being the opposite of music, changes
his tune, incorporating not only the musical sound of the hip-hop generation, buts its clothing style, with A & T donning yellow bandanas, at the
Classic, and its languages, telling them "let's get crunked." Their success is
the result of Dr. Lee's own growth and his willingness to bridge the gap, but
only after his pupils demonstrate their willingness and ability to change as
well. He tells the band, "People say the band is just a reflection of its director.
But I want you all to know that you have influenced me as well. And I'm very
proud of you." Although addressing the entire band, his sentimental speech,
similar to *Drumline's* end, and that of most of the genre, embodies the film's
effort to redeem Devon.

Devon's early failures, his ego, his brash masculinity, his selfishness, and
his hip-hop identity (he eventually begins to correct his own use of Ebonics
toward the end of the film) are lost as he works with Shawn: he helps Jayson
find his rhythm despite no longer being a member of the team; he teaches the
line although he has nothing to gain from his participation. He becomes the
true leader of the team, learning how to follow in order to lead. The film's
disturbing overall vision (especially read in context of increasing levels of
state violence directed at youth of color), that the process of disciplining and
controlling the hip-hop generation is needed in the black community's quest
to find happiness and secure the America Dream, replicates the themes and
message of the rest of the genre. At the same time, it advances dominant discourse regarding crime and the problems with today's black youth more than
the others. Through discipline and hard work, Devon is able to transcend the
limitations of a ghetto (cultural) existence, fulfilling the ultimate American
Dream of individual success, educational attainment, and grounded assimilation. Not limiting itself to tropes of the American Dream, and discipline,
Drumline equally fulfills dominant assumptions about race, offering a clear
narrative of the insignificance of race beyond culture, which of course can be
practiced (positively or negatively) by anyone regardless of class, race, and
geography. Devon ultimately finds a productive way to embody a positive

black masculinity, one that any and all can identity with, especially given the elements of hard work, discipline, team, and accommodation (i.e., middle-class values), each of which is so prominent in this film, as well as in *Love & Basketball* and *Brown Sugar*.

LOVE & BASKETBALL

Like *The Wood, The Best Man,* and *Brown Sugar, Love & Basketball* (Gina Prince-Bythewood, 2000) explores the inner workings of black relationships in telling the story of Monica (Sanaa Latham) and Quincy (Omar Epps), who's lifelong friendship materializes and disintegrates and rematerializes into one of love and passion. Using basketball as both a subplot and meta-phor for the characters' roller-coaster love life, which spans the 1980s and 1990s, *Love & Basketball* once again challenges dominant representations of the black city experience. Focusing on relationships, the gendered aspects of basketball, and the black middle class, *Love & Basketball* challenges the veneer of the dominant narrative, although offering little resistance of domi-nant discourses regarding race, racism, and the American Dream.

Responding to Cynthia Fuchs regarding how *Love & Basketball* is different from what its viewers might have seen before, Omar Epps summarized both the strengths and weaknesses of both this film and the wave of middle-class African American films: "It's a new slice of African American life, with basketball as a backdrop. It's refreshing in that it's part of that new movement in black films, looking at the middle class, both the kids come from two-parent household, so it's not against all odds, or basketball or die. And for me, the major draw was that the girl got to have her cake and eat it too" (2000). The film most cer-tainly recenters the black middle class, telling the story of a young black female (although Quincy is a prominent protagonist) and her struggles against patri-archy, sexism, and double standards inside and outside the world of sports. It also documents a world of intergenerational and gender divisions, where fathers and sons teach each other how to become men, and mothers and daughters challenge each other's definitions of femininity. Through each part of the nar-rative, *Love & Basketball* documents the power of love, its importance and the difficulties of securing love with friends, family, and partners. In chronicling a world often erased by Hollywood, where representations tend to pathologize single mothers, youth of color, and absentee fathers, *Love & Basketball* falls into the trap of flat positivity. It replicates what Kobena Mercer warns about in terms of responding to racism with what appears to be "positive images" (1994). It thus reflects a "social engineering approach to black cultural productions, which views black image making as practice that should be devoted to promoting posi-tive representations of African Americans." The overtly positive trajectory of the film de-centers the struggle of the characters over both individual obstacles and those resulting from societal institutions such as racism and patriarchy; yet moments of subversion can still be found in *Love & Basketball*.

From the initial moments of the film, it is clear that Gina Price-Blythewood is up to something different with *Love & Basketball,* her first feature and one of few current Hollywood films written and directed by a black woman. With Al Green's "Love and Happiness" forming the backdrop, the camera brings the audience to unfamiliar territory, Los Angeles's upper middle-class suburb, Baldwin Hills—large houses with plush green lawns, long drive ways, ample trees, kids shooting hoops, peace and quiet. Yet this world is not a white community that drives visions of the American Dream, thereby challenging dominant representations and stereotypes of the black community being one of decay, poverty, and despair. "By constructing an urban space defined outside the more common parameters of poverty, criminality, and drugs," Price-Blythewood "provides a view of a community that is more diverse than the majority of representations of black city space so far would have one believe, and in doing so, [s]he changes representation of the inner city away from earlier spatiotemporal constructions of the ghetto" (Massood 2003, p. 130).

Through the film, Monica's family is clearly marked as middle class, as a challenge to the stereotypical inscription of contemporary blackness: their large house, expensive furniture, suburban neighborhood, family pictures, and even the deployment of gender roles inscribes a middle-class existence. With Dad working at a bank and Mom tending the house, the film goes to great lengths to link traditional gender roles to middle-class status, concluding that once families are able to prosper on a single income, women return to their rightful place within the home. The film's narrative does not necessarily problematize this idea, but documents tension, whether through Monica and her mom, or Q and Monica, as to how to transgress these proscribed gender divisions of middle-class life.

While the film paints both Monica and Quincy as the embodiment of today's black middle class, it leaves the audience believing that both Monica and Q can attend college only with an athletic scholarship, through their basketball. In a film that renders race and blackness as little more than aesthetic markers, its inscription of stereotypical visions of blackness where ballin' represents the only path to academic success is particularly troubling. In fact, the film's narrative emphasis on basketball being one of the few means to secure a college education for black youth reflects an erasure of class, of the privileges that middle-class black men and women have within America's educational system. To say this denies the effects of race on the black middle class and questions how *Love & Basketball* plays on stereotypes by chronicling how even those black youth with privileges need athletics and a scholarship to secure an education. At the same time, it denies the importance and significance of race within contemporary America. The film's overall erasure of the ways in which race and racism affect the black middle class represents a defining characteristic of *Love & Basketball* and the entire genre of film.

The tendency of middle-class-oriented African American films to construct a world without problem, as one of happy people with happy problems, not only challenges prevalent popular representations in Hollywood, but also validates a post-Civil Rights America. In portraying Africans as having made it, as having fulfilled the American Dream, *Love & Basketball* erases the 1 million black folks in prison, the 18.1 percent rate of unemployment among African Americans, and the 44 percent of black youth living in poverty. At the same time, it erases the struggles and relevance of racism within lives of the black middle class.

Joe Feagin and Melvin Sikes (1995), in *Living with Racism: The Black Middle Class Experience,* found that the black middle class faces the pervasive sting of white racism—often subtle and covert, at times blatant—on a daily basis. According to their study of 209 middle-class blacks, the black middle class experience racism in the form of discrimination on the job in salary, evaluations, and promotions; prejudice against black renters and homebuyers by white landlords, real estate agents, homeowners and neighbors; the channeling of black students into vocational "tracks"; physical assaults and institutionalized racism on college campuses; and daily hostility blacks face in restaurants, stores, and other public places. In other words, the black middle class has not transcended race; it has not secured entry into the greatest place on earth where racism and stereotypes no longer affect life's opportunities. Whether in dealing with police brutality, the legacies of racism, or segregation, racism still plays through the lives of the black middle class.

In watching *Love & Basketball,* viewers see no such world, but rather a colorblind world. For example, both families live in Baldwin Hills, a community with a long history of racial segregation. In dehistoricizing the formation of this community, one that came into existence through struggle, resistance, and bloodshed, *Love & Basketball* imagines progress as natural, as the result of hard work and perseverance. Beyond this historical erasure, the film imagines a world in which the problems of the black poor have little relevance to the lives of the black middle class; *Love & Basketball* paints Baldwin Hills, a community adjacent to Los Angeles's poorer black and Latino communities, in isolation to the black poor. Moreover, although both Monica and Quincy attend Crenshaw High, there is little reflection about the historical and racial context of their high school years. In fact, the late 1980s and early 1990s saw an increased amount of policing within schools like Crenshaw, with cops and metal detectors, and the declining investment from the state within inner city schools. With state expenditures focusing on the mass incarceration of communities of color at the expense of education, health care, welfare, job training, and other social services programs, inner city schools catering to black and Latino students saw dramatic changes during this period. Such changes, as with increasing incidences of racial profiling as part of America's war on drugs, did not elude the black middle class, affecting all, especially those living adjacent to and attending schools within America's ghettos.

The effort of *Love & Basketball* to tell an alternative cinematic narrative to that of the ghettocentric imagination, one of the middle class, contributes to the film's effort to kill the audience with kindness, erasing the problems that define the black middle class within post-Civil Rights America. Whether racial profiling and being followed at the store or glass ceilings within the business world, discriminatory teachers, or racist curriculum, the black middle class continues to face the burden of blackness. In constructing a world devoid of race, one that appears to be colorblind, *Love & Basketball* goes beyond telling this untold story, bringing to life an all-too-familiar story of hard work, perseverance, of class trumping race, of progress, of an America where race does not matter, and one of the American Dream.

In bypassing the realities of contemporary racism, its effects on the black middle class, and the persistent place of state violence within the black experience, *Love & Basketball* tells a story of women's experiences, "in relation to and separate from those of the men in their lives." While surely a story of Monica, Camile (Alfre Woodard, her mother), and Nona (Debbi Morgan, Quincy's mom), privileging no experience over another, it avoids the trap of heaping praise onto Monica because of her independence, because of her will to challenge existing definitions of femininity from society and her mother, and because of her desire to trade an apron for a jersey. Rather, the film seeks to contextualize (mostly through generation) each woman's identity, their struggles, as different yet also connected to larger ideologies and institutions—masculinity, patriarchy, double standards, and discrimination. "Camille, Nona, and Monica have very different experiences, to be sure, but each is represented with a similar respect, and Monica's is clearly shaped by her understanding of what was available to her mother's generation," writes Cynthia Fuchs. "Where the girl faces hurdles based in discrimination against women as professionals and as athletes, her mother and Nona embody the long term cultivation of a 'woman's place,' their simultaneous internalization and resentment of such limits. Where Nona waits for her husband at home, priding herself on raising a decent and sensitive son, Camille is caught between two hard places: she fears her daughter's independence, but she also admires and encourages it" (2000).

The film's effort to challenge societal double standards and the ways patriarchy constructs the home as a "woman's place," forcing women to push aside dreams for good of family, is an important feminist statement. Unfortunately, the film's decision to tell a universal story, to avoid race through rendering class as the ultimate trump card, not only negates the power of the narrative, but also limits its contribution of African American cinema. White supremacy has long denied black woman access to traditional definitions of femininity, pushing (forcing) black women out of the home and into the workplace, further delegitimizing their femininity by denying their claims to productive motherhood (those who stay home are the good mothers). It has also limited definitions of beauty and womanhood to white women. The film's effort to reconstitute patriarchy and sexism outside a context of racism, where generational and gender conflict mediate questions of whether women can wear jerseys and also be women, smacks in the face of the complexity of black female identity.

While attempting to construct a colorblind raceless world, *Love & Basketball* enters into a series of dominant discourses regarding race and basketball. *Love & Basketball*, like the WNBA itself, attempts to capitalize on the backlash against the NBA. Denounced as not offering "real basketball" as full of me-first, selfish (black) players, the popularity of the NBA waned in the 1990s. Wrapped in the cloak of amateurism, or the limited financial reward of women's sport, *Love & Basketball* imagines an ideal world where the values (love and adoration of sport/fan/community, hard work, team) of sports are firmly entrenched in the organization of sport. The links between gender, colorblindness, and love of the game transcends the gender and racial mediation of these celluloid athletes, but is visible within the context (discourse) to which these discussions exist. *Love & Basketball* offers a "breath of fresh air for an American public 'tired of trash-talking, spit-hurling, head-butting sports millionaires'" (Cole and Andrews 2001, p. 72). More specifically, it offers an alternative black female hero to "African American professional basketball players who are routinely depicted in the popular media as selfish, insufferable, and morally reprehensible" (Cole and Andrews 2001, p. 72).

Whereas women and white athletes play out of love/respect for the game, black male athletes are imagined as playing because of selfish needs and economic benefits. *Love & Basketball*, thus, deploys widely seen images/tropes of black male athletes, eluding the simplicity of whiteness with the inscription of black female athleticism as its counterpoint, simultaneously entering into a discursive field that envisions white and female athletes as heroes that overcome adversity through hard work, determination, and faith, as opposed to the gifted (genetics) black male athletes who care little beyond self and compensation.

Following in the tradition of a film like *Hoosiers* (1986), *Love & Basketball* offers an alternative entry into the world of basketball through the women's game. This attempt to construct a world of basketball through a narrative of middle class colorless blackness seeks to reclaim basketball for its beauty, for its focus on team, and for its discipline. While avoiding questions of contemporary basketball and its surrounding racial discourse by nostalgically debating narratives of the late 1980s and early 1990s, where we are led to believe bling-bling, long shorts, trash-talking, and selfish players were rare, the film offers a few signifiers (stereotypes) of blackness. Throughout the film, Monica is hot-headed, temperamental, and unsportsmanlike. The film infers that Monica's propensity to talk trash comes from the influence of black masculine basketball culture. As within the larger societal project, the film clearly disapproves of these behaviors. It illustrates the destructive consequences of keeping it street on the court (technical fouls; Monica initially not getting recruited) and reclaims the importance of disciplining and punishing black bodies.

Early in the film, Monica is benched because she taunts another player and receives a technical fowl. Although a college recruiter was scouting her at this game, her coach sends her (us) a message about discipline. Positioned as deserving this punishment, Monica does not learn her lesson until her white coach at the University of Southern California (Christine Dunford) intervenes. During a heated scrimmage, Monica finds herself matched up against Sidra O'Neal (Erika Ringor), her competition at the starting point guard position. Monica seems to have the upper hand, ripping Sidre to start a one-on-one fast break. Rather than conventionally driving the ball to the basketball for an uncontested lay-up, Monica pulls up for a 3-pointer, holding her hand in the air as the ball swishes through the net. Monica basks in her glory with her pose, but the game continues and Sidre scores without resistance from Monica, her would-be defender. This causes the coach to stop the action.

Coach: Monica, while your busy, your man just scored. Show me again.

Monica: What?

Coach: You like to pose so much, lets see it again (Monica laughs). You think I'm funny (team laughs as Monica raises her arm to recapture pose). I want you to stand like that for rest of the practice.

Monica: Coach?

Coach: You stand like that so you get sick of it, because I don't want to see it again; you hear me?. . . . You better step off the court.

Love & Basketball not only replicates widespread discourses that attempt to police and demonize the intrusion of showboating and trash-talking into the world of sports, it sees such behavior as destructive. The coach (and others, including her parents) shows Monica the error of her ways, disciplining and eventually eliminating such behavior. On the other hand, Quincy is unable to overcome these cultural practices and is engaging in some destructive behaviors. Without his father, he falls into the cultural traps of blackness, whether with his decision to turn pro or his practice of showboating.

One of the important ways in which *Love & Basketball* engages contemporary racial discourses regarding sport is through Quincy's (bad) decision to turn professional after only one year in college. *Love & Basketball* makes its contempt clear for young black males skipping college for NBA riches and its lifestyle. The film suggests that Quincy's decision is a self-destructive move that leads toward a failed career. Entering the game with the other reserves late in the LA Lakers game (his fourth or fifth team), the camera emphasizes Quincy's failures in the league, with Chick Hearn (the Lakers' legendary announcer) announcing his unfulfilled potential in the league. After missing a jumper, the camera shows a less brash Quincy moving up and down the court, eventually making a steal, resulting in a break-away dunk. Rather than going for a lay-up or a simple dunk, he goes for one with flair and style, landing awkwardly and hearing his knee "pop." Quincy's ultimate failure comes through a break-away dunk, the signifier of a career wasted by bad decision making, both on and off the court. His failure to undo the problematic manifestations of a black masculinity based on arrogance and a flashy on-the-court approach ended his career, just as his decision to leave college early proved to be detrimental to his professional and personal growth.

Through both decisions—turning professional and showboating—*Love & Basketball* gives voice to much of contemporary discourse of demonization regarding today's NBA and documents these decisions as self-destructive. Like today's media coverage of the NBA, *Love & Basketball* constructs authentic masculine blackness as menacing and threatening, as a pollutant that requires surveillance and control, whether with increased rules or more prisons. More specifically, its denunciation of younger black males entering into the league reflects a widespread backlash against the infusion of hip-hop and efforts to police "authentic blackness." The efforts to push those young black men who have jumped straight to the league reflects the desire to regulate bodies in the league (and send symbolic messages to fans) and to push future players into conditions and spaces that will ultimately produce a still commodifiable, yet controllable installment of today's hip-hop baller. Although complicated with elements of gender and the limited popularity of women's basketball, *Love & Basketball* constructs the on-the-court Quincy as undesirable and Monica as an embodiment of a controlled and still commodifiable inscription of blackness.

Although *Love & Basketball* seems to want to function as African American film transcending race, its construction of Quincy and Monica embodies dominant stereotypes of black masculinity. Its effort to construct a narrative of gender strife and tension comes through its reliance on dominant representations of black male athleticism. Quincy as a natural talent, as a great athlete, appears to have been born to play ball. He takes the game for granted and uses it to become a star, a millionaire, and desired commodity.

On the other hand, Monica works at the game—she practices, lives and dies with the game, rarely traveling without ball in hand. She resists the teasing and questions about her identity, persevering because of her love for the game. In an effort to show the double standard that leads Quincy to NBA riches and Monica to play for a pittance in Europe, *Love & Basketball* relies on racial and gender stereotypes. The film leads audiences to believe that Monica works hard because she, as a girl, lacks the natural ability of Quincy, the genetically advantaged (NBA father; black masculinity) ball player. Worse, society praises Quincy and demonizes Monica, in both monetary and other ways. In offering this important argument about gender and sports, *Love & Basketball* deploys widespread stereotypes of race, failing to see the interplay of race and gender.

Another inscription of black masculinity via stereotype comes through the film's representation of Zeek (Dennis Haysbert), Quincy's father. A former professional athlete, the film portrays Zeek as upwardly mobile, yet unable to outrun his true identity. Despite his attempt to play the part of a business-man (always wearing a sports coat and expensive jewelry), he cannot secure any job after basketball except for a "shitty scouting" gig. More important, Zeek is unable to transcend his own faulty black masculinity, one that leads him to lie to his son and cheat on his wife. As noted by Patricia Hill Collins, "Like their female counterparts, men of African descent [are] also perceived to have excess sexual appetite, yet with a disturbing additional feature, a pre-dilection for violence" (2004, p. 32). Zeek embodies the stereotypical black male athlete, who despite having secured the American Dream, cannot stay true to this dream because of his insatiable sexual appetite. Justifying his affairs to his son, Zeek tells Quincy after confessing infidelity: "When you're in the NBA there are 100 girls in every city; 20 make it past security." Playing on widespread assumptions of the primarily black NBA, the film—even as it tells us that race does not matter—fulfills those visions of the NBA, reifying dominant constructions of a valueless NBA and problematic black masculin-ity. Even as *Love & Basketball* attempts to construct a world where race does not matter, a narrative that purports itself to be colorblind, it relies heavily on fetishism of black athleticism and stereotypes of black identity, whether it is those of college students (athletes) or black male sexuality.

While *Love & Basketball* paints the struggles and tensions of the black middle class as one of generation and gender, rather than race and one con-cerned with structural inequality, its resolution follows suit. Unable to find satisfaction without a heteronormative, patriarchal relationship, Monica gives up basketball overseas to return to the United States in pursuit of Quincy, a family, and a "normal" (middle-class, heterosexual, nuclear) relationship. Unable to continue playing basketball, she chooses acceptability from family and community in trading "in Nikes for a pair of (high-heeled) shoes" that she can't even walk in. Monica attempts to become a "lady," to become more traditional in hopes of winning back Quincy. Whereas in college, she "didn't know how to do that (being a good girlfriend) and be about ball," the film's fourth quarter reveals a transformation where Monica tries to be that good girlfriend, with or without basketball. Her efforts to win him, even though he is engaged to Tyra Banks's character, leads to their settling the issue like most couples: on the basketball court. Although Quincy wins their one-on-one match for marriage, which should have resulted in Monica giving up on her pursuit of Quincy, he instead challenges her to another game, resulting in the ultimate victory: their reuniting.

The fulfillment of this American Dream did not come through Monica merely winning back her man or through her performance on the court, but because of her efforts to become a "true woman," to finally figure out the proper balance between "ballin" and being a girlfriend, wife, mother, and woman. *Love & Basketball,* thus, concludes at the Great Western Forum in Los Angeles, with Monica now married, with a child, playing for the Los Angeles Sparks. With Quincy and her young daughter sitting on the sidelines in support, the film illustrates the possibility of being both a basketball player (traditionally seen as a male space) and a woman, of working outside the home and being a faithful wife and mother. By the end, Quincy and Monica not only figured out their relationship and what constitutes healthy (black) masculinity and femininity, but the ways in which black families can successfully integrate into modern America. Although apprehensive to engage the racial context of basketball or contemporary America, and the effects of racism/race on relationships, family, community, education, sport, or assimilation, instead focusing on deracialized gendered narrative, *Love & Basketball* provides a template for *Brown Sugar,* which offers a far more nuanced and complicated understanding of race, albeit still mired by dominant discourses of the American Dream, individualism, and colorblindness.

BROWN SUGAR

After a screening of *Brown Sugar* (Rick Famuyiwa, 2002) in my African American film course, students were quick to point to its similarities to *Love & Basketball.* Both films chronicle loves stories that emanate from childhood and through 20 years of friendship. Each documents the experiences of the black middle class as one of success and opportunity, where race determines little in terms of life chances. Specifically, *Brown Sugar,* even more than *Love & Basketball,* chronicles how African Americans of the hip-hop generation have used popular culture as a path to the American Dream. Both Tre (Taye Diggs) and Sidney (Sanaa Latham) possess all the trappings of financial and professional success: the ability to attend fancy cocktail parties with celebrities, expensive business suits, designer furniture and art work, dinners at fancy restaurants (although the hip-hop roots in Tre mandates an occasional hot dog), $50,000 wedding rings, and a bridal shower of cucumber sandwiches and gifts from Tiffany's. Clearly, the world presented within the cinematic imagination of *Brown Sugar* is alien to much of popular culture, with the exception of those seen in *Love & Basketball.* As with other films, *Brown Sugar* explores what it means to be black in contemporary America, offering a sometimes powerful narrative about the complexities of blackness—being gulley or hip-hop does not require a gangsta lean, a jersey, or a diamond-crusted pendant; it can come with a business suit, a phat crib, or in being a cab driver.

The complexities and diversity of blackness, as well as the processes of commodification, performance, and defining all of which exist outside a black community, reflect the limitations of a discourse focused on an authentic blackness. Notwithstanding these oppositional elements, as well as the film's sometimes powerful commentary on assimilation, accommodation, and "keeping it real," the film's tendency to mirror the ideological and discourses of other middle-class oriented films not only limit its power but contributes to dominant understandings of race, embodying the realities of new racism.

While following in the footsteps of *Love & Basketball* in its concern the erasure of the daily and institutional racism that the black middle class faces in contemporary America and its tendency to inscribe a narrative of "happy people with happy problems," *Brown Sugar* deviates from the raceless and colorblind worlds presented in both *Drumline* and *Love & Basketball*. Its limited recognition of racism and meek voice to the persistent effects of race in the streets and boardroom is not matched with its successful treatment of black identity in the twenty-first century.

Unlike *Love & Basketball*, which privileges gender over race in chronicling the experiences of the black middle class through a world of basketball, *Brown Sugar* offers a more complex rendering of black assimilation and acceptance. Using hip-hop, a cultural forum often labeled as outside the mainstream, as a lens to explore growth and cultural change, as well as the proliferation of the black middle class, *Brown Sugar* asks: what is lost with assimilation? Who/What is left behind (and gained) through acceptance in mainstream America? What compromises are invariably tied to financial gains and cultural acceptance? The film's situating of these dilemmas within a world of hip-hop offers a powerful commentary on the long-standing issue of double consciousness within the black community. In "Of Our Spiritual Strivings," the initial chapter of *The Souls of Black Folk*, W.E.B. DuBois argues for the existence of a fragmented African American consciousness, which he describes as "twoness." According to DuBois, the histories of enslavement, segregation, and state violence resulted in a "double consciousness—two souls, two thoughts, two unreconciled strivings, two warring ideals in one dark body" (p. 3). In other words, the desire to remain black and be accepted politically, economically, and culturally within the American landscape represents a desire "to satisfy two unreconciled ideas" that cannot be reconciled (p. 5). James Weldon Johnson, with *Autobiography of an Ex-Colored Man* (1995, 1912), offers a similar assessment of black identity formation, describing it as "a sort of dual personality," where African Americans are forced to reconcile a "desire to help those I considered my people or more a desire to distinguish myself" (21–22, 147). Although both DuBois and Johnson oversimplify the question of identity in relying on a false binary of personal and political liberation, their ideas continue to permeate public and private discourses, academic and popular conversations, as evident in the narrative of *Brown Sugar*.

Brown Sugar opens with a series of short, tightly framed film shots of the New York subway, graffiti, and others signifiers of an urban setting. With a series of old cuts playing in the background, the opening shot not only sets the stage of the film's narrative of hip-hop, but also marks its nostalgia for this historical moment as the film's point of departure. Followed by a series of interviews with the O.G.s and new, but true, voices of hip-hop—Pete

Rock, Russell Simmons, Jermaine Dupree, Talib Kweli, Doug E. Fresh, De la Soul—each of whom crystallizes the film's nostalgia for a hip-hop lost in speaking how and when they fell in love with hip-hop.

The film's opening scene make clear that *Brown Sugar* isn't simply a narrative of the black middle class or one that attempts to capitalize on the popularity of hip-hop. Rather, it is a history of street art, a story of a somewhat failed cultural resistance movement, of the ever-changing meaning and place of blackness, hip-hop, and the black community within post-Civil Rights America. Packed with nostalgia for a time when hip-hop was pure and real, and limited by its masculine imagination that privileges the old and new voices of male hip-hop artists, *Brown Sugar*, in its opening moments, offer a powerful commentary on how hip-hop has long been a source of freedom and liberation for the black community. As the film's part-time narrator, Sidney sets this tone, announcing on the conclusion of the last interview with these real hip-hop artists, that "hip-hop was my first friend, the one to talk to us, to understand." Establishing the cultural and political importance of hip-hop, as an art form that gave voice to the struggles of black youth, while also providing hope in the face of decreasing opportunities and increased levels of state violence, *Brown Sugar* offers an important commentary as to what happened to hip-hop, to the black community, as part of its music lost its roots—as its roots were ripped from ground by corporate interests, material aspirations, and cooptation.

In spite of being a product of hip-hop's beginnings, Tre represents those undesirable changes evident within the rap game. Enticed by the luxuries provided by transnational corporations, Tre has lost sight of his (the music's) roots. Working at Millennium Records, Tre embodies everything that is wrong with hip-hop: image over substance, a lack of soul, and moneymaking over consciousness. Although dissatisfied with his role in the industry— so much so that he hopes to sign a new artist, Cabby (Mos Def), because he is what hip-hop needs to be about—Tre has to toe the company vision when it signs Ren and Ten: The Hip Hop Dalmatians. Exaggerated to the highest level, Ren and Ten represent everything that the film (and Tre and Sidney) sees as wrong with hip-hop: all gimmicks and no skills; driven purely by money; a fake, corporate vision of hip-hop, with their bling, black and white mink coats, and exaggerated street vernacular.

Once again reminded that he is not being true to his love of hip-hop, its roots, his self, or his true love of Sidney, who continually calls for a return to the goodness of hip-hop, Tre is enraged that he has to produce the hip-hop Dalmatians and not real music. Hoping to change the system from the inside, Tre approaches Simon (Wendell Pierce), Millennium's CEO, yearning to plant hip-hop's true roots inside its new corporate headquarters. Hearing Tre's apprehension to work with the Hip-Hop Dalmatians and desire to produce "authentic hip-hop," Simon is less than pleased, reminding Tre that they work in the music business: "Simon: I am trying to sell records to those who buy records. Get me MTV rotation." As Tre stands in disbelief to the CEO's decision to sign the Hip-Hop Dalmatians, it is clear to him (us) that reform isn't possible and that the music he loves has lost its ways:

Simon: They the future. Eminem, he paved the way. Now they gonna be like Paul McCartney and Stevie Wonder. Ya know. Paul McCartney and Michael Jackson; woo.

Tre: They can do a remake of the "Girl is mine."

Simon: Oh shit! Hell yeah. See that's why I got you. That's gonna be tight. I'm gonna be able to call it, "That ho is mine."

Tre: Are you serious?

Simon: Yes, if you want to work for Millennium Records that's what we do here. We make hits. If you want to keep it real go to Rauckus. We keep it profitable. It is too hard to do both.

Frustrated by his inability to reconcile the demands of profit and his yearning to keep it real, Tre retreats from his corporate office to take solace in Sidney. Confessing that he wants to leave Millennium, he is torn because of the allure of "money, upward mobility and suits." He wants to make real music, but he can't imagine giving up the perks of corporate hip-hop. Sidney shows compassion despite her trueness to hip-hop and contempt for the music of Millennium, giving voice to the struggle of doing business within corporate America. "We all sell out a bit in business. That's how we survive." Unsure if he does anything but sell-out, he tells Sidney that he wants something else. "I want to make music. All I do is make money."

While Sidney does not disagree with Tre that he has "punked out" by accepting compromises that render hip-hop as no longer hip-hop, Tre knows that he has not only failed hip-hop and the black community but Sidney. He has failed to give that which he loves the lover they deserve.

Tre's struggle to find acceptance and co-exist within the corporate power structure in spite of his yearning to remain true to hip-hop is not merely reflective of the allure of his bougie lifestyle but also to the demands of Reece (Nicole Arie Parker), his wife. Unlike Sidney, Reese is not hip-hop, but rather an embodiment of a soulless black middle class. While a lawyer with what seems to be her own professional power (in telling us very little about Reese, the film demonizes her as a pollutant to Tre's effort to be true to self and community), Reese loves Tre (and hip-hop) as much for the diamond rings and beautiful apartment as for him. Upon confessing his dissatisfaction with his role at Millennium, intimating his thoughts about leaving the company, Reese is less than sympathetic and supportive. Believing that Tre was happy working at Millennium and certainly content with their lifestyle, she makes clear that she would have tried to talk him out of quitting his job had he asked. This is why Tre made the decision independent of his wife. His love is of hip-hop/Sidney and not Reese and her materialistic middle-class existence.

As to emphasize the beauty (internal and external) of Sidney and the disconnect between a confused and contradicted Tre and Reese, who seems unfazed by the demanded double consciousness, *Brown Sugar* concludes this sequence with Sidney once again expressing her love and angst for hip-hop (and blackness and Tre).

The union of hip-hop to the mainstream is a hard thing to imagine. Hip-hop was always this personal, regional thing that belonged to just me. Starting with Fab Five Freddy and Yo MTV Raps!, anyone with a television set and a cable box could get a piece of hip-hop. I knew I was gonna have to share and that was hard to get use to.

Beyond the mainstreaming of hip-hop, the film's struggle is one of moving forward without leaving behind that which made hip-hop special. It is about the compromises that come with success. Once again Sidney gives voice to the essence and conscience of hip-hop, demonstrating its value and why Tre truly loves Sidney and hip-hop. She is real and uncompromised, driven by her own love and sense of self. She has found the proper balance to move forward without severing roots.

The efforts to give voice to the history of hip-hop, chronicling a narrative highlighting its resistance origins to its commodified corporate cooptation by the mainstream, take on a particularly gendered tone. While both Tre and Cabby represent hip-hop (as evident in Sidney's love letter to hip-hop doubling as a love letter to him; Cabby keeping it real with his lyrics, by working in a cab and through repelling "Shiny suits and bling" and by "keepin it gulley"), Sidney embodies its roots and aesthetics. Cabby and Tre represent hip-hop, but Sidney is hip-hop. In the film's opening scene, while the camera and narrative privilege the voices of several hip-hop legends, Sidney's importance becomes clear. Beyond the surfaced centering of these men, the scene ostensibly renders Sidney as hip-hop. As she asks several rappers when they first fell in love with hip-hop, it is she they seek to impress with their answers. As Gwendolyn Pough notes, within *Check It While I Wreck It: Black Womanhood, Hip-Hop Culture and the Public Sphere,* "She might as well be saying so when did you first fall in love with me" (2004, p. 96).

Throughout the film, with her writing, her descriptions of hip-hop, and her encouragement to Tre to remain true to hip-hop, Sidney is positioned as the authentic, real-deal, embodiment of hip-hop culture. As Tre seeks to return to his (hip-hop, black, street) roots, to make "music rather than money," he also works to garner the approval of Sidney, "who is like hip-hop" (Pough 2004, p. 96). During a New Year's Eve party, Tre raises his glass to Sidney, and not his wife, Reese, whose light skin, bourgeois/assimilated lifestyle, materialistic aspiration, and lack of respect for the rap game, render her as not hip-hop. As he toasts Sidney, he describes her as "the perfect verse over a tight beat." With glass raised, he then announces "to hip-hop." *Brown Sugar* is not just a love story of Tre and Sidney, but of their love affair with hip-hop.

Reflecting the widespread practice within hip-hop that effectively symbol-izes the virtues of the music and culture through femininity, *Brown Sugar* fol-lows the "practice of gendering hip-hop as feminine" (Pough 2004, p. 94). In Common's "I Use to Love H.E.R," he raps about the history of hip-hop, from her (its) origins as an Afrocentric, pro-black, opposition art form to its less lovely stage. Common mourns the co-optation of hip-hop, chronicling the ways in which commercialization and mainstream audiences betrayed his youthful love.

At face value, such inscriptions appear to be celebrations of black womanhood—that which is sought and desired is black femininity, which serves as a stand-in for the virtues of hip-hop. Yet she is the source of betrayal as well, having left her man in search of the virtuous woman. Moreover, the practice of gendering hip-hop as feminine, evident in A Tribe Called Quest's "Bonita Applebaum," The Roots' "Act Too (The Love of . . .)" and Erykah Badu's "Love of My Life (Ode to Hip-Hop)," which appears on the soundtrack for *Brown Sugar,* all deny the agency of black women as artists, as practitioners, as activists, and even as fans. "Hip hop gendered feminine has no agency. She is something acted upon. She does not do; she is done" (Pough 2004, p. 94). While *Brown Sugar* challenges this practice in certain ways, by providing Sidney with voice and by positioning her as the conscience of hip-hop that we witness through her writing and conversations with Tre, it is ultimately Tre and Cabby that save hip-hop in their effort to win the love and respect of Sidney and community.

With the inspiration and financial assistance from Sidney (and without input or support from Reese), Tre ultimately leaves Millennium to start his own label. During a studio session with Ren and Ten: The Hip Hop Dal-matians recording "That Ho is Mine," Tre finally realizes that he cannot reconcile these two worlds, symbolically removing his tie, which shackles him inside the corporate world and outside hip-hop. Beyond quitting his job, starting his own label, and trading in his Armani suit for a Starter jersey, Tre returns to his roots by attempting to sign Cabby. Yearning to make truthful (true) hip-hop, Tre swallows his pride (Cabby had previously called him a sell-out), basically begging Cabby to sign with him, despite his past collabo-ration with Millennium, going as far as cleaning Cabby's taxi to demonstrate that he is indeed "gulley" and true to the game of hip-hop. He confesses to Cabby: "I left Millennium because I was tired of making bullshit and calling it hip-hop." But Cabby wonders if his returning is possible given that the he and others had already sold the music to the highest bidder. "The industry has already exploited (corrupted) the music and artist," as to remind us about the difficulty of revitalizing already torched roots. We are left wondering if his (our) love for hip-hop can be recaptured in spite of changes; Sidney, however, provides needed hope: "Just when you think you know hip-hop, it surprises you." Her voice as narrator once again propels her as the conscience of hip-hop and a glimmer of hope as to its possibilities.

The narration, and overall significance of Sidney to the film, is just one example of the challenges *Brown Sugar* poses to dominant narratives of hip-hop, self, and selling out in the music game. Unlike in other productions, a series of rap songs, or even contemporary black social movements (as evidence by the Million Man March), which center patriarchy and old style of black masculinity as source of possible redemption and the authentic soul of the black community, *Brown Sugar* defines hip-hop through Sidney, through her understanding of music and community, challenging those that feminize hip-hop as needing a male savior. In reconstituting a revitalized black cultural community through Sidney, *Brown Sugar* also successfully offers an alternative rendering of black masculinity.

Brown Sugar brings a new vision of hip-hop onto the big screen that challenges that which demonizes hip-hop as a source of spiritual and moral corruption; it reduces the societal problems of sex, violence, misogyny, and drug use to hip-hop. In chronicling the history and beauty of hip-hop, and the increasing power of multinational corporations (money) as the corruptive force, *Brown Sugar* provides context for understanding the hip-hop generation.

Likewise, the film challenges the persistent efforts to link hip-hop to the black underclass, telling a story through a black male executive and female hip-hop intellectual. At a certain level, the strength of the film lies with its efforts to repel stereotypical inscriptions of black masculinity (and femininity to a lesser degree). While both Tre and Kelby (Boris Kodjoe), Sidney's boyfriend, work within industries—hip-hop and professional sports—traditionally connected to a narrow vision of black masculinity (thuggish,, hyper-masculine, hypersexual), neither fits the stereotype. Neither looks hip-hop in the terms of dominant imagination. Tre wears business suits, speaks with "proper English," and otherwise plays the part of an upper middle-class executive or at least a BUPPIE with mad love for the beauty and Afrocentric elements of hip-hop. Kelby, too, lacks the aesthetic and performative markers so often associated with (and demonized) today's black NBA star: no earrings or bling, soft spoken and monogamous, no crew or overt masculine bravado. Instead he is a romantic who sends what seems like 12 dozen roses after his first date with Sidney, and then cooks a gourmet meal for her at a restaurant he rents out for their second date.

Brown Sugar successfully offers an alternative vision of black masculinity (less developed and less complex visions of femininity with the perfect Sidney and the overbearing, money-driven Reese) and hip-hop, at least challenging many of today's racist representations inside and outside of popular culture. At its core, despite its erasure of racism, state violence, and its rendering of life's choices as one of individuals, *Brown Sugar* provides a template for cinematic works on black masculinity. Although not perfect and limited by its failure to understand intersectionality, *Brown Sugar* offers a representational rendering of Mark Anthony Neal's vision of NewBlackMen: "A NewBlackMan is not so much about conceiving of a more 'positive' version of black masculinity . . . but rather a concept that acknowledges the many complex aspects, often contradictory, that make up progressive and meaningful black masculinity. . . . NewBlackMen is for those willing to embrace the fuzzy edges of a black masculinity that in reality is still under construction. . . . NewBlackman can be best captured in a line from HBO film Boycott where Bayard Rustin (Erik Todd Dellums) says 'I am a man of my times, but the times don't know it yet'" (2005, p. 29). *Brown Sugar* most certainly captures these "fuzzy edges," whether in the nervousness of Cabby, the sensitivity of Kibby, or the passion/sophistication/complexity of Tre. It is successful in imagining an alternative black masculinity, one of heterogeneity and difference, one of depth and meaning, of transcendence and one "still under construction."

Simultaneously, the film's inscription of a kinder and gentler world of hip-hop follows the pattern set by *Love & Basketball* in imagining a world of the black middle class as one of happy people with happy problems. The effort to tell a story of the middle class through nonthreatening representations that virtually render the blackness of its characters meaningless leaves the film with a lot of unfulfilled potential. By choosing the safe path—middle-class and universal characters within the highly racialized and commodified world of hip-hop—the film attempts to capitalize on the popularity of hip-hop. It chooses moneymaking over creating a transformative and oppositional film; it selects mass appeal over "keepin it real." Nowhere is this more evident than with *Brown Sugar's* Hollywood ending. While waiting for Cabby's single to hit the airwaves, Tre instead listens to Sidney on the air, confessing her love for hip-hop. Dedicating her book, and Common's "I Use to Love H.E.R.," which plays in the background, to hip-hop, Sidney announces her love for the music, for black cultural expression and for Dre, as she says "To hip-hop. I use to love you. I still do. And I always will."

Determined to announce to the world that he does indeed love Sidney, Tre confesses his love for her at the same time that his return to authentic hip-hop becomes official. The film, thus, brings the story of their relationship and hip-hop's devolution with the short-sided conclusion that we can choose to return to our roots, to balance two competing worlds, whether it be an artist demanding authentic hip-hop or those seeking to rekindle childhood romances. The reduction of all things to choice, especially considering the ways in which race and racism affect identity formation for communities of color, not only embodies a happy ending, but reflects its tendency to imagine the black middle class as being a community of happy people with happy problems. The film's overemphasis on choice and its erasure of the realities of racism, global capital, and patriarchy result in its betrayal of the double consciousness and all the complexity it entails, ultimately producing art that resembles those money-making projects that the film so appropriately challenges.

The dominant representation of hip-hop centers America's black ghettos; gangstas; a violent black masculinity; a culture of bling, materialism, and misogyny; and a cultural form (lifestyle) that should elicit fear and surveillance from white America. *Brown Sugar* successfully intervenes, if not destroys, this dominant narrative, exploring processes of commodification of hip-hop and its overall history. Yet in telling this story, *Brown Sugar* challenges this powerful mythology. It elucidates a world of hip-hop defined by a powerful and sophisticated black femininity. It represents black masculinity not in terms of violence or hypersexuality, but conscience, passion, and community. It tells a story of hip-hop not defined by materialism and excess, but by art, politics, and the difficulty of reconciling its roots with its future. It does all this without mentioning racism, or the state violence that emanates from the same ideological and discursive space that fosters the corporate take-over of hip-hop. In the end *Brown Sugar* offers something new in terms of its representation of hip-hop, black masculinity and femininity, art and politics; yet it tells an all-too familiar story where blackness holds little meaning beyond a cultural signifier in its erasure of racism and state violence. Providing a greater amount of complexity than *Drumline* and *Love & Basketball*, *Brown Sugar* falls into many familiar traps of happy people with happy problems, and in doing so constructs a class fissure within the black community. Successful in elucidating the historical and cultural links within the black community, *Brown Sugar* never moves beyond the individual. Unlike *Good Fences*, it ignores the bridge of racism, police brutality, job discrimination, the prison industrial complex, new racism, processes of commodification, and identity, all of which define hip-hop as much as the difficult search for its roots.

GOOD FENCES

I conclude this chapter with a discussion of Ernest Dickerson's *Good Fences*. While never intended to be a feature film, *Good Fences* was a made-for-television film, shown originally on Showtime. This fact is important given the differences between films distributed to theaters and those shown on the small screen. Obviously, the fact that a film like *Good Fences* does not need to generate box office revenues and cater to the desires of consumers (middle-class white suburban consumers) provides a certain amount of freedom that is reflective in the film's narrative and cinematic approach. Although still a commodity and source of revenue for Showtime and others, it takes a very different form because it needs to be less in tune with consumer wants and desires. It can be niche-oriented, and as such *Good Fences* (and most cable films) seeks out a more educated, middle-class, older, and in this case blacker, audience, thereby offering more complex and provocative examinations of the (upper) middle-class black experience.

The individuals who participated in this film, from Whoopi Goldberg and Danny Glover to Ernest Dickerson, Spike Lee (executive producer), Terry Ellis (writer), and Erika Ellis (writer), all of whom are equally prominent within black Hollywood, demonstrate the important connections between the film and television media. In a sense, cable television has offered black artists a forum for more risky—in form and content—cinematic projects that provide a more complicated and critical insight into black cultural practices, experiences, and their place within the history of America and its racist past, present, and future.

Although a production for the small screen, *Good Fences* represented an important step forward for black representation, offering an important counter-narrative to those of *Brown Sugar, Love & Basketball*, and *Drumline*, but demonstrating the persistent meaning of race regardless of class and dispelling the mythology of the black middle class being a community of happy people with happy problems.

Good Fences chronicles the struggles and difficulties of an upwardly mobile black family's movement into a prestigious white community of Greenwich, Connecticut. The father, appropriately named Tom (i.e., Uncle Tom) Spader is a promising lawyer determined to pull himself up by the bootstraps to provide his family opportunities he did not experience by himself while disproving racist logic and actions. He will go to any length to secure the American Dream, accepting all cases, especially those deemed undesirable by the rest of the firm.

The power of the film's narrative rests not only with its complicated rendering of this process, but with its effort to challenge popular assumptions about upward mobility. The film initially focuses on the happiness and realness of the Spader family, who seem comfortable and happy in their lower middle-class existence. They attend BBQ's with family and friends: Tom (Glover) and Mabel (Goldberg) are seen as a loving couple that talk and comfort one another. Tom even paints Mabel's nails in the most sensual way. All of these signifiers of happiness dissipate once Tom initiates his family's ascent into America' elite in accepting a case that proves to be financially and professionally beneficial, but disruptive to the family's overall happiness.

As the only black lawyer at his firm, Tom is asked to represent a white man who set fire to a building that resulted in the deaths of two black youth. Despite the racial realities of the case and the widespread protests from the black community, Tom sees an opportunity for himself and his family in representing this racist arsonist. Their American Dream would have to come through defending racism, through protecting a man who continued a 300-year history of racial terrorism through arson. He continuously reminds Mabel and his children that such a case would be is his only means to get interviewed on TV, to get recognition, and eventually to secure a partnership in the firm. That is, the logic of racism mandates that the financial opportunities would come only if he aided the efforts of white supremacy. The racial nature of the case provided him with an opportunity, as his blackness finally became an asset to him and the firm. Having been passed over for promotions for almost 10 years, Tom felt as if he was given the simple choice of representing this racist or remaining in a professional basement. Bringing to life the realities of racial discrimination and powerful effects of race on economic/professional opportunities for people of color, *Good Fences* additionally elucidates the larger consequences of this racist system.

Tom does not merely represent this man and the manifestations of a racist system. He becomes everything he hates in the process: "a bougie Moron from Harvard," that spouts the most racist sentiments. Amid protest against his client, Tom denounces the protestors as "trashy rascals," children in need of discipline. In response to harassing calls, Tom refers to those who protest as "ignorant chimpanzees hangin from trees."

At one level, *Good Fences* represents a world of job discrimination and sacrifice, but it also shows how Tom rationalizes his decision by advocating the racist ideologies central to white supremacy. He demonizes black youth and celebrates notions of meritocracy and hard work, attributing his own status to the result of his own doings rather than his deal with the white devil. In other words, he made it because of hard work while those black youth on the streets faced poverty and unemployment because of their own failures and laziness.

In the end, Tom wins the case, receiving much media attention and financial compensation, which allows the family to move into a wealthy, white neighborhood. He has won the ultimate prize: the acceptance of white America. In one scene, a white stranger pays for his family's dinner, offering him thanks for a job well done. Offering a powerful juxtaposition for Tom having betrayed the black community at the same time that he garners support from the white community, *Good Fences* leaves the audience wondering why this man and others are thanking Tom—for his legal skills, his willingness to save a white male, or his eagerness to support a racist system.

Tom is driven by his desire to transcend racism and to secure power not even available to those racists who had harassed him in the past, but he and Mabel are equally driven by a desire to secure the financial wealth associated with the American Dream. They are, in fact, almost obsessed and determined to secure material possessions. In one instance, during an awkward sex scene early in the film, Mabel screams with passion that she plans to buy shoes with their new-found riches, while Tom aggressively makes love to her. With each thrust, he announces his professional plans as if his pleasure comes as much from the fantasy of running a trial division in the law firm or becoming a judge as the actual sex. His work and the prestige, power and possessions that come with professional mobility are the ultimate turn-ons. The dreams and pleasures of Tom and Mabel thus come from their desire and eventual fulfillment of traditional gender roles that racism has denied to them: Tom moans with the dream that one day he might be able to climb the corporate ladder and garner professional power so that he is able to provide for his family; for Mabel, excitement comes with the thought of his securing true masculinity by enabling her to become a true woman in her imagination, one that consumes and represents oneself through material possessions. This is reinforced further when the Spaders move into their new home, where Mabel joyously gazes at her beautiful kitchen. The sight of a massive refrigerator and top-of-the-line appliances is the fulfillment of her dream, one that takes her back to her childhood where she joyously cooked and tended to the house without even the prospect of leaving her impoverished ways. Tom saved her then with marriage, and again by moving her into an upscale house with an immaculate kitchen tended to by her black maid. To her, this is pleasure, and this is her source of excitement.

Despite standing at the gates of the American Dream, the Spaders are unable to find happiness or a world in which the content of their character truly means more than the color of their skin. Not only failing to find acceptance from their neighbors, who are less than enthralled about potential diversity on their block, the Spaders soon discover a whole world in which they aren't accepted. The film's close-ups of Tom and the use of red lighting throughout the film to highlight his inner struggles repels the assumptions about both the American Dream and successes of the black middle (upper) class.

One of the most prominent themes of the genre of black middle-class films (and colorblind discourse) is the notion of racial transcendence. Whether because of profession, education, celebrity, or financial status, the ascendancy of African Americans into the middle class supposedly allows blacks to transcend the burden of racism. *Good Fences* puts this ideology into serious question by chronicling the inner struggle and the persistent levels of racism experienced by the Spaders upon their movement into an all-white neighborhood and their securing of the American Dream. In fact, no member of the family is able to escape racism in the outside world.

In his first few weeks at school, Tommy II, the family's older son, is grilled by his white classmates as to whether he knows "Walt Frazier, Kareem Abdul Jabbar, or Miss Jane Pittman," treating him as a lovable mascot rather than a classmate. For Stormy, the young daughter, things aren't much different. Her classmates ask if they "can touch her hair." The film powerfully illustrates how race continues to mark them as different, as outside, which impacts their daily interactions, whether with teachers, classmates, or others (Tommy II's first sexual encounter is driven by his Asian friend's mother's fetish for black male sexuality).

When the family initially arrives at their newly purchased mansion, the symbol of their American Dream, in the midst of unpacking Mrs. Bonner stops by to introduce herself to the new neighbors. Assuming Mabel to be the maid, she asks, "When is the family going to arrive?" all the while speaking slow to make sure that Mabel can understand her.

Assumptions about intelligence and profession were not limited to the neighborhood. Mabel's first trip to the supermarket demonstrates that their

move, her money, and the status of Tom within the community did not necessarily translate into equality and a colorblind experience. When Mabel goes
to the supermarket, the white patrons gaze at her with mistrust, just as the
few black customers, all maids, stare with shock at the presence of a black
woman who is not a maid living in the neighborhood. Even those working
in the market treat Mabel as an outsider, as someone unworthy of service.
Standing in line waiting to order some meat, she is ignored as the other white
patrons are served, even though they arrived after her.

Mabel's first meeting of the community wives is a no less disconcerting
reminder that Connecticut is still the United States. These women sit in her
home making racist comments in her presence. To Mabel's embarrassment,
one of the women discovers a copy of *Afro*, an all-black magazine resembling
Jet. Looking at the cover, with a picture of a dark-skinned woman donning
a large afro, she announces to the group: "Who knows where they would be
if they didn't spend money on trash." Remaining silent, Mabel is rescued by
another woman, who retorts, "5 cents won't break them. God knows they
work hard enough for it." Even though all of the women have black maids,
this comment prompts laughter as the original bigoted woman contemptu-
ously announced, "Aren't you a liberal?" leaving her and Mabel all alone to
their thoughts about how race matters even within the American Dream.

The power of this narrative resides not just with its chronicling of these
hostile experiences, but its efforts to show the constancy of racism for the
Spaders. That is, the family's efforts to accommodate the white majority,
to break down social distance and deny or at least minimize the incursion
of their blackness into the community, did not result in acceptance or transcendence. For example, in the middle of a test during school, a teacher tells
Stormy that she can leave early so that she can catch the bus to make it back
across town. To the teacher, her race overshadows the realities of her class
status; others in the classroom find this comment funny.

Tommy II also never gained acceptance. In the days after the family watched
Roots on television, a car approached him as he was mowing the lawn. The
occupant yelled: "Keep mowing Toby."

The power of *Good Fences* resides in its effort to document the daily meaning of race and how racism continues to matter even for the black elite. The
story of the Spader family and their attempts to integrate or assimilate, to
buy into hegemonic ideologies, particularly those of materialism and white
supremacy. did not lessen the burden of race, eliminate the obstacles, or
result in the true fulfillment of the American Dream. Rather it resulted in the
family's pain and suffering, as they realize the ever-present, unjust obstacles
posed by modern American racism.

Just as *Good Fences* repels the common representations of the black middle-
class or elite experience as one free from the shackles of racism, or one without obstacle and struggle, *Good Fences* elucidates the complex ways in which
race operates within the characters' lives. As part of their ascendancy into

America's elite, Tom, Mabel, and Stormy all begin to identify with ideologies of white supremacy. Referring to other blacks as "trashy rascals," "savages," or just plain old "nigger," Tom not only becomes all those things he used to loathe (racist, sellout, bougie, Uncle Tom), but begins to articulate dominant understandings of blackness, race, and American opportunity. Wanting to believe in the American dream, in the idea that his sacrifices would ultimately result in improved opportunities for himself and his family, Tom imagines those black folks who hadn't succeeded as inferior, as those who brought down black people because of their own failures and inability to take advantage of opportunities. During a Thanksgiving dinner, Tom lectured the kids about a colorblind world that would provide them unlimited opportunities:

Tom: When I look around my table, you know what I see?

Stormy: What, turkey?

Mabel: Stormy!

Tom: As I look around this table, I see promise. I see unlimited horizons. I see Princeton [looking in the direction of Tommy II].

Stormy: Well, I'm gonna study abroad in Spain next year.

Mabel: Spain, that's very far away, isn't it dear?

Tom: well that's the most sense that girl's spoken in a while. Paris, Spain, Moscow that's where all these little white kids will be studying.

Stormy: Race, race, race. Can we get through one meal without you obsessing on it. All that nasty stuff doesn't matter like it did back in the olden times.

Mabel: Its Thanksgiving

Tom: Though I did not appreciate the tone, young lady, I think we were actually making the same point: opportunity, promise, those are the watch words of the day. Too many of our people are struck in the olden times convinced that the master's shackles are still around their necks. That's why I'm talking about Princeton. We don't have to just settle for Negro colleges, like Morehouse or Howard. The sky is the limit.

Whether beginning to believe in the logic of white racism, doing its dirty work, selling out, or merely trying to convince himself and his family that the sacrifices they have made are worth it since with them have come opportunity, it is clear from this scene that none of the Spaders have transcended race in either the world or within their own internal identity struggles.

So often in the films discussed n this chapter as well as the others that have and continue to represent a black middle-class experience, the desire to secure the American Dream among African Americans is constructed as a single-minded goal. They seek to become part of the American middle class and the procurement of all the material possessions associated with upward mobility without any struggle or question. These desires to move into a (white) middle-class neighborhood and ultimately garner the acceptance of the white majority are imagined as a source of complete happiness. *Good Fences* challenges such representations and the latent ideological assumptions that drive these cine-matic constructions of blackness, documenting what is lost, what is sacrificed, and what pain is felt by the Spader family, all of which is part of the process of upward mobility. More than this, the story of the Spader family reveals the inner struggles and pain that comes along with a big house, a well-paying job, "better" schools, "safer streets," and increased opportunities, as long as race is a factor in America. The burden of white supremacy is that regardless of whether the Spaders lived within a black community or a white community, whether they professed racist ideologies or work toward the elimination of rac-ism, whether they interacted with other black families or ignored even those on their block, race still mattered and racism still affected them. Their belief that "selling out" would result in opportunities and a race-free existence proved to be false, demonstrating that fancy houses and nice cars were not emblematic of the fulfillment of the American Dream for this family, but another dream deferred.

One particular scene is extremely important in this regard. The film uses the historical importance of the initial showing of *Roots* not only to mark the historic moment that the film seeks to document, but to give life to the internal struggles that face the Spader family: the corruptive force of upward mobility and racism to their sense of self, to their identity, and connection to community.

After Tom Spader berates his children about the opportunities he has pro-vided them (through his sacrifices) and imploring them to "reach for the sky," the film jump cuts to the family attentively watching *Roots*. As Stormy sits on the couch reading *Seventeen*, suggesting her disinterest in her black-ness, the rest of the family attentively watches until Tom is unable to stand watching its representations and narrative, which seem all too familiar to him. Tom finds it difficult to watch because he obviously sees himself in the film. He sees the black slave doing the master's work, whipping Kunta Kinta for his refusal to say his new name, Toby, for his resistance to the "season-ing" process. This powerfully renders Tom as replicating the historical tra-dition of the "House Negro," of those African Americans who have been afforded privileges because of their willingness and ability to advance the cause of white supremacy, while also documenting Tom's own recognition of this historical constancy. Unable to handle the parallels between his work in the criminal justice system, where he receives privileges for sending so many black youth into jail, and slave overseer, who was responsible for beating and abusing African slaves, Tom walks out of the room, admonishing the fam-ily for watching a film that rehashes the past. Capturing inner struggles and difficulties with identity formation and the meaning of blackness within the black middle class, *Good Fences* brings to life the powerful ways in which race, history, and racialization operate within the life of Tom and his family. The choices he makes and the dilemmas he faces cause much anguish, resulting in even more difficulties.

He is not alone in his struggle, as both Stormy and Mabel make choices and decisions that eat away at their soul and erode their identity and their sense of self, history, and community. Although less conscious, Stormy struggles with her own sense of beauty, with her desire to become a model in a world where blackness is not imagined as sexy or beautiful. Stormy's reaction is not to try to change the world but to change herself by dying her hair blonde and otherwise accentuating her features so that others might see the whiteness within her.

Mabel, too, struggles with sense of self, with a comfort in her newly formed blackness, following Tom's proscribed path to the American Dream and acceptance in their white neighborhood. At first, she merely loses touch with her friends, with those she used to attend church with and the larger black community. In fact, it seems that her interaction with black people is limited to those who are maids, waiters, and others working for her and her new white friends. While certainly disconcerting to her, Mabel follows this plan so that her family will mesh with those other families in the neighborhood, a desire that she and Tom eventually learn is impossible.

When Ruth Crisp, a single black woman who struck it rich with the lottery, moves into the neighborhood, Mabel knows that Ruth has faced prejudice in the new neighborhood and wants to befriend her. But Tom does not want Mabel to associate with Mrs. Crisp because the new neighbor reinforces dominant stereotypes, whether through her colorful clothing or her loud BBQs. Fearful of how it might look and of the consequences of being too close to this black woman (and her blackness), Mabel does not befriend Ruth, as this might accentuate the Spaders' own blackness. Mabel, thus, joins the others in the neighborhood to shun and ostracize Ruth, maintaining her stake as the acceptable token of the neighborhood while also aiding and abetting America's racism. Bringing to life such harsh realities and the painful (and disgusting) choices made by the Spaders "to distinguish" themselves "from these Niggers," *Good Fences* challenges notions of happy people with happy problems—their money, their big house, their closeness to white folks, their opportunities bring additional problems and less happiness. Fighting their own identity dilemmas and the struggles associated with assimilation the Spader's rise to the top; their effort to secure the American Dream is not without pain and contradiction. Wishing race did not matter, as it did when his victory at the Alabama Spelling Bee almost resulted in his lynching, even Tom is forced to confront the persistent effects of race even as he denies its impact on his life because of that yearning to celebrate his own talents and fortitude.

In one of the film's most powerful scenes, *Good Fences* makes clear how race impacts even the most upwardly mobile family, resulting in conflicts and contradictions of self, identity, and beliefs. As the camera pans first around a courtroom, it gazes at Tom, donning his judge's robe, the black defendant, and an all-white jury, it quickly cuts to a modeling agency; the camera focuses on Stormy and several young white women waiting in anticipation. As each woman disappears to presumably take part in an interview, Stormy is left alone, eventually told that she doesn't have the right look—she is just too black for a world selling beauty. Despite Tom and Stormy's belief in the system, in meritocracy, and that race and racism are no longer relevant obstacles, the film not only demonstrates its importance through such representations, but reveals the pain that it causes to those who see or dream of a colorblind world only to taste the sourness of American racism.

Good Fences' power lies not just with its rendering of the complex and contradictory meaning of race and racism to upwardly mobile African American families, but through its illustration of the effects of these realities on these same African Americans. *Good Fences* chronicles a confused and spiritually empty Stormy, obsessed with becoming beautiful in the eyes of white America. It brings to life a depressed, saddened, and somewhat deranged Tom, who has dedicated his life to disproving racist assumptions, to work hard in the face of racially limited opportunities, and to playing their game by their rules, all the while buying into their vision of the world, yet never able to find happiness. His uneasiness with his compromises, with illusions and deferred dreams, manifests itself in his near obsession with disproving American racism. He even burns down Ruth's second house, which she had bought on the same block, sending Tom into a panic about white flight. The enactment of racial violence against Mrs. Crisp, once again mirroring the violent efforts of the KKK to drive black families out of white neighborhoods through racial terrorism, is too much to handle, sending Tom into a state of depression. He has finally crossed over, embodying a virulent racism that carries out racial terrorism, yet remaining a black man in America. The film makes this explicitly clear as Tom stands gazing into the fire, only to see a silhouette of a noose, crystallizing the fact he was nothing more than a modern-day house slave, doing the dirty work of white racism, enacting violence for his white master. His actions did not result in his freedom or acceptance, he remained instead a slave. This fact and his actions pushed Tom over the edge, resulting in a nervous breakdown.

Only Tommy II, who follows his own dream by attending Morehouse (we only get a quick shot of Tommy, with his newly grown Afro, a dashiki, beads and a clearly Afrocentric girlfriend), and Mabel, who finds happiness by reconnecting to her blackness through finally finding a friend in Ruth Crisp, seem able to remain true to self, to feel comfortable in their identity, and taste a real American Dream.

CONCLUSION

Mark Reid concludes his chapter on the black family film in his most recent work, *Black Lenses, Black Voices,* with a discussion of the range of contemporary films centering on the black family. He notes that the more common production acknowledges the existence of racial discrimination and poverty, but provides a limited gaze to the "demoralizing effects" of these social forces on the black community. He cites *Soul Food* (1997), *The Inkwell* (1994), and *Eve's Bayou* (1997) as contemporary examples of films that situate the realities of racism, poverty, and violence within narratives of the black family, albeit in limited and peripheral ways. On the other hand, he celebrates films such as *Crooklyn* (1994), *He Got Game* (1998), *Straight out of Brooklyn* (1991), and *Clockers* (1995) for their willingness to challenge the hegemonic practice of decentering family and the narratives around family from representations of racism, poverty, persistent inequality, and state violence. In his estimation, these films:

Do not shirk their responsibility to dramatize the existence of class divisions in African American families. In their dramatization of interfamilial class discord, the films indicate a general problem in post-Civil Rights era America. They do not indicate an American that is now post-black or postracist. They point to the diverse political affinities, class differences, and individual experiences that exist in the postNegritude world view. (2005, p. 34)

Unfortunately, the recent wave of middle-class oriented films, to varying degrees, imagine a post-black and colorblind America, where blackness signifies a meaningful and profitable cultural difference, but little else. The demoralizing and actual impact of segregation, poverty, police brutality, job discrimination, and everyday acts of racism are all but absent from *Drumline, Love & Basketball,* and even *Brown Sugar,* which offers a far more complex rendering of the middle-class black experience. Instead, these films reduce blackness to a cultural marker, to spice or source of exoticism, for otherwise universal narratives of the middle-class experience. They safely package the black middle class in pleasurable narratives of progress, universality, the American Dream, and universal desires for upward mobility; yet they simultaneously use race as a marker of difference or hipness to sell the film.

The efforts to imagine a raceless middle-class world, especially in conjunction with a discourse that demonizes and pathologizes the black working poor, and the projects that reduce blackness to a commodifiable black cultural practice embody new racism. Imagining a black world without black people, thus, embodies new racism or the hegemonic practice of racism without racists. In other words, these films "reproduce and disseminate the ideologies needed to justify racism" (Collins 2004, p. 34). With the exception of *Good Fences* and *Brown Sugar* (to a lesser degree), which successfully constructs a middle-class world as one of struggle, conflict, personal pain, and continuity, these films reify dominant discourses that celebrate colorblindness, racial/black progress, and personal responsibility and choice. They celebrate a population that has it "made it," that has transcended the limitations (and pathologies) of blackness, noting that the success of Devon, Tre, or any number of celluloid black middle-class characters comes from their discipline, hard work, and determination. In telling these stories through a world without race, these films not only perpetuate a racist system that blames poverty on the poor, the blames crime on those incarcerated, that blames family disintegration on the absentee black father and welfare mother, that pathologizes, demonizes and polices black bodies, but denies the racialized experience of the black middle class. Such representations deny the persistent difficulty that middle-class African Americans have securing a cab in New York, or the problems that middle-class black youth have with police who "mistake" them as delinquents. These films erase the racism that college students experience at many universities or inequalities that members of the black middle class face within the criminal justice system. None of this is to argue that these films needed to address these issues, but rather that their cinematic imaginations, their celebration of the black middle class being one of racelessness, their presumption that positivity means colorblindness, embody the dominant themes and ideologies that reproduce and disseminate the ideologies needed to "justify" (or erase) racism.

In discussing *Drumline* and *Love & Basketball* in one of my classes, I asked the class how each film presented the black community and American race relations, and how it compared to other contemporary African American films. With little deviation or hesitancy, the majority of the class heaped praise on both of these films for their positive representations of the black community and for their hopeful representations of contemporary race relations. In their estimation, unlike other films, these films challenged stereotypes, whether the clownish characters of black comedies or the violent and hypersexual gangstas of so many ghettocentric films. One student described *Drumline* with such a celebratory analysis: "It represented the black community very positively, and the theme of community is prevalent throughout the film. [It shows] the Black community in a positive, nurturing environment." In his estimation, compared to other films, its imagery is "positive." "The film is devoid of the negative stereotypes that mainstream 'black' films made by white people usually contain."

The widespread celebration of these films as "positive" and therefore "oppositional" is problematic on several fronts: First, the tendency to challenge "negative imagery," those negative representations of Hollywood and beyond, ultimately reinscribes those "negative representations." In other words, the films discussed here don't unsettle the foundational representations of new racism—the gangsta, the black underclass, and the welfare mother—but rather inscribes them as a point of departure. The "positivity" of *Drumline* is that it tells the story of Devon, who is not Jody; the "positivity" of Michael Jordan comes from the fact that he is not Mike Tyson or Ron Artest. The processes of demonization and pathologizing are never disrupted so that "positive" is little more than saying, through various representations, that "there are some good black folks." As Stuart Hall notes,

The problem with the positive negative strategy is that adding positive images to the largely negative repertoire of the dominant regime of representation increases the diversity of the ways in which 'being black is represented, but does not necessarily displace the negative. Since the binaries remain in place, meaning continues to be framed by them. The strategy challenges the binaries—but it does not undermine them. The peace-loving, child-caring Rastafarian can still appear, in the following day's newspapers, as an exotic and violence black stereotype. (1997, p. 274)

In other words, the representations offered in these films don't eliminate those stereotypes visible in *Baby Boy* or *Soul Plane*; nor do they challenge the processes of demonization of the black underclass. In fact, by denying the relevance of racism, and reducing all to individual choice, these films exacerbate those other stereotypes. Even worse, they perpetuate a system of racism, albeit through codes and celebrations that define new racism. The construction of positive representations (positive to whom?) does not erase racism or even challenge its existence; to do as many middle-class films fall victim—to celebrate the reduction of blackness to a commodifiable cultural practice; to praise the American Dream; to reduce the black middle class to happy people with happy problems; to heap praise onto cinematic inscriptions of black middle class as "professional," family-oriented, as individual successes—is not positive per se. Each embodies a representation of new racism, which of course is positive to no one within the black community. *Good Fences* points to an alternative possibility, one that challenges the hegemonic reduction of blackness to the urban poor in need of discipline and policing, yet does not erase race, racism, and community from the discussion. Unfortunately, these cinematic ruptures are increasingly more infrequent, as certainly evident in post-9/11 black comedies.

4

BLACKNESS AS COMEDY: LAUGHTER AND THE AMERICAN DREAM

The history of black cinematic comedies is a story as long as Hollywood itself. Unfortunately, stereotypes and otherwise degrading racist imagery define this history as much as the genius of black performers. If you take Thomas Bogle's claim that the history of African American film is one of "Toms, Coons, Mammies, Mulattos, and Bucks," it is clear that it is equally a history of comedies; the bulk of those characters, especially, "Toms, Coons, and Mammies," have found their "home" inside of comedic films. The Tom character was the black character, although initially portrayed by a nameless, slightly overweight white actor in black face. In most films, the tom character was often chased, harassed, bounded, flogged, enslaved, and insulted. Eliciting laughter through the absurdity of his behavior, the Tom remained faithful and loyal through anything and everything. Beyond concretizing the natural racial difference and inferiority of African Americans, the Tom revealed black satisfaction with subordination and stupidity, as who else would be happy within such situations?

Likewise, the Coon or Black Buffoon has long existed to provide laughter and levity to whites. Normally a male, he is known for single-mindedness, childlike behavior and his inability to delay gratification. More specifically, there have been three comedic uses of the coon character:

1. The Pickaninny, children who are harmless little screwballs, with eyes popping out of their heads and hair a mess. Like the other characters, the performative power of the pickaninny rests with the pleasantry and diversion of antics that otherwise confer difference and inferiority.

2. The Pure Coon—a stumbling and stuttering idiot, who is often defined by unreliability, craziness, shiftlessness, limited mastery of English language, a lack of intelligence, and an overall lack of humanity.

3. The Uncle Remus, who is a hybrid of the coon, because of his stupidity and the Tom, given his naiveté and loyalty to white folks. With each character, films have exploited exaggerated racialized stereotypes to elicit laughter and pleasure from audience members, all the while confirming white superiority/black inferiority and the natural racial differences that necessitate separate, surveillance and control.

Finally, the Mammy has long served as source of laughter, further demonstrating the need for cultural and institutional control of black bodies. The Mammy reminds viewers of the beauty and appropriateness of a time when black women served as maids in white households. More specifically, the mammy, while finding multiple representations, was often dowdy, dark, angry, cantankerous, bossy and asexual. She was everything that white women were not. Both in look and behavior, the mammy has long embodied dominant racial discourse and ideology. She signifies the supposed backwardness of the black community given the dominance of black women over black men (weak)—the opposite of what is supposedly normal. As evident through this history, Hollywood has long deployed racist caricatures of blackness as the basis of its comedic projects, not merely replicating stereotypes for sake of laughter and pleasure, but conferring and disseminating dominant and broader ideologies. While the hegemony of our colorblind moment precludes a replication of these representations, the vestiges and ideological inspirations continue to penetrate the surface of contemporary cinematic representations.

More recent films do not duplicate the grotesque images of Amos and Andy, or Step n' Fetchit, but films like *Held Up* (1999), *Kings of Comedy* (2000), *Queens of Comedy* (2001), *Two Can Play that Game* (2001), *The Wash* (2001), *Daddy Day Care* (2003), *White Chicks* (2003), *Bringing Down the House* (2003), and *Soul Plane* (2004) contain numerous stereotypes, reminiscent of Hollywood racism of years past. This chapter investigates ways in which recent black comedies conceive and construct blackness, African American culture, sexuality, gender relations, and masculinity, while centering a discussion of the long-standing stereotypes in these films. More specifically, it examines the ways in which films like *Bringing Down the House* and *Soul Plane* deploy overt racialized stereotypes. Acknowledging how these films have left behind the Coon characters of the era of minstrelsy or even the popularity of black comedies in the 1980s, this chapter demonstrates the powerful ways in which stereotypes and racial tropes continue to guide "black comedies." More important, it takes up the newness of these productions, connecting them to a broader cinematic and discursive moment in terms of their promulgation of ideologies of a colorblind America, where the American Dream and cultural traveling is within everyone's reach. In demonstrating the heterogeneity and homogeneity of contemporary black comedies, from those with more overt stereotypical inscriptions (*Soul Plane*) to more coded and subtle projects *(Barbershop)*, this chapter examines the continuity and homogeneity of these films that ultimately advance the racial status quo. Whether in reifying difference or justifying inequality, these films, even more than those in the past, teach lessons of difference, progress, culture, and individual responsibility.

Although not arguing for a conspiracy, the chapter consciously situates the *Barbershop* series within a broader context of mostly overt black comedies, such as *Bringing Down the House* and *Soul Plane*, which comfortably deploy mocking stereotypes of blackness. Their uses of longstanding and explicit racialized tropes render films like *Barbershop* (2002) and *Barbershop 2* (2004) as "positive" and "innovative" within the dominant imagination, particularly the middle-class, black community, given its propensity to a discourse of respectability. Praised as "empowering" and a "breath of fresh air," because of the constancy of pejorative representations of blackness available within Hollywood, the reactionary and conservative politics of the *Barbershop* films went relatively unnoticed. Moreover, the controversy that followed these films further erased its conservative and new racist orientation. The media and critics constructed *Barbershop* as another hip-hop film that bespeaks to the larger problems of black youth.

Although imagined as "innovative" and "respectful," ultimately *Barbershop 1* and *2,* as well as *Soul Plane, Bringing Down the House,* and the numerous black comedic films not discussed here, follow a similar recipe that celebrates the American Dream, colorblindness, cultural commodification, and bootstraps American integration, all the while denying and erasing persistent inequality, poverty, and state violence. In each film race is deployed in distinct and different ways, depending on the transparency of racial tropes and ideologies, but in the end each offers a similar fulfillment to a new racist cinematic moment. Each embodies a broader and societal fear, love, and loathing of a post-Civil Rights, colorblinded, commodified blackness that jointly reinscribes racialized difference all the while pointing to the possibilities of successful personal integration and assimilation into the mainstream. In absence of racist institutions and legal barriers, these films focus on the cultural and individually imposed obstacles to securing the American Dream within the black community. Their success in this regard comes not in spite of their comedic elements but because of the genre of comedy and through vehicles of laughter. More important, challenges to both stereotypes and the reactionary politics that emanate from this recent wave of comedies are invariably met with clichéd responses of "it's just a joke," or "relax and don't take things so seriously," both of which are defining elements of the current racist moment. Such issues, questions, and representations form the crux of this chapter, interrogating the ways in which the common elements of a colorblind moment fixated on the availability of the American Dream because of the obsolete nature of American racism.

Although focusing on the ways in which these films follow suit with those previously discussed, this chapter also highlights the number of missed opportunities present in contemporary African American comedies. More than the other genres, the recent wave of comedies, even the most problematic and troubling (*Soul Plane, White Chicks*), have shown glimmers of transformative power, offering alternative representations, cultural understanding, and narratives to that which celebrates the donning of a colorblind America, where the American Dream is available to anyone who chooses to make it happen. In the vast majority of cases, however, these opportunities are merely lost, as the reliance on racial tropes and dominant narratives, discourses, and ideologies undermine any possibility of opposition. *Undercover Brother* (2002) and *Bamboozled* (2000) demonstrate the transgressive possibilities of two films that challenge both conventional representations and dominant understandings of race and American progress. They reveal the immense possibilities of comedy to reach beyond the boundaries of dramas and documentaries to give voice to the vestiges and persistence of inequality. These films, however, also illustrate the failures of the vast majority of African American films that merely continue longstanding practices of commodification and demonization for the sake of pleasure, profit, and the perpetuation of privilege, poverty, and persistent inequality.

SOUL PLANE

I sought to start this chapter with a film that took racist representations to an extreme, an all-too-familiar place, one of Step 'n Fetchit, coon shows, the blatant racism of Hollywood's past. *Soul Plane* represents the brand of comedy that emanates from a Hollywood that merely seeks to commodify blackness within the white imagination. In doing so it legitimizes white supremacist representations and ideologies (as opposed to those films that use comedy to distort and conceal conservative politics through presumably black narratives, and those that use parody as a place of opposition).

With this agenda in mind, I sat down to watch *Soul Plane*. At first glance, I wondered what more needed to be said beyond the fact that *Soul Plane* represents a mere continuation of the likes of Amos and Andy, promulgating representations that simultaneously render blackness (and black people) as a source of laughter and contempt. Its inscription of long-standing racialized stereotypes fulfills hegemonic projects that reduce blackness to sources of laughter and legitimizes the inferiority of character and culture. At a certain level, my colleagues are correct in that little more discussion is needed regarding this film and its place in Hollywood, which is clearly not the idyllic racial promised land projected within popular discourses, especially those that have celebrated the progress of black artists. Despite these reservations and my bewilderment about what else needs to be said about this film, there is a need to dissect (quickly) this awful film. To understand the dialectics of commodification and racism, to comprehend the consequences of popular culture as a source of dominant ideologies, whether in examining claims about the banality of racist jokes, denunciations of hip-hop, demonization of black sexuality, or theories regarding cultures of poverty, it is crucial to examine the worst and most extreme offerings of contemporary Hollywood.

Soul Plane chronicles the story of NeShawn (Kevin Hardy), who through sheer luck secures the American Dream. While traveling across the country, NeShawn gets stuck in the airplane bathroom (in fact, his ass gets stuck in the toilet). During the flight, the cargo door accidentally opens and his dog dies in a mid-air collision. Struck with grief from the murder of his dog by a white airline, and emotionally devastated as a result of the trauma of being stuck in the bathroom, NeShawn files suit against the airline, winning $100 million. The initial portions of the film offer some prominent cultural frames of reference:

1. NeShawn does not secure the American Dream through hard work or talent but through his luck and his ability to "work" the system, especially in regard to accusations of racism.
2. NeShawn convinces the jury to vote in his favor through a speech about his poor single mother.
3. *Soul Plane* makes clear that NeShawn is ultimately successful within the court system because of his ability to "play the race card," and elicit compassion from the jury.

Given the realities of the American justice system, the film's biggest, yet untold, joke is its premise that a poor, young, black male could successfully defeat a major American corporation with a $100 million verdict—now that *is* funny! Its inscription of dominant ideologies, however, is not funny, nor new. *Soul Plane* merely promulgates hegemonic ideologies regarding the children of single black mothers and the widespread belief that blacks can secure the American Dream only through a stroke of luck, whether it be God-given athletic talent or a $100 million verdict.

With $1 million, NeShawn purchases NWA Airlines, which has only one plane in its fleet: a big, fat, purple plane, with massive spinners (rims), a banging stereo system, a hydraulic system, and its own departure point in Los Angeles, from Malcolm X Terminal. The terminal offers waiting passengers pornography and basketball courts (their inclusion are merely representative of this film's blatantly racist representation and its connection to a history of minstrelsy within popular culture).

The film's second half chronicles the first flight of NWA Airlines, as the crew of the plane dies in flight, leaving NeShawn in the captain's chair, where he not only ultimately lands the plane, taking on responsibility for the first time in his life, but wins back his ex-girlfriend, who happens to be a passenger on the flight. Beyond this, there is little narrative or plot to *Soul Plane*. Instead, the film relies on the comfort of racist jokes and otherwise demeaning representations. In fact, the film's DVD captures the essence of the film. On the menu page, hip-hop blasts as young, scantily clad, big-breasted black women excitingly dance. Like this teaser, *Soul Plane* offers little beyond accepted representations of blackness as hypersexual, shallow, thuggish, and without culture beyond hip-hop.

Soul Plane does not merely promulgate stereotypes through flat racialized representations. It also deploys the themes as a central part of its narrative. Specifically, the film offers the spectrum of racialized stereotypes: the Arab passenger who (humorously) experiences harassment and racial profiling; the loud, aggressive, incompetent, and hypersexualized black female airport security guards; the black pilot (Captain Carter played by Snoop Dogg) who not only learned to fly in prison but smokes weed while flying; the series of black football players and soldiers on the plane who seek out the company of Heather Hunkee, the just turned 18-years-old white woman on the plane (interestingly, their only purpose in film—in life— is to sexually pursue white women); the gay black flight attendant, who reflects all the trappings of an "unmasculine" man; the hypersexual black couple that cannot seem to keep their clothes on because of their almost desperate need to have sex on the plane (and in the terminal); the black, Asian, and Latino strippers/flight attendants, whose mere job description (purpose) is to provide visual pleasure to both passengers and viewers; the blind black man, who fulfills the stereotype of black male sexuality in his incessantly talking about sex, eventually "fingering" some mashed potatoes that he mistakes for the vagina of the woman sitting next to him, resulting in his reaching orgasm; and the lone white passengers, the Hunkee (Honky) family, whose goofy nervousness serve as the basis of their prejudices (purse clutching).

Of course, Mr. Hunkee's girlfriend and his daughter become increasingly obsessed with black male sexuality through the flight, particularly fixated on their bodies and the size of black male's genitals. The Hunkee son finds a similar change through his contact with blackness, as he dons a velour suit, a chain, a tilted hat, and otherwise embraces all the trappings associated with hip-hop culture. Their experience on NWA Airlines was life changing, with the women generating a "taste" for black men, and the boy finding a love for blackness through clothes and style.

The Hunkee family is representative of the white fetishization and commodification of blackness, particularly the embedded privileges whiteness facilitates, if not encourages racial transgression. Their place in the narrative brings to life important cultural and racial issues, ones that hold the possibility of offering a transformative racial commentary; yet the film's inability to move beyond racialized stereotypes and conservative politics limits this possibility. In fact, its reduction of everything to a joke, whether the commodification of hip-hop (blackness), white fears of black criminality (the site of an NWA plane leads passengers on an all-white Texas airline to lock doors), and racial profiling/police harassment (one of the black security guards justifies her harassment by telling a passenger: "We feds now, we can violate every civil right," all the while sexually harassing him) reflects the serious problems with *Soul Plane*. It does not merely promulgate stereotypes; it reduces social injustices and societal problems to a joke, in turning everything into a punch line. *Soul Plane* successfully devalues the importance of rectifying persistence of state violence, while simultaneously erasing crucial discourses of race.

Such an approach, as with the film's reduction of racial difference to cultural difference, albeit through its presentation of a mainstream sanitized version of hip-hop, ultimately fulfills dominant racial discourses. In the same way, my students and others respond to racist cartoons or sexist statements on the radio with claims of "it's just a joke," thereby dismissing critics (haters) who just need to develop a thicker skin and stop playing the race card.

Furthermore, the film and many contemporary black comedies reify arguments of racial difference, being little more than a cultural difference that can be easily bought and exchanged between communities. Race identity is not so much about community, history, state processes, but about cultural practices, whether proficiency in Ebonics or a tilt in one's hat. Dismissing racist discourses, such as those that go down in *Soul Plane,* and the reduction of difference as a mere "culture thing" is more than an act of disengagement with the rhetoric. Rendering something, even a notexactly-brilliant film like *Soul Plane,* as just a joke not only normalizes racist comments, but through this normalization gives consent to "real life" verbalizations of racist thought. Nowhere is this truer than with the recent commentary of William Bennett.

In the wake of Hurricane Katrina, former Secretary of Education William Bennett stated on his radio show during a discussion about abortion and security that, although undesirable and reprehensible, if someone desired to lower crime rates, aborting every black children would be successful to that end: "But I do know that it's true that if you wanted to reduce crime, you could—if that were your sole purpose, you could abort every black baby in this country, and your crime rate would go down. That would be an impossible, ridiculous, and morally reprehensible thing to do, but your crime rate would go down. So these far-out, these far-reaching, extensive extrapolations are, I think, tricky."

Outraged by his equating crime to blackness and his presumed call for genocide, black leaders and others took to the airwaves, demanding an immediate apology from Bennett. A few commentators withstood opposition, coming to his aid, denouncing his critics as racist and misguided. For example, Jesse Lee Peterson, on the September 30, 2005 edition of Sean Hanity and Alan Colmes told Fox News that:

Colmes: Wait, I want you to answer to my question. Is the root cause of crime race or is it poverty?

Peterson: The root cause of crime is a lack of moral character. You know, we saw a good example of that in the New Orleans situation in the inner cities. I've done a lot of work in the inner cities, and I have to tell you that crime and out-of-wedlock birth, black folks having babies without being married, and stuff like that is out of control. And it's not because they lack material things but because not all, not all, not all.

Rich Lowry (guest co-host and National Review editor): Right.

Peterson: But most of them lack moral character. Look what they did to the Dome. In three days they turned the Dome into a ghetto.

Although Peterson supposedly represents a peripheral voice of the Republican Party, his assessment of the black community and his claims that a degenerative black urban culture was the root of problems within the black community is not so peripheral; in fact, it resonates in *Soul Plane.*

Through the stereotypes and juvenile comedy, *Soul Plane* articulates an argument that identifies a culture of poverty, one without morals, class, and values, as a sign of inferiority. On flight 069, few African Americans sit in first class, where Moet and filet mignons are available to every passenger. Even in this upscale space, black passengers represent a pollutant. Whether through uncontrolled hypersexuality, or the intrusion of strippers and gambling within business class, *Soul Plane* makes clear that you can take a person or a culture out of the ghetto, but you can't take the ghetto out of hip-hop or black folks, for that matter. Worse yet, the majority of passengers aboard this flight reside in low class, defined by the presence of rap music, malt liquor, gambling, strippers, and fried chicken. In reducing those in low class to a mere group defined by cultural deficiencies and savagery, *Soul Plane* mirrors the claims of Patterson, Bennett, and others. The rates of poverty, incarceration, or unemployment are not the result of structural racism, or the legacies of slavery, but the consequence of faulty values manifested in hypersexual behavior, alcoholism, and an overall degenerative set of cultural values.

Earning almost $14 million in box office receipts and close to $2 million more in rentals, *Soul Plane* was a modest financial success. Still, its deployment of long-standing stereotypes that Spike Lee lamented in *Bamboozled,* its narrative that moved little beyond a flying minstrel show, and its articulation of dominant discourses and ideologies demonstrate its cultural and racial "success" in legitimizing a white supremacist status quo within and beyond Hollywood. *Soul Plane* represents the trajectory of today's black comedies, films that consistently ridicule and demonize the black poor. These films see racism and state violence as the next joke and they legitimize dominant claims about racial transgression as a source of racial liberation, all in the name of progress and colorblind discourses.

Legitimating such claims through such representations in the name of desiring a colorblind America is not limited to over-the-top films like *Soul Plane*. Similar normalizing projects can be seen in contemporary reincarnations of the biracial buddy comedy, a popular formula that peaked in the 1980s with film series like *Lethal Weapon* (1987) and *48 Hours* (1982), in which a black character is responsible for uplifting and redeeming his or her white counterpart. *Bringing Down the House* is the marriage of these ideas, reducing and normalizing state violence through comedy while praising supposed acts of racial transgression.

BRINGING DOWN THE HOUSE

Bringing Down the House chronicles the story of Peter Sanderson (Steve Martin), a divorced, uptight, wealthy white attorney, who seems stuck in a perpetual mid-life crisis. Still in love with Kate, his ex-wife (Jean Smart), and unable to understand why she left him, despite his obsession with work and his inability to put down his cell phone, Peter sees little hope for a future relationship. That is until he finds "Lawyer girl," a woman he meets on the Internet. Given his own social awkwardness and his inability to talk to people, Peter is forced to turn to virtual reality with hopes of finding a woman. Through their conversations, he begins to fall for "Lawyer girl," who he believes is a brainy, blond bombshell lawyer. When they meet, however, Peter finds that his brainy blond bombshell lawyer is nothing more than a fantasy or a fraud, as she is not an Ivy League lawyer, white, or blond. Instead, he meets Charlene (Queen Latifah), a prison escapee, who is in search of Peter's assistance to prove her innocence and clear her name. Initially, Peter is unwilling to help, partially because of his own racialized assumptions about Charlene's guilt. Eventually, Charlene forces Peter into helping her when she causes a scene on his front lawn by accusing him of abandoning her and their little child, "Kareem," who knows that he has a "white daddy." Peter is fearful of what his neighbor, Mrs. Kline (Betty White), who happens to be his boss's sister, might do, especially after she emerges from her home, golf club in hand, shouting, "I thought I heard a Negro." Peter still wants nothing to do with Charlene, so she disrupts his luncheon with Mrs. Arness (Joan Plowright), an important client whose racial politics resemble those of Mrs. Kline. Once Peter gets to know Charlene and can see beyond her color, he eventually comes to her aid, allowing his once ordered, yet unhappy life, to turn upside down. He jeopardizes his lifestyle, job, relationship with his wife, and his whiteness all in the name of proving Charlene's innocence. As stated in the film's tagline, Peter found "everything he needed to know about life," from what "*she* learned in prison."

Although *Bringing Down the House* is unlike the other films discussed in this book, in that it does not have a black writer or director, it reflects a number of core themes and concepts of contemporary Hollywood. Its reduction of blackness to a source of laughter and ridicule, its commodification of blackness, its vision of racism, its static understanding of racial identity, its deployment of racialized tropes of redemption, and its use of racialized stereotypes are found in numerous films whether those by white directors (*Bringing Down the House*), black directors (*Barbershop; Love Don't Cost a Thing*), or Latino directors (*Soul Plane*). Moreover, despite having a white director, probably because of Queen Latifah's current popularity within Hollywood and her prominent role in the film's production (as its star and executive producer), *Bringing Down the House* has been consistently linked to a wave of African American cinematic projects since 2000. The effort to define African American film through individual personalities and a film's cultural aesthetic (i.e., its use of hip-hop) is problematic and rooted in racist ideologies.

The many failures of *Soul Plane* and *Bringing Down the House* brings into question the issues related to new racism, demonstrating the importance of discussing such films within this project. It is within this larger context that we include *Bringing Down the House,* not in an effort to deny the importance of cinematic authorship, but to illustrate the oversimplification of any approach that denies the power of race and racism across communities, the power of Hollywood and dominant discursive fields in determining the ideological and political trajectory of commercial films, and the importance in moving beyond authorship and celebrities to politics and aesthetics in exploring the meaning and importance of the cinematic images of blackness.

Unlike so many contemporary films with interracial themes and casts, *Bringing Down the House* does not shy away from the theme of racism. Unfortunately, giving voice to the persistence of racism is not inherently transgressive or oppositional. In this film racism is a thing of individuals, as something practiced by ignorant rich folks (a different approach from using poor white Southerners as the embodiment of racism but reflective of the same problems) who are either crazy (odd) or out–of–touch with reality because of their age or tendency to live behind gates and fences. In the first moments of the film, Mrs. Kline (Betty White), Peter's neighbor, questions him about a new Latino family who had just moved into the neighborhood. Shocked by their moving into her wealthy white community, Mrs. Kline scoffs at the thought that they could afford to buy a house, as all of them "have nothing but leaf blowers." This is not an isolated moment; Mrs. Kline is the embodiment of racism in the film, uttering prejudicial comments throughout the film, making clear that she sees people of color as inferior. Although pretty explicit in her racism (prejudices), reflecting the film's argument that racism embodies ignorance and that ignorance (racism) manifests itself because of social distance fostered by elitism (but not segregation), the film intertwines examples of racism throughout its narrative to serve the basis of its theme of racial redemption and also as the basis of laughter and comic relief.

Like Mrs. Kline, Ashley (Missi Pyle), Peter's ex–sister-in-law, is explicit and extreme in her racist thoughts. Ashley is even more racist than Mrs. Kline and she is a reprehensible gold digger, who sleeps with senior citizen men in hopes of securing cash and gifts. The film centers Ashley's racism as a symptom of both her anger and her evilness; she is angry and this contributes to her racism, which is symptomatic of her being an evil person. Elitist and prejudice, she is a cliché of the stereotypical white bigot. While at her exclusive club, the mere sight of Charlene prompts her to comment on this unacceptable intrusion, asking Charlene to get her a drink, which Ashley's views as the only acceptable role for a black women inside an elite club. (Notice how Ashley is constructed as the racist while the other members of this exclusive white club are positioned as outside this understanding of racism). In another instance, Ashley ridicules Charlene for pushing a broom, calling her Aunt Jemima. Finally, in describing Charlene to her sister, in an effort to warn her against the corruptive influence that this black woman would invariably have on her children, Ashley deployed the common description of black women as being "full of 'tude and welfarish."

In each instance, the film does not provide a character as a voice of opposition, using neither dialogue nor narrative to effectively intervene and undermine Ashley's racism. Rather, it renders both Mrs. Kline and Ashley as absurd, laughable, and clichéd, as to make sure audiences understand the contempt for these characters. Yet in constructing racism through their bodies (and the identities that they represent), the film reifies dominant discourses that tend to locate racism in those ignorant and absurd individuals common on today's talk shows. It is the angry and stupid individual who promotes racist ideals, thereby maintaining hope in the possibility of a colorblind society—we merely need to "treat" or change those who harbor prejudices.

All of this is not to argue that *Bringing Down the House* reduces racism exclusively to its extreme—bigoted/ignorant folks—forms. The film hints at the manifestations of racism within Peter, who for all intents and purposes is presented as a good, middle-class white man, whose worst quality is his lack of involvement in his children's lives. As Peter meets Charlene on the Internet, he is unaware that she is a black woman, stuck inside prison. Instead, he falls in love with someone whom he believes is a gorgeous white blonde lawyer. On meeting Charlene for the first time, Peter quickly realizes Charlene is not who he thought she was. He feels a sense of betrayal not just because Charlene deceived him, but because of his own prejudices against African Americans. The mere sight of Charlene at his doorstep pushes Peter into a panic, in which he hides knives in his house, while calling her a criminal type. He is startled not just because she is not a blond lawyer, but because her blackness scares him.

Although he embodies the film's understanding of racism, Peter represents a much more nuanced and complex rendering of racism than the characters of Mrs. Kline and Ashley. The film uses Peter's supposed prejudices as a marker of his own flaws and one of the places to which he seeks redemption. The narrative development of Peter provides viewers (even if not part of film's intended message) the opportunity to think about colorblind racism, to think about the ways in which Peter naturalizes whiteness within his own imagination and works from assumptions about both whiteness and otherness.

The film's effort to show racism in multiple forms challenges dominant (and even its own) tendencies to pathologize racism does not represent the only transgressive potential of the film. *Bringing Down the House* equally shows possibility in challenging dominant racial discourses within and outside Hollywood with its commentary on racial performativity and the universality of this process. In *Gender Trouble,* Judith Butler explores the ways in which the body is discursively constructed and controlled within society. Butler's concept of performativity is used to describe the repeated acts of constructing and normalizing an identity. The "performing" of these identities, through a series of acts, fosters an understanding, acceptance, and knowledge about societal norms and constructed ideas associated with gender or race. According to Butler, one does not voluntarily choose an identity, but is forced to display it through the normalization of this identity as a daily occurrence. "There is no gender identity behind the expressions of gender; . . . identity is performatively constituted by the very 'expressions' that are said to be its results." In other words, race, gender, and sexuality are all a performance: it's what you *do* at particular times, rather than a universal *who you are*. Performativity means that we play multiple identities at any time, that institutional demands and various levels of privilege impact our ability to perform identity. In the course of conversations with Peter, Charlene reveals that she embraces hip-hop and that she dons the costume of a gangsta, whether through clothes or the use of Ebonics not because she's ignorant, but by choice. While reducing racism to stereotypes and denying the importance of institutional racism, the film's lessons regarding racial stereotypes and its dialectics with performativity and identity formation are instructive. Of course, its failure to differentiate between the racial performances of Charlene and Peter or recognize power and privilege differentials in this regard embodies the immense failures of the film.

Specifically, the film makes clear that both Peter and Charlene are performing their (and society's) understanding their own racial identity, one that is affected by societal expectations/demands (stereotypes) and structural realities. As a businessperson seeking to find acceptance within the white elite, Peter not only embodies a particular version of white masculinity (absentee father dedicated to work), but also sees (constructs) his own identity in opposition to his perception of blackness. Through the influence of Charlene, and because of Peter's eventual desire to save her (as any good white man would do, especially one of privilege), the end of the film brings an alternative racial identity, one where Peter dons a personal blackness with a new identity of hip-hop. Although the film does not problematize the neo-minstrelsy of Peter performing blackness in the white imagination, which reflects its overall inability to reflect on power or privileges of whiteness, not the film's own commodification of black identity, it offers some insight into the performative pitfalls of racial identity. Charlene is not immune, in that throughout the film she seems to perform the blackness that Peter, Howie (Eugene Levy), Ashley, and even the audience expects, whether manifesting in her 'tude, her clothing, her sexuality, her propensity to swear and engage in violence, or her aggressiveness.

Notwithstanding her intelligence, Charlene acts stupid; notwithstanding her innocence, she acts like a thug. The film successfully demonstrates that the performative aspects of racial identity are not simply a matter of choice, but are connected to larger institutions and practices. In order to protect herself and protect Peter from loosing his job, she has to pretend to be a maid, embodying a subservient black identity acceptable to white racists. Here lies the film's greatest potential in that Peter forcing Charlene to be a maid (clear who's has power), to return to the plantation, to protect him, to save home from his racist bosses, thereby demonstrating that while all racial identities are performative, there are different contexts and consequences for white racial identities and those of people of color. However, the film doesn't make this fact explicit, nor does it illustrate through its narrative the power and privilege embedded in whiteness; that in America, whiteness transversing the boundaries of whiteness warrants celebration, as evident in Peter saving Charlene inside the black nightclub, as opposed to Charlene, who faces ridicule and opposition for her attempt to enter a white world. Its failure to reflect on these differences and its tendency to use racial performance and cross-dressing as a source of laughter rather than a vehicle of generating understanding of race and racism represents a major shortcoming in the film. Worse yet, in celebrating racial performance as something that occurs in all communities and linking redemption and progress to racial cross dressing the film appropriately reinscribes dominant discourses of contemporary race and colorblindness.

A WHITE MAN'S BURDEN? REDEMPTION IN POST-CIVIL RIGHTS AMERICA

As already mentioned throughout this text, racial redemption remains a prominent theme in Hollywood, fulfilling dominant discourses about the possibilities of racial harmony and colorblindness. More important, this racial trope reduces racial conflict and racism in general to social distance that can easily be traversed through contact, cooperation, and possibly cultural (racial) absorption (cross-dressing), resulting in both improved race relations through eventual colorblindness and increased happiness throughout society. In *Bringing Down the House,* both Peter and Charlene grow from their interracial interaction, where Charlene secures freedom, and also matures, finds confidence in herself, and seems to figure out her life because of her relationship with Peter. Equally important, Peter grows as well, reconnecting with his kids and rekindling his relationship with his ex-wife, seeing the beauty in life beyond materialism and professional advancement. The reduction of racial difference and conflict to qualities and cultural attributes that hold the potential to teach, enlighten, redeem, or better the lives of others is problematic to say the least.

Worse yet, the narrative use of cultural difference and celebration of cultural clashes as source of growth and redemption emanates through its deployment of long-standing racialized stereotypes. For example, Charlene threatens Peter on numerous occasions in her attempt to prove her innocence. Moreover, her blackness, or better said, the inscription of stereotypical renderings of blackness, elucidates the film's articulation that when cultures clash, growth and redemption are not far behind. After Peter's daughter sneaks off to a party, Charlene is forced to rescue her from a threatening boyfriend by hanging him on the balcony. When Gregory (Peter's son) struggles with reading, to the dismay of his parents, Charlene intervenes by teaching him to read through the use of sex magazines. Most important, Charlene teaches Peter how to love life and family, whether through her philosophical speeches or her dance lessons that include instructions on how to "ride" his sex partner. In the end, Charlene's worth to the Sanderson family and society emanates from her displaying stereotypical characteristics of blackness and from her teaching those of privilege the lessons she has learned.

Bringing Down the House reduces racial difference to these redemptive qualities, celebrating Peter's ability to help and enhance the life choices afforded to Charlene. To save Charlene, Peter talks with DL (Steve Harris) at a club, where white boys are either "cops, corpses, or crack heads." Although he quickly figures out how to "talk gangsta," he ventures into their foreign territory despite the perceived danger. To improve his chances of helping Charlene, he does not stop with his learning of Ebonics; he buys clothes off the street so that he can fit in this all-black club. With his hip-hop gear (clothes), gaited walk, and bling/ice (diamonds) in hand, Peter goes to great length to transcend his whiteness for the greater good. Unable to pull it off, instead acting whiter than usual given the absurdity of his appearance, he still solves the crime, saving Charlene from the police and prison, where she doesn't belong, and from her boyfriend, who does belong in prison. By his willingness to go to the ghetto and by his ability to transcend his own whiteness, Peter saves Charlene and gives her the greatest gift: freedom. His whiteness—intelligence, ingeniousness (he tapes their conversations), courage—provides the necessary keys to secure Charlene's freedom. In the end Charlene also frees Peter, not just from his unhappiness and his restrictive job, but from his whiteness (the source of his unhappiness).

Peter: Fellas, did I tell you, I am going out on my own.

Bob (Peter's boss): You don't have the resources.

Peter: Well, I have one multi-billion dollar client, so that is a start. And a partner!

Howie: I am all over it "G."

Peter: Let's go, excuse me.

Ed: Peter, we can talk about this.

Peter: Ed, you can kiss my natural black ass.

By using the lessons and courage Peter he has learned and received from Charlene, he finds courage to leave his stuffy—white—firm for the hopes of a more free professional existence. In celebrating his decision, and his 'tude directed at his bosses, *Bringing Down the House* does not merely link Peter's new outlook on life—whether in his professional choices, his improved relations with his children, or his willingness to put family ahead of his cell phone—to his friendship with Charlene, but to new found blackness.

Moving into his beautiful office overlooking the Pacific Ocean (with his kids and black secretary right by his side), Peter learns the film's ultimate lessons from Charlene. Wearing a bright red dress (compared to the torn up prison-issue clothes she wore during their initial meeting as to signify the changes that she has undertaken), Charlene offers Peter thanks for his help, for her courage, and for his whiteness:

Charlene: I really wanted to tell you again how much I appreciate what you did for me!

Peter [shaking head]: If I could only give you half of what you gave me.

Charlene: We'll call it even. Now, give me a hug.

Peter: White people don't hug.

Charlene [embracing Peter]: You ain't white.

Peter: Well, I'm off white.

Leaving the audience with a clear understanding of redemptive possibilities of cultural exchange, albeit through Charlene teaching Peter the lessons of prisons and attributes of blackness in an effort to elicit his help in clearing her name, this scene is made more powerful by linking these transformations to love. Both Charlene and Peter find love not with each other, but in Howie and Kate.

As Kate and Peter kiss to solidify their love that resulted from Charlene "shaking" things up through her lessons on courage, fighting, and sexuality, the film concludes with an even more explicit celebration of culture clashing. With hair braided and uttering phrases, like "holla at your boy," Howie does not merely find love and a partner to match his freakiness in the bedroom in Charlene, but a guide to a new outlook on life.

While replicating dominant tropes of racial redemption and overcoming social distance as the panacea for societal problems, *Bringing Down the House* offers a new vision of contemporary racial politics, concluding that everyone is happier when they are black. In this way it reinscribes widespread processes of commodification (fetishization) of blackness. More important, the film's conclusion legitimizes the often-uttered belief that if we all were mixed, race wouldn't be an issue and in turn we would all be a bit happier. Embodying stereotypes and hegemonic racial discourses of colorblindness, redemption, commodification, and the notion that difference has little material consequence, this comedy offers a powerful commentary on race, mirroring numerous other comedies that use jokes and laughter to conceal their conservative message, while erasing the pain and violence that define contemporary American racial politics.

Notwithstanding its illustrative rendering of the performative aspects of racialized ideal and embedded in its deployment of racialized tropes and those centering racial redemption, at its core *Bringing Down the House* is an immensely conservative film, reifying dominant understandings of race, privilege, and contemporary politics. While attempting to sell itself as hip-hop, as a counter-narrative that paints a happy face on a hip-hop world, through centering a female character and constructing an interracial world, *Bringing Down the House* offers both old and new representations, ideologies, and racial tropes that collectively embody a new racist project. In using blackness and Charlene as sources of comedy and audience pleasure, *Bringing Down the House* resembles its predecessors with its use of a comforting and comedic blackness. Yet as part of the wave of films that embody a new racist cinematic aesthetic, the film also uses white racist bigots as additional sources of laughter, which in the end works to confine racism to its logical extreme, leaving whites inside the theater as having little to do with a system of racism.

Its definition of racism, its usage of comedy as a source of comfort and pleasure (rather than opposition and discomfort), and its ultimate conclusion about the possibility of racial reconciliation through cultural exchanges, leaves *Bringing Down the House* as a reactionary and immensely racially conservative film. Such failures are disappointing given the possibilities of this film to offer a transgressive narrative. But like *Soul Plane* and the *Barbershops,* the deployment of new-old racial tropes and its ultimate celebration of the American Dream make *Bringing Down the House* no more than another missed opportunity. As will be seen, it is not alone; both *Barbershops* hold a significant amount of potential, as films that held the possibility of unsettling dominant discourses and decentering hegemonic representations, yet its celebration of the American Dream, bootstraps politics, and colorblind discourses destroys any possibilities for a transgressive narrative. Notwithstanding controversy, or the commodification of hip-hop, both *Barbershop* films, like *Soul Plane* and *Bringing Down the House* are conservative (reactionary) cinematic productions that legitimize white privilege and rationalize inequality. Each, in its own way, demonstrates the newness of colorblind projects that use blackness and the related aesthetics of hip-hop not merely as a source of commodification but as a marker of difference, all the while rearticulating dominant understandings of race, racism, progress, and the arrival of the American Dream.

BARBERSHOP

When it seems black cinema is preoccupied with excusing the worst elements of the African-American experience, "Barbershop," has taken the novel approach of celebrating its best elements. It features a lively and very likeable cast exchanging intelligent dialogue in an entertaining story with a message. Yet, it is controversial.

In the movie, rapper Ice Cube is a surprisingly nice fit as a family man and struggling business owner. Other cast members range from female rapper Eve to Cedric the Entertainer, who conspires to deliver uplifting messages about the value of self-respect, personal responsibility, entrepreneurship, community, family and diversity. Barbershop communicates its positive messages with wit, style and optimism. It displays images of African-American culture that have unfortunately gone missing in many recent offerings.

In Barbershop, you meet an ambitious expectant father and his pregnant wife who are working together to build their future. There is also a young African-American woman demanding the respect to which she is entitled. Throughout, African-American characters also give themselves permission to be diverse in their opinions. Furthermore, the movie shows tolerance of those who are not African-American.

Barbershop is not a movie about blaming "the man" or "the system" for every ill in the African-American community. It is not a movie about poverty, pity or despair. It is, however, a movie about history, hope, ambition and optimism that attempts to show the connection between the struggles of previous generations and the challenges facing the current generation. In short, it's a movie about black people, their concerns, opinions and ambitions told without gratuitous foul language, sex or violence.

With so much working in its favor—including being number one at the box office for a few weeks—it seems inconceivable that Barbershop could be at the center of controversy (Agnes Cross-White and Sherman White 2002).

The release of *Barbershop* in 2002 elicited more than controversy of massive proportions, which is discussed later; it also garnered a significant amount of critical praise, much of which celebrated it for its decency and positivity. Describing it as "special" and a "breath of fresh air," critics lauded the film for its willingness to offer something other than the dominant images of contemporary Hollywood. They celebrated the film for its challenge to liberals and those of the hip-hop generation who talk too much about race and racism. "What was also so refreshing was the anti-reparations message articulated by a 'three-strikes' candidate skillfully played by Michael Ealy," wrote Bob Parks. "This had to have really irked [Jesse] Jackson as well. 'Barbershop' celebrates the work ethic and strong family, a place where Jackson has been absent for some time."

Steve Sailer, a conservative movie critic, offered similar praise for the film; he also used his review to denounce the problems induced by a culture of poverty and a larger culture obsessed with race and racism (especially Hollywood) rather than promoting values and morals. "The movie is for the African-American audience, but its appeal could be broad—at least to non-blacks who can decipher the dialogue. (It took me about twenty minutes before I could understand more than half of the lines.). 'Barbershop's' conservative moral and social messages and unhip style (complete with Laurel and Hardy-style slapstick) have left ill at ease many white critics—the kind whose highest term of praise is subversive." To Sailer, the film's brilliance lies with its message: "about African-Americans getting their acts together morally." Others focused not just on the message of the film, but on its willingness to challenge the hegemony of liberal and progressive thought regarding African Americans, which many see as part of the problem, one that enables black failure. Agnes Cross-White and Sherman White, leaders of Project 21, a national network of African American conservatives, concluded their praise of the film with the following statements:

One cannot help but wonder where Jackson's protests are when popular black cinema celebrates illegitimacy, violence, criminality and ignorance. Tom Joyner condemns the movie while proudly proclaiming he won't see it. Perhaps the insensitivity of the movie's creators should be the issue, but rather the intolerance of Jackson and his supporters.

For a long time, the African-American political left has served to remind us of the importance of diversity. It is both disappointing and unfortunate that their definition of diversity seems not to include diversity of thought or opinion. In the end, I hope people will give themselves permission to do what the African-American characters in Barbershop gave themselves permission to do: To think for themselves, form their own opinions and share their opinions with others through open, honest and constructive dialogue.

Barbershop is a special movie that everyone—left, right and all places in between—should see. (2002)

Such analysis and celebration were not unique; much of the critical reception focused on the diversity found in *Barbershop* as a challenge to the monolithic vision and understanding of the black community in white America.

Although certainly offering a broad range of characters and ideas that hint at the diversity of the black community, *Barbershop* does not challenge conventional Hollywood inscribed racial stereotypes; rather it reifies many longstanding representations. In fact, *Barbershop* offers no depth to its characters, presenting stock characters that play on numerous racist assumptions and stereotypical understandings of blackness as both part of its narrative structure and its effort to secure laughter.

Barbershop chronicles a day in the life of Calvin's Barbershop. Calvin (Ice Cube) has inherited the shop from his father, but he is unable to keep the it afloat, despite its importance as a place of gathering within the community. Too focused on quick get-rich schemes and the acquisition of material possessions (he carries a picture of Oprah Winfrey's guest house in his wallet), Calvin lacks perspective and an understanding of the broader picture. In fact, his financial struggles have more to do with his own failed business ventures than the financial struggles of the barbershop. Unable to make things work to his satisfaction, Calvin eventually sells the shop to Mr. Wallace (Keith David), the neighborhood loan shark, for $20,000.

The least stereotypical character of the bunch, Calvin embodies the often uttered belief about black men being more focused on material possessions and making money than on hard work and empowering community. So while Calvin embodies the grown-up elements of hip-hop and challenges dominant conventions of a hip-hop aesthetic, his unwillingness to work, his almost obsession with securing the trappings of wealth, and the spontaneity in which he makes decisions (he sells the shop on a whim, without consulting his wife or those who work inside the shop) all render Calvin as a more nuanced stereotype of black masculinity. More than this, the film's effort to make him positive through erasing any connection to hip-hop (he even institutes a rule in the shop limiting hip-hop until after 10 A.M.) and minimizing displays of sexuality (or his underdeveloped relationship with his wife) leaves Calvin a nonthreatening, modernized, hipper Uncle Tom. He is good and positive because he is not like the others; he is unique compared to those outside the walls of the barbershop, meaning that ultimately Calvin reinforces dominant stereotypes of dangerous, criminal, pathological black men so rampant in today's media. The limited depth available to Calvin, however, is not available to those other characters that make up Calvin's barbershop.

The cast of characters in *Barbershop* not only offers a range of personalities and social locations. It presents a series of long-standing racialized stereotypes: there is Dinka (Leonard Howze), the heavy-accented, fat, asexual, African janitor, who often serves as the butt of many jokes uttered inside the barbershop. Referred to as "jumbo Mutumbo," Dinka secures the respect of his peers only after he affirms his masculinity by punching out Jason (Jason George), Terry's cheating boyfriend who continuously mistreats her.

Terry (Eve) is the lone woman in the barbershop. She is a typical angry black woman, offering attitude in every instance, threatening to beat down those who cross her path. Part sexual object, and part bad-ass woman, Terry fulfills many of the common stereotypes of young black women within contemporary popular culture.

Terry finds her male counterpart in Ricky (Michael Early). A two-strike offender, Ricky has found "the straight and narrow," after gaining employment at the barbershop. Yet Jimmy, the police, and others continue to question whether Ricky has truly reformed himself. With cornrows, a bandana, and his saggin Sean Johns, Ricky still embodies the aesthetic vision of the hip-hop generation, leaving his peers to wonder whether he truly can become part of the mainstream; he looks, walks, and talks as any hip-hopped black youth might. Despite his fulfillment of widespread stereotypes, Ricky, more than any other character, challenges the often flat construction of today's

hip-hop youth. Through his conservative politics, his contempt for reparations, and his vast knowledge of shellfish, Ricky defies audience expectations
of a hip-hop, ex-felon, and black youth. The effort to construct Ricky as
"positive"—as not like the rest of today's gangsta black youth—ultimately
legitimizes such stereotypes in that Ricky becomes the exception, a unique
individual to the rest of them, thereby legitimizing existing stereotypes of
black youth as dangerous, uneducated, hypersexual, and otherwise deviant.

Still the most blatant and classic racialized stereotypes were reserved for
three other characters: Jimmy (Sean Patrick Thomas), Isaac Rosenberg (Troy
Garity), and Eddie (Cedric the Entertainer).

The film first introduces the audience to Jimmy while he orders his morning coffee on his way to work. Dressed as any middle-class businessman,
Jimmy seems to be fronting his not-yet-attained middle-class status. His
effort to pass as part of the black elite, something other than a barber, to act
as if he is better than others in the community, is evident in this initial meeting. He condescendly orders his triple, nonfat, half decaffeinated caramel
French Roast cappuccino, with just a hint of hazelnut and orange extract,
"with foam in a separate cup because I'll have to spoon it on myself because
y'all never get it right." Not merely a stereotype of the arrogant, sellout, and
bougie black male who snubs his nose at those he sees as beneath him, Jimmy
is reminiscent of the classic buffoon characters so prominent in the 1920s and
1930s. Just as Amos, Andy, and other buffoon characters (Kingfish, Step 'n
Fetchit) of past years, Jimmy does not merely act like something that he is
not; he does so in such an absurd and foolish manner that it's clear that he
is both a fraud and laughable. His coffee order, which is not actually a drink,
his propensity to make up phrases ("ocular proof"), and his willingness to
disseminate misinformation amid his elitist ignorant arrogance embody his
status as an updated version of the classic black buffoon character.

Isaac Rosenberg, the lone "white" character inside the barbershop, is also
a buffoon. Although white, Isaac walks and talks as if he is "black," at least in
a stereotypical buffoonish manner, displaying all the trappings of the stereotypical "wigger:" he speaks Ebonics, he dons a velour sweat suit and do-rag,
he drives a pimped out Cadillac Escalade and has a black girlfriend. More
than this, he works in a black barbershop and displays heightened levels of
sexuality. When he has to say goodbye to his girlfriend, he squeezes her ass
and sloppily kisses her entire mouth, all of which points to the film's representation of stereotypical black masculinity through inscription of the wigger
character. Rather than using Isaac to problematize contemporary constructions of blackness in the white imagination or challenge the clichéd inscription of whiteness (even those said to represent blackness through whiteness)
within contemporary black films as the minority, Isaac legitimizes the notion
that hip-hop is indeed the authentic black body and voice. The film further
gives voice to the idea that blackness, as a commodified cultural practice,
can be bought and worn by whites without any questions. Worse yet, his

character doesn't simply justify stereotypes of blackness, but those efforts to construct white bodies inside black spaces as minorities. In each instance, Isaac fulfills dominant expectations regarding blackness, whiteness, and contemporary race relations.

The third character, Eddie, resembles the classic Uncle Remus character. Eddie is trained as a barber, but we never see him work or cut one strand of hair. Instead he spends his days talking trash and lecturing the youngsters inside the barbershop about values and history. Part cantankerous, part curmudgeon, and the rest comedian, Eddie provides those in the barbershop and audience with a source of laughter. Although he offers important historical lessons, often correcting the ignorance of those inside the shop (and within the audience), he is offered little respect. For example, he rightly points out that Rosa Parks was not the first African American to refuse to move to the back of the bus, nor a pioneer in this respect, given that others had ended up in jail because of their own protests. Yet, positioned as a cantankerous, crazy, loud-mouth grandpa, neither those in the barbershop nor the audience take him or his statements serious, reducing him to a laughable old man in the tradition of Uncle Remus.

While each of these characters reflects stereotypical representations of blackness that continue traditions of racialized Hollywood imagery, no two characters embody these troubling elements more than J.D. (Anthony Anderson) and Billy (Lahmard Tate). Serving as a source of comic relief, J.D. and Billy are modernized coon characters. Having little to do with the narrative about Calvin, the story of the barbershop, or even the film's tendency toward reactionary preaching, J.D. and Billy are clowns, buffoons in the tradition of Amos 'n Andy. The bumbling twosome steals an ATM machine in the initial moments of the film, and we follow their attempts to retrieve the money throughout the film. During the robbery, their foolishness is made clear as they drag the ATM machine with their truck. Incompetent even as criminals, J.D. and Billy initially find difficulty stealing the ATM machine, as their bumper rips off the truck. Their bumbling and stumbling criminality does not end with their initial failures, as neither J.D. nor Billy is able to break into the ATM to secure the cash. The entire film chronicles their failed effort to finish off the robbery, which they are never able to do because of their incompetence, their childish behavior, and their laziness. Whether dropping the machine on J.D.'s foot, crushing his hand during an attempt to pass the clichéd fat man on the stairs, failing to break into the machine with an ax and a blow torch, or merely setting their room on fire, J.D. and Billy are laughable at best. At worst, they are slight reworkings of racist characters of years past.

Despite the rampant stereotypes both reminiscent of past images and those that reify dominant representations of today, critics praised *Barbershop*. Limiting its criticism to Eddie's "disparaging" remarks about black leaders, critics celebrated its positivity, its racial politics, and its vision of contemporary America. "*Barbershop* is not a movie about blaming the man or the system for every ill in the African American community. It is not a movie about poverty, pity, or despair." This review captures much of the critical praise for *Barbershop*. The positivity that critics and fans celebrate in *Barbershop* resides not so much with its humor, narrative, or even character development, but rather with its politics, its challenge to those ghettocentric films with its erasure of racism, "poverty, pity, and despair." Likewise, in erasing the realities of racism, *Barbershop* is not a movie about "blaming the man" or the system, but one about blaming black youth for failed choices, about demonizing the hip-hop generation for contributing to their own sassed steps. While the film's practice of blaming black youth, in a similar vein to contemporary politicians, is commonplace, Eddie often serves as the source of condemnation. In one instance, Eddie lectures the young people in the shop about their (lack) of work ethic and sense of history.

The problem with y'all is you don't know nothin. Sit up, watch too much TV and listen to that . . . hippy-hopty nonsense. . . . In my day a barber was more than a person setting around in his FUBU shirt with his drawers hangin out. In my day, a barber was a counselor; he was a fashion expert, style coach, a pimp. But the problem with y'all cats today is you got no skill, no sense of history and then with a straight face got the never to want to be somebody. Want somebody to respect you, but it takes respect to get respect, understand?

Although sounding like the child of Bill Bennett and Daniel Moynihan, *Barbershop* craftily inserts such ideologies through a comedic vehicle. Notwithstanding laughter and the insertion of aesthetics of hip-hop (dozens of Mama jokes, music), this passage embodies the widespread demonization of youth of color. Focusing on individualism and cultural failures, such rhetoric is emblematic of both its celebration of the American Dream and its place within a wave of new racist cinematic productions.

Although Eddie, despite his laughable, clownish demeanor serves as both the conscience and source of tough love for a lost generation of black youth, the film's conservative bootstrap politics is not limited to Eddie or even those older characters within the film. During a discussion about reparations, Ricky (notice that part of film's humor comes from the irony of Eddie and Ricky telling others how to act) gives voice to these same ideologies, providing an ironic moment in which Ricky, the hip-hop ex-con of the barbershop, scolds the others for their focus on race and past injustice rather than personal responsibility, restraint, and respect.

Customer #1: I heard on BET that we're suppose to get some money. . . . Black people to get some money; reparations or something.

Jimmy: I am sure everyone in here would love to get a handout.

Customer #1: I mean if they're handing it out, I ain't gonna turn down nothin but my collar.

Ricky: Not everyone thinks reparations are a good idea. Reparations is stupid.

Jimmy: I am surprised to hear you say that; I figured you make a case for how slavery got you all oppressed and how the white man got us.

Rickey: Given us money ain't gonna do nothing.

Billy: Man, slavery ruined my whole life.

Customer #3: Man, I don't know what all you say, but I ain't taken no reparations because as a black man I got pride and my dignity.

Jimmy [laughing]: That's bull. And you know why? Because you got bills.

Eddie: We got welfare and affirmative action; is that not reparations?

Ricky: So everywhere you look there's opportunity.

Billy: I had this opportunity to get this job last month and this crack ass cracker gonna tell me I need a diploma. Now right there, that's racism, classism, eroticism. Come on man, I am talking about isms.

Ricky: We don't need reparations, we need restraint!

Billy: Restraint?

Ricky: Restraint!

Billy: Whatever.

Ricky: Some discipline. Don't go out and buy a Range Rover when you are living with your mama. Pay your mama some rent. And can we please try to teach our children something other than the Chronic Album. And please black people be on time for something other than free before eleven at the club.

The power of this scene resides not just in its deployment of conservative or reactionary ideologies, or even with its opposition to reparations, but through its use of Ricky as the voice of reason and Billy—the criminal—as the embodiment of a lost generation of today's black youth that sees race and racism as the source of its problems. More important, the juxtaposition of Ricky, who has turned his life around, advocating these political positions compared to Billy, who remains on a path of criminality, serves to legitimize Ricky's conclusions regarding the fulfillment of the American Dream.

Erasing the realities of unemployment, racial profiling, structural adjustment programs, the prison industrial complex, and a host of other practices that impact the life chances (and choices) of youth of color, *Barbershop* replicates widespread conservative discourses that blame black youth and hip-hop culture as the true cause of today's problems within the black community. Interestingly, the film certainly attempts to capitalize on the popularity of hip-hop, whether with its soundtrack that is saturated with hip-hop artists from P. Diddy to Ginuine, or the marketing of the film through Ice Cube and Eve, its two hip-hop stars. More important, the film rides the wave of a market driven by hip-hop culture, in that the popularity of *Barbershop* reflects its aesthetics, and its place within a larger milieu of hip-hop productions. Reflective of societal practices that both demonizes and commodifies black cultural styles (hip-hop), *Barbershop* offers a sometimes-scathing critique of contemporary black youth, identifying hip-hop and not racism as the obstacle to securing the American Dream.

Barbershop not only embodies the widespread demonization of black bodies and cultural aesthetic so commonplace within our new racist moment. It also demonstrates the ubiquitous and simultaneous practice of commodification. Moreover, its articulation of reactionary and new racist politics reveals the links between processes of demonization, policymaking, and other institutions, and to new racism, which together generate an understanding of twenty-first century racial logics that seeks to profit off of blackness while simultaneously denouncing and controlling these same cultural and communal manifestations.

The film's focus on personal responsibility and the need for corrective behavior is not limited to this exchange on reparations. Nor does it limit the discussion to individuals, instead focusing on the important role black institutions must play in facilitating needed change. Emphasizing boostrapism, family values, and entrepreneurship, *Barbershop* celebrates not only the individual work ethic but the importance of black businesses as the source of black stability and progress. It makes clear that a barbershop is more than a place to receive a haircut. It is a place of gathering, a site in which old and young come together, where history, values, culture, and morals are taught and maintained. According to Eddie, the barbershop has been in the past and needs to be in the future a source of pride and liberation for the black community. "This is a barbershop. The place where being a black man means something; the cornerstone of the neighborhood. Our own country club. . . . That's the problem with your whole generation, you don't believe in nothing."

By the end of the film, Calvin and his crew of hip-hop barbers have learned this message, making better choices for themselves and the larger community. Calvin, having sold out to Lester Wallace, works to make amends, so that he can retain control of the barbershop and do a better job providing for the community. He uses the money he had received from Lester Wallace to bail Ricky out of jail, who was wrongly arrested for the ATM robbery. Calvin's choice, his good will to Ricky, and his willingness to give Lamar a haircut free of charge so that he can get a job symbolize how Calvin is putting Eddie's words into practice. He is not alone, as Ricky chooses not to seek revenge on his cousin, J.D., whose actions landed Ricky in jail. Instead, he uses his head, throwing the gun in the river to avoid trouble. Calvin and Ricky make "the right choices" further emphasizing the film's reactionary orientation in that success and failure are directly linked to individual choices and values. To make matters more clear, Calvin received a $50,000 reward for finding the ATM machine, offering the conclusive piece of evidence that not only does crime not pay, but working with the system, making righteous choices, and looking beyond self pays off, assisting Calvin in transforming the barbershop into his American Dream and the ultimate black man's country club.

The conservative nature of *Barbershop's* racial politics is not reserved to questions about black assimilation, success, liberation, or even to the demonization of hip-hop and black youth. It also finds resonance in the film's deployment of Isaac. In using Isaac as the minority within the barbershop, as someone who has to prove himself because of the prejudices of others (no one will allow him to cut their hair because he is white), *Barbershop* erases the persistent realities of white supremacy, and more important the salience of white privilege. White privilege, according to Peggy McIntosh, exists as an "invisible package of unearned assets that I can count on cashing in each day, but about which I was 'meant' to remain oblivious. White privilege is like an invisible weightless knapsack of special provisions, maps, passports, codebooks, visas, clothes, tools and blank checks" (in Rothenberg, 2005, p. 109). For Isaac, his whiteness does not represent a privilege, but an impediment, an obstacle toward his fulfilling his dream. In imagining race through such a device, *Barbershop* denies the existence of this knapsack, concluding that we can all be part of majority and minority at some point and time.

The film's failure here reflects not merely its inability to give voice to the realities and importance of white privilege within contemporary America or its connection to a history of racial appropriation, but also its effort to minimize the importance of these issues. In a powerful exchange between Isaac and Jimmy, *Barbershop* renders racism as something that goes both ways, concluding that there is nothing inherently problematic in cultural appropriation, in Isaac "acting black" because he is being true to himself, instead leaving the audience to believe that racial progress can come through the blending of cultural practices and values across communities *and* the acceptance of this process.

Jimmy: What you laughing at Kid Rock?

Isaac: Don't hate on me because I'm not a sellout.

Jimmy: You got the black girlfriend; you got the pimped out ride and I'm the sellout? You ain't nothing but a minstrel show turned on its ear. Al Jolson in a FUBU hate; blackface for the new millennium.

Isaac: You got so much education, so how come all you talk about is me.

Jimmy: Because you don't belong here. The white barbershop is uptown.

Isaac: You know what I think: you wish you were me. You wish you had my fly ass girlfriend, and my pimped out ride. Man, you wish you had my clothes, my style, my walk; why you think my fly ass girlfriend ain't with you? Cause your little bitch ass can't compete!

Jimmy: I got news for you white boy . . . you're not black!

Isaac: Jimmy, I'm blacker than you. And what's messed up; in your best day you could never be.

At this point, the other inhabitants of the barbershop do not intervene by coming to Jimmy's rescue by putting Isaac in his place, but rather mediates the conflict by turning on some music, the anecdote to all problems.

While the scene gives voice, albeit on the surface, to issues of appropriation and commodification of an imagined blackness, in the end it sides with Isaac and those who deny the racial implications of his performative identity. Jimmy eventually comes to his senses, not only apologizing, but in asking Isaac to cut his hair—he has seen the error in his ways, allowing Isaac to demonstrate his authenticity by entrusting him with his hair. Moreover, as the film uses Jimmy, the arrogant yet unknowing wannabe, and Eddie, the ignorant, but lovable, grandpa, as those who give voice to claims of minstrelsy, appropriation, and racism, it delegitmizes their analysis given their place in the film. It misses the opportunity to explore racial appropriation in the twenty-first century and how minstrelsy in its myriad forms perpetuates racism within contemporary America (as done in a film like *Bamboozled*). In writing on white appropriation of hip-hop Bill Yousman argues that:

White youth adoption of Black cultural forms in the 21st century is also a performance, one that allows Whites to contain their fears and animosities towards Blacks through rituals not of ridicule, as in previous eras, but of adoration. Thus, although the motives behind their performance may initially appear to be different, the act is still a manifestation of white supremacy, albeit a white supremacy that is in crisis and disarray, rife with confusion and contradiction. (Kitwana 2005, p. 103)

To Yousman and others, such practices facilitate the perpetuation of racism rather than usher in a new vision of racial politics defined by colorblindness (Kitwana 2005; Wynter 2002).

The desire to "be black" because of the stereotypical visions of coolness, difference, and sexual potency all play out within the construction of Isaac. bell hooks explains the widespread process of "eating the other," evident in the popularity of hip-hop as a space of commodification and appropriation of blackness, as being the result of white yearning to experience something "more exciting, more intense, and more threatening. The lure is the combination of pleasure and danger" (1992, p. 26). Hence, the popularity of hip-hop culture and an imagined black urban aesthetic, as evident in a film like *Barbershop* or a character like Isaac, embodies the racialized yearning for pleasure and danger derived from commodifying and eating the other. It is not as the film argues through Isaac that he is just being himself, but rather performing a particular racial identity that both mocks and exploits black cultural styles. As hooks argues, "Black youth culture comes to stand for the outer limits of 'outness.' The commercial nexus exploits the culture's desire (expressed by whites and blacks) to inscribe blackness as 'primitive' sign, as wildness, and with it the suggestion that black people have secret access to intense pleasure, particularly pleasures of the body . . . It is the young black male body that is seen as epitomizing the promise of wildness, of unlimited physical prowess, and unbridled eroticism" (1992, p. 26).

Isaac embodies this reality rather than a new white identity that embraces blackness toward the formation of a new individual and collective identity.

As either clichéd buffoon or transformative white racial identity, Isaac offers little toward understanding the complexity of white identity and racial performativity. Rather, as the film constructs Isaac as offering greater authenticity, because of his car, clothes, talk, and girl, it offers a very narrow and problematic understanding of both hip-hop and blackness. More important, the opportunity to critically engage white appropriation of blackness, which of course would have potentially left audience members uncomfortable, or even imagine the possibilities of hip-hop as the basis of a new racial politics is lost.

Barkari Kitwana offers hope in his provocative *Why White Kids Like Hip Hop* when he explores the potential of hip-hop as a site of radical racial transformation. He notes that "My belief is that rather than being resistant, many white hip-hop kids have yet to realize that is up to them to create such anti-racist programs" (2005, p. 104). In contrast, *Barbershop* provides little hope in this regard, celebrating Isaac as evidence of the American and Martin Luther King Jr.'s dreams, whereupon hard work and racial (cultural) integration will ultimately lead all to the promised land, even for a white kid living in the south side of Chicago.

The importance of *Barbershop* is not limited to its narrative or even its cinematic construction of blackness. It can be seen with the controversy that surrounded the film's release. In several instances, Eddie, the cantankerous barber who rarely works, but often criticizes, offers his understanding of African American history, challenging the accepted mythology, communal identity, and leadership within the black community. At various points in the film, Eddie calls Martin Luther King, Jr. a whore, questions the contributions of Rosa Parks, and tells Jesse Jackson to fuck off. Even though the rest of the barbershop denounces Eddie for his comments in each instance, and although the film uses these moments to emphasize the heterogeneity of the black community and the dynamic nature of a black barbershop, these comments soon became the basis of discussions concerning *Barbershop*.

These few lines prompted a wave of outrage, much of which emanated from the established Civil Rights leadership and older African Americans. "The filmmakers crossed the line between what's sacred and serious and what's funny," said Jackson during a press conference. "I could dismiss the comments about me, but Dr. King is dead and Ms. Parks is an icon. There are some heroes who are sacred to people, and these comments poisoned an otherwise funny movie. Why put cyanide in the Kool-Aid?" James Meeks, Vice President of the Rainbow/Push Coalition, agreed, noting that "There are certain things we should choose not to joke about. With a major film like that, there is an obligation to teach these kids everything is not funny. There will be many young people who don't know the Rosa Parks story" (Hall 2002).

Reverends Jesse Jackson and Al Sharpton specifically called on MGM to remove the offensive scenes. While unsuccessful in this regard, the film's producers did issue an apology. George Tillman told the Associated Press that they "did not mean to offend anyone. [We] wanted one individual in the shop saying something funny and we wanted everyone to disagree with that person" (AP, 2002). While Jackson and Sharpton found some satisfaction in the apology, others saw it as insufficient and unacceptable. Throughout the black press, editorials called for a widespread boycott of the film. Vernon Jarrett encouraged blacks to show the world through a boycott that they would not "pay for or snicker at crude insults" (2002). He remarked further that a "boycott is the only course for Black moviegoers who still claim any level of the racial/personal pride that made it possible for our ancestors to survive and for us to prosper today in America." Jarrett's understanding of progress and belief in a hegemony of colorblindness are reflective of much of the condemnation of film. Columnists saw Eddie's speech as one that might erode America's racial progress and one that spit on the efforts of those who secured the freedom and success that defines the black experience in the twenty-first century. Moreover, his comments embody the efforts of critics to reduce the problems of *Barbershop* to these remarks rather than the rampant racial stereotypes and its reactionary social/racial commentary. Perhaps, in fact, its conservative values and its tendency to condemn black youth are what these critics found redeemable in the film despite Eddie's commentary.

Others saw the film as equally problematic, but concluded that the debate and subsequent critique of the film and its hip-hop generation of supporters was healthy. "The *Barbershop* debate is a healthy one! Misseducated younguns need to hear King and Mrs. Parks defended," wrote Bill Alexander in *USA Today*. "They need to understand how a mass-marketed movie can 'trivialize' giants. The white critics have been glowing over the movie because it is non-threatening and taps into stereotypes. My barbershop used to be like that years ago, but I switched to another where views are enlightened and the background Jazz is cool" (2002). Ironically sounding like Eddie chastising the youth in the barbershop for their ignorance and terrible taste in music, Alexander's comments are reflective of a larger segment of the debate which both denounced the film and saw it as a teachable moment to curtail the destructive and disturbing behavior of the hip-hop generation.

Still others disagreed, warning that Eddie's speeches were indeed dangerous and that was part of its appeal to white critics and audience members. It was the denunciation of King and the stereotypical barbershop banter that enticed white audiences into the seats and elicited praise from white critics, and not the reactionary, conservative, and colorblind ideologies rampant within the film.

Although these perspectives represented the loudest segments of the debate, much of the controversy and public discourses focused less on the film and the implications of the controversial scenes and more on the debate itself and what it revealed about the state of African American cinema, the black community, and race in the twenty-first century. To many, the controversy and debate reflected an ongoing generational struggles between black America's old guard—those reared before and during the Civil Rights Movement—and the hip-hop generation. "You have seen some individuals from the civil rights movement, Jesse Jackson and Al Sharpton, who are utterly offended that some of their icons have been criticized," noted Todd Boyd, an associate professor at the University of Southern California. "You have another generation who finds no problem whatever in criticizing anyone who they see appropriate for criticism. They have rejected the idea of the sacred cow, instead keepin it real" (Kong 2002). Specifically, those of the Civil Rights generation continually expressed concern not just with the film's effort to ridicule black icons, those individuals supposedly respected and valued within white America, but the willingness of the hip-hop generation "to air dirty laundry" and pay to be insulted. Aldon Morris, a sociology professor at Northwestern University, saw the film as potentially damaging in this regard, wondering about its effects on the black psyche. "I believe that this just comedy routine is naïve and short-sighted. During the Jim Crow period, black people exacerbated their own oppression and negative stereotypes in art that reinforced their oppression" (Caputo 2002).

Although overly simplistic given the reduction of film production and consumption to individual choice, much of the media and black leadership's response focused on the dangers of the film in arming whites with evidence and false justifications for their prejudices as well as further perpetuating those identity issues that plague the black community. Interestingly, these same critics and commentators have remained silent regarding other films and popular cultural mediums (video games, TV) regarding their damaging effects on the black community and their arming white racists, rather taking this opportunity to publicly excoriate the hip-hop generation through a public discussion of *Barbershop*. In other words, the outrage prompted by *Barbershop* had little to do with the specifics of the speech, or the possibility of its negatively impacting race relations. Rather it reflected the larger struggle between the Civil Rights and hip-hop generations over the future leadership and direction of the black community. That is why so much of the public discourse focused on the film as an expression of the problems facing the hip-hop generation, those who represent the future of the black community.

Such fears were enhanced by polls that revealed how little support Jackson, Sharpton, and others denouncing the film had within the black community. In a survey by *Black Voices,* almost 85 percent of respondents thought Jesse Jackson and others were "too up-tight" over *Barbershop* jokes. At BlackAmericaWeb.com, e-mails ran 9 to 1 against the stance of Jesse and Al, with a majority dismissing the controversy as "just a joke." Still, the black media and much of its leadership, once again obsessed with questions of respectability, saw a major issue at work within the film.

An editorial within the *Chicago Weekend* not only captured the outrage many had toward the film, but reflected the larger concern about the state of the black community in light of the film's message: "As a people who in serious trouble BECAUSE [note my emphasis] today's youth does not respect its elders and many elders fear today's youth," noted one commentator. "Rosa Parks is acknowledged in Black history as the mother of the Civil Rights movement and thousands of other people marched, endured physical abuse and, in some cases, murder, so that those who followed them could enjoy the opportunities racism denied them. And this is how they say thanks? Sadly, today's emphasis on being hip, fast, and financially 'phat' has caused too many black people to disrespect those who cannot or will not keep up" ("Is Everything Funny" 2002).

Sounding much like a speech Eddie or Ricky would have given in the film, the public denunciation of the film focused on the failures of black youth to hold up the legacies of the Civil Rights Movement, and how their own personal choices, values, and cultural practices posed a threat not only to themselves but to the entire community. The focus on the generational divide and the absence of values, respect and sense of history within the hip-hop generation is not surprising given its prevalence within both Hollywood films, as evidenced by our discussion of *Drumline, Brown Sugar,* and *Love & Basketball,* and larger public discourses.

The practice of blaming societal problems on youth, particularly youth of color, and hip-hop are longstanding practices through which both *Barbershop* and its critics engage in with their mutual efforts to demonize the hip-hop generation. Both those celebrating and hating *Barbershop* were joined together by their reactionary and conservative vision of the world, as well as their mutual contempt for the hip-hop generation. Equally important, all sides were linked by their basic denial of racism and focus on how individual choices impact the opportunities afforded to the black community. As previously noted, a central element to a new racist politics is the practice of blaming societal inequities and those institutionally rooted problems on individuals and the supposed dysfunctionality of culture. To the narrative and message of *Barbershop,* the articulation of such racialized discourse is equally important, as the failures of youth and their adaptation to a hip-hop identity is constructed as the reason for communal problems. In a sense, the focus on communal pathologies and widespread demonization of youth of color, whether in *Barbershop* or within the U.S. Congress, is central to the American Dream, as inequality and poverty unsettle the hegemony of rhetorics around the American Dream; those who don't live the Dream do so because of their own failures, and not those of America or because of racism. Its invoking of such discourses is evidence of its reactionary message and its deployment of the rhetorics of the American Dream and colorblindness.

Despite the reactionary politics and ubiquitous deployment of long-standing racialized stereotypes, *Barbershop* still shows a lot of potential as a film, as a political statement, and as a racial/social commentary. In fact, many of the scenes that elicited outrage and criticism from the Civil Rights establishment embodied the best that the film had to offer. More than those instances, *Barbershop* revealed possibilities through its engagement with hair politics. The opening scene, in which Tim Story, the film's director, pieces together a montage of black hairstyles, reflects the immense possibilities of *Barbershop*. This powerful cinematic montage captures the diversity of the black community and the importance of hair politics in understanding black identity. In this instance, *Barbershop* pushes viewers to think about black cultural styles and the importance of the barbershop within the black community as a cultural, social, economic, and political institution. Although missing the opportunity to provide insight into the history and cultural importance of the black barbershop, it does illustrate how barbershops continue to serve as a place of gathering, as a "black country club." Despite integration and because of persistent inequalities, barbershops continue to be an important site of resistance. Finally, *Barbershop* successfully challenges dominant representations of both popular culture and news media that imagine America's ghetto as places of despair, poverty, and crime. It dispels the narrow and hegemonic vision of inner city spaces as ones without family and working people. In centering the narrative within the barbershop, it successfully represents inner-city Chicago as racially diverse, inhabited by the working class, the unemployed, and the middle-class. It is too bad that with this backdrop, *Barbershop* replicated the cinematic racism and reactionary ideologies that continue to limit the possibilities of African American cinema.

BARBERSHOP 2

The commercial and critical success of *Barbershop* inspired several follow-up projects including a Showtime television series and the release of *Barbershop 2: Back in Business* in 2004. Taking a cookie-cutter approach, despite having a new director (Kevin Rodney Sullivan), *Back in Business* not only has all the same characters of its predecessor but also replicates its message and narrative structure.

As with *Barbershop*, *Back in Business* chronicles the financial struggles facing Calvin and his barbershop. Once again, Calvin battles to maintain control of his barbershop. In the original, Calvin overcame personal difficulties to eventually secure his American Dream. This time the incursion of a Nappy Cutz, a flashy, modern barbershop franchise across the street poses a new threat to the barbershop. Offering a bit more historical commentary and insight into the effects of gentrification within the black community (although at times feeling like a black version of *You Got Mail* (1998) without the love story), *Barbershop 2* provides a much more complex rendering of a black social reality, albeit through a less fresh, appealing, and enjoyable narrative.

Barbershop 2: Back in Business begins with a short historical lesson to establish the communal importance of the black barbershop in the development of the black community. With fireworks serving as a backdrop, the film's initial street scene is titled: "July 4, 1967, Southside Chicago," to establish a time-and-place orientation for the narrative. A staggering Eddie is on the run from the cops, after stealing meat from a store so that he could participate in America's dream. He could join in on the celebration by having a BBQ with his family. Before entering what we learn to be Calvin's barbershop, Eddie runs into a man dressed up as Uncle Sam, as to further symbolize the ongoing struggles for black America. The symbol of U.S. freedom stands in the way of Eddie's freedom and his desire to celebrate Independence Day, notwithstanding the absence of freedom in his own life; however, the barbershop proves to be a source of safety, of freedom, for Eddie. Without much thought or questions as to why he has entered his job in such a hurry, Calvin Sr. (Javon Johnson) helps him hide from the police, cutting his hair as part of his disguise protecting him from the police. This historical retrospective not only serves the narrative by explaining Eddie's relationship to Calvin Sr. and the barbershop, which he calls his home, but to solidify the importance of the barbershop as a space of community cohesion and family; it is a place away from white America that has historically protected the black community from the foot of American racism.

This historical flashback, as with the film's depiction of the 1968 riots after the assassination of Martin Luther King Jr., works to establish the importance of the black barbershop, providing some needed historical context, which was absent from the first film, and establishing a lens to understand the film's examination of gentrification and the erosion of black communal institutions within the contemporary moment.

While defining gentrification is somewhat difficult, given its local specificity and the varied ways it materializes, it is important to grasp the basics of a working definition of gentrification. Gentrification reflects the process in which rising housing costs, public policy, and others forces connected to an influx of new wealthy and usually white residents displace poor and minority residents, along with small businesses, often resulting in dramatic shifts in the aesthetics, demographics and "flavor" of particular neighborhoods. Neil Smith further clarifies and complicates the essential elements of gentrification in arguing that gentrification is "a dirty word" (Smith, 30–31). Regardless of the definition and the varied nuances of this social issue, gentrification always encompasses three essential elements: (1) displacement of original neighborhood inhabitants; (2) systematic upgrading of the neighborhood, especially with its housing and business; (3) a dramatic change in the character of a particular neighborhood.

The term *gentrification* was initially coined in the 1960s. British sociologist Ruth Glass coined the term to describe the movement of London's middle class ("gentry") from more expensive neighborhoods to those deteriorating communities. As these newcomers upgraded their homes, and businesses opened to cater to these new residents, housing values tended to increase, thereby leading to the displacement of low-income residents. As noted, gentrification, while usually associated with housing, is equally linked to commercial businesses. Beyond the shift in types of businesses, commercial real estate owners found ways to take advantage of the increasing financial capital of a neighborhood's residents by increasing lease rates, equally contributing to displacement. Finally, this process leads to the closure of small businesses and the opening of chains/large businesses, further injuring the small business owner.

Barbershop 2 does a pretty good job of bringing gentrification into the spotlight, giving voice to the myriad issues at work within many inner-city communities. First of all, it demonstrates the reality of corporate power within contemporary black communities so evident today in Chicago, Oakland, Harlem, and Washington D.C. In the film, Nappy Cutz, as part of a larger corporate endeavor, appropriately named Quality Land Development, has access to capital that allows it to provide goods and services otherwise not available at Calvin's barbershop. This new establishment offers a fancy Web site, milk baths, shiny new haircutting appliances, a basketball hoop, a massive fish tank, and all the fancy coffee you can drink. What it lacks in substance and history, it makes up for it in flash and "bling-bling." The film's commentary is particularly important because it aptly reflects on how these new joints, which are backed by corporate power, are not only appealing to middle-class patrons at the exclusion of working-class residents, but facilitate the annihilation of family business and communal establishments that cannot compete.

Along these lines, the narrative treatment of gentrification puts into question the supposedly foundational principles of capitalism—that competition is good for businesses, consumers, and the overall economy. The inequity of power between Calvin's and Nappy Cutz demonstrates that no competition exists between the two businesses, but as the Porsche-driving developer of Nappy Cutz tells Calvin, the relationship between the two stores is nothing but annihilation or destruction; they are competing because Nappy Cutz will invariably destroy Calvin's barbershop. Because Nappy Cutz has financial power and political backing, competition does not exist, which ultimately isn't good for Calvin's shop or the entire community because of the loss of history, communal power, and control, all of which would reside outside the community if corporate power displaced the likes of Calvin. The film makes this point clear in its unwavering opposition to gentrification through a dramatic speech given by Calvin during a City Council meeting dedicated to the proposal of Quality Land Development.

My name is Calvin Palmer. I own Calvin's Barbershop over on 79th. We've been there since 1958 and all I'd like to say is all change isn't bad; who can argue with progress? Better schools, cleaner streets something we need on the Southside. And I want the best for my son just like my parents wanted the best for me. Some change on 79th is well-needed and well-deserved. Also, I'm happy that people outside our community are starting to find the value in the neighborhood. But, if that means sellin our soul to make a quick buck, I ain't with it. That's why I'm not selling out, like some people I know. . . . We gotta realize that people make this community. Not five dollar coffees and twenty dollar mugs. It's the people. And once you lose the people, you lose the neighborhood. So, if I had a say, I would deny Quality Land Development's proposal to tear up 79th because it just ain't worth it.

While a bit clichéd and part of the film's tendency toward corny drama, Calvin's speech and the film's larger narrative focus on gentrification gives voice to the human, cultural, and communal costs of the corporate take-over of inner-city communities, despite the incursion of lattes and smoothies, a fact that outsiders often describe as progress or needed change. It also demonstrates how power and greed operate within this context. Unfortunately, *Barbershop 2,* like its predecessor, misses a significant opportunity to document the full picture of gentrification, because it erases race from the discussion. Like so many of today's films, *Barbershop 2* reduces gentrification to an issue of class, to the often-constructed and narrowly defined conflict between those African Americans who, in post–Civil Rights America, have secured the American Dream and those whose dream has yet to be realized. The battle to control 79th Street according to the film is a battle between Calvin, the other barbers, and the residents with Quality Land Development, which is run by Quentin Leroux (Henry Lennix), a black businessman more interested in personal profit, and Lelo Brown (Robert Wisdom), a black alderman more interested in reelection and bribes than in representing the people. The problem of gentrification, which the film rightly imagines as a crisis, is constructed as an inner problem of the black community, as an unfortunate outcome of the class divide of black America. Beyond the film's erasure of transnational capital and the ways in which major corporations capitalize on the degradation of ghetto communities, the open markets and its exploitable land, its narrative, like so many that come from Hollywood, constructs conflict through class rather than race, in spite of the historical and contemporary reality where gentrification is clearly a racial phenomenon.

While not inherently a racial phenomenon, gentrification tends to take on a racial element. The reality of income and wealth gaps, which are tied to the historical and contemporary practices of racism, results in a process whereby whites are able to systematically displace low-income residents of color. While the norm, the paradigm of white-minority gentrification can be limiting, in that America's shifting racial make-up complicates our understanding of gentrification. For example, San Francisco's Bay View/Hunter Point, a longtime African American community, saw an increasing number of Asian American newcomers during the 1990s. Their presence has led to rising rents and the systematic displacement of longtime African American residents. With an increasing visibility of middle-class families of color, it would be easy to assume that gentrification reflects a class hierarchy in America. In other words, those without financial capital, who are unable to compete with incoming residents to pay rent, are forced out of certain neighborhoods.

Class status certainly plays a role in the process of gentrification. Those with money are able to secure certain properties, but the reality of white privilege, the intersectionality of race and class, and the political power afforded to white Americans (as opposed to immigrants) mandate that we situate our understanding of gentrification within a larger context of race.

The numbers, reflective of rates of poverty and unemployment among communities of color, and the history of gentrification, being mostly of whites seizing control over communities from minorities, reveal the centrality of race. As more and more Americans reap the benefits of the information age, while changing existing neighborhoods, the majority of the United States is getting poorer and poorer. The richest 1 percent of the population in the United States control more than half the nation's wealth; the richest 10 percent controls nearly 85 percent. The poorest 20 percent of the population, some 60 million people, are sharing less than one-half of 1 percent of the wealth. Currently there are nearly 40 million people living in poverty in the United States, another 40 million are one paycheck away, a 200 percent increase from 30 years ago. As many as 10 million people are homeless or near homeless, most are women and children and half are black; one of four Americans does not have basic health care. For all of these statistics people of color are, of course, disproportionately represented. Blacks and Latinos make up nearly half of all those in poverty. While politicians and news media lament the strength of the economy (by which they usually mean the financial speculations of those wealthy enough to play the stock market), unemployment for some groups is upwards of 25 to percent. One of five children are born into poverty in the United States; one of two black kids and American Indians, one of three Latinos. Under such worsening conditions, the likelihood of gentrification increases, as the divide between the haves and have nots widens. In constructing gentrification between the black-run Quality Land Development and the black community, between the black haves and have nots, *Barbershop 2* presents gentrification in an acceptable way that, like much of contemporary Hollywood, reifies colorblind discourses and reduces conflicts and tensions within the black community to those driven by class divisions.

Films, whether African American cinematic productions or those dedicated to giving life to the experiences of white Americans, don't have an obligation to provide a gateway into social/cultural reality; but the failures of *Barbershop 2* to uncover the entire picture of gentrification not only represents a missed opportunity, but a shortcoming within the film given its effort toward critiquing the corporate takeover of inner-city communities.

Barbershop 2: Back in Business, even more so than its predecessor, is a film of unfulfilled potential. While less original, compelling, and even enjoyable than the first, it possesses far greater potential with its emphasis on community, institutional power, and diversity. For example, the film's opening scene mirrors that of the first, with a montage of various black hair styles, yet it marks hair as a site of cultural resistance through inscribing those styles of 1960s and 1990s, providing a powerful commentary on black hair politics, of both change and continuity, of the ways in which black culture, rage, and identity has been, and continues to be, visible within hair styles. Unfortunately, the film offers little more commentary on these issues, instead offering little more simplistic clichés, reducing difference to cultural signifiers, as evident in the diversity of hairstyles.

Like so many comedies, the potential for a counter-narrative, one that not only offers counter-representations but greater understanding to contemporary racial politics and racial formation, is there, but is erased through clichés, traditional racial tropes, and the reduction of race to cultural differences. The missed opportunities that define *Barbershop 2: Back in Business* are emblematic of the nature of a new racist cinematic production.

Even the film's critiques of capitalism, which are absent from *Barbershop*, with its focus on gentrification, and its denunciation of corporate power as a pollutant to the black community, are ultimately undermined by the film's conclusion—yet another missed opportunity in offering an oppositional narrative and one that gives voice to both contemporary problems and struggles for resistance. Ultimately, despite financial incentives to support big capital, Calvin decides to oppose the development of the neighborhood. The prospect of a major national corporation taking over his community, despite his being offered $300,000 dollars and receiving a promise that his shop would be the only barbershop in the neighborhood, was not enough to entice him to sell out his community. Beyond his rejection, Calvin additionally demonstrates his resolve with his effort to return the shop to its rightful and authentic look (he had bought fancy paintings and art as part of a plan to change the look of Calvin's in hopes of competing with Nappy Cutz, replacing them with posters of the community).

In both cases, *Barbershop 2* falls short, with its conclusion embodying the film's simplistic reduction of gentrification and communal development to personal choice. Whereas Calvin and Jimmy, who quits his job with the Alderman, choose community, history, and the preservation of the shops authentic character over money and power, Quentin and Calvin's cousin (Kenan Thompson), who had worked at Calvin's barbershop before leaving for Nappy Cutz, choose profit and personal gain over all else. In the end, the film leaves its audience with belief that life is about choices, and we each have choices to make, whether in the direction of our community or own values.

The emphasis on personal choice (responsibility) and keepin' it real in the absence of a sustained discussion of institutional realities, politics, and power differentials reflects its unfulfilled potential and its liberal understanding of race and inequality. Its reconstitution of resistance as individualized acts of opposition and dramatic speeches, notwithstanding the efforts of numerous organizations dedicated to protecting poor inner-city communities from gentrification and corporate power, embodies the failures of *Barbershop 2* (and its predecessor). The omissions of grassroots organizing combined with its political trajectory render these two film as liberal comedies at best and at worst conservative commentaries working to the advancement of a racist status quo.

COMEDIES AS TRANSGRESSION

Throughout this chapter, I have focused on the missed potential of many recent comedies that use their comedic elements as sources of pleasure and laughter rather than opposition. These films ultimately serve the interests of the status quo and white privilege through their celebrations of the American Dream, demonizations of the black poor, reduction of race to cultural aesthetics, and deployment of racialized tropes. Yet each film also demonstrates the potential of comedies in using laughter and the presumption of humor as a point of entry into political, social, and racial issues. As such, I have continually described this set of films, to varying degrees, as one of missed opportunities, as a series of failed chances to challenge both hegemonic representations and the structural realities of contemporary racism. All that being said, I end my discussion of this recent wave of comedies with an examination of *Undercover Brother* (2002) and *Bamboozled* (2002), both of which demonstrate the possibilities of comedies to both entertain and challenge, to garner pleasure for those in the seats and those in the streets, in challenging the hegemonic narrative of a colorblind post-Civil Rights America.

UNDERCOVER BROTHER

The first several times I saw previews for *Undercover Brother* I could only shake my head with both amazement and disgust. Resembling *Soul Plane* and *Bringing Down the House,* both films that struck me as neominstrel shows, it appeared to be yet another Hollywood attempt to mock, ridicule, and commodify a racist vision of blackness all the way to the bank. Initially reluctant to spend either time or money on the film, despite the critical praise of trusted peers and colleagues, as well as celebrations from various communities, including those of the worlds of entertainment, academia, and black artists, I eventually relented with its DVD release.

During the initial portions of the film my fears were unfortunately affirmed, leaving me to wonder if I was watching the same film as others had described to me as progressive, oppositional, and innovative. To me, it was inundated with racist stereotypes that mirrored the representations of minstrel shows in the past. Without much depth, it replicated many of America's most absurd, prejudicial, and disturbing racial assumptions that have long dominated America's racial politics and popular culture. Nowhere is this more evident than with the film's main character: *Undercover Brother.*

Although the film takes place within the modern era, *Undercover Brother* (Eddie Griffin) resembles a throwback to 1970s Blaxploitation antiheros, such as *Shaft* (1971), *Sweetback's Baad Assss Song* (1971), and *Superfly* (1972), all of whom helped define an oppositional identity during the tumultuous period. With his Afro, colorful leisure suits, gold Cadillac with "solid license plates," black power medallion, and his embodiment of Afrocentrism, the film constructs Brother as the truest of uncompromised and unassimilated brothers. Lisa Guerrero, in "Racial representation and the Ironic Reponses in African American Popular Culture" (2005), describes *Brother* as one who "Fights the racial injustice of modern-day America with the direct simplicity of the Civil Rights movement and the style of 'Soul Train's Don Cornelius.'" His blackness is not merely embodied by his style, his black power salutes, and his constant utterances of "Solid," but through his actions.

Early in the film, we witness Brother carry out his work as a "black Robin Hood," as he erases bank records in an effort to assist low-income families exploited by the man. Beyond his activist work and his challenges to "the man," Brother's blackness is continually and stereotypically confined by his performed identity. The film does not represent his effort to help low-income families in resisting gentrification and capitalist exploitation as a manifestation of his politics or his understanding of racial politics, but merely as a marker of his coolness and his desire to oppose authority, in other words the film's stereotypical construction of blackness. "His 'authentic blackness' is never at issue for audience because they can identity him by his platform shoes, snakeskin pants, and hip language," writes Guererro. "The security camera outside the Brotherhood headquarters verifies what we already know about Undercover Brother when it declares: 'Blackness confirmed. You've got soul,' after he successfully greets the simulated hand with a convoluted, syncopated, and choreographed series of handshakes" (2005, p. 6). More than this, the audience's assured laughter and the film's rendering of the Afro, black power handshake, and even his clothes, which are all historically replete with racial and political meaning, as a source of laughter and coolness, as well as an embodiment of the film reduction of Brother to a racial caricature, left me wondering if *Undercover Brother* was a minstrel show in hiding. It left me questioning what my friends and colleagues saw in the film, and how Malcolm Lee, the film's director and Spike Lee's cousin, could produce such a racially troubling film. Unwilling to give up on the film, I continued watching with hopes of a change in the film's racial politics.

The audience's introduction to the B.R.O.T.H.E.R.H.O.O.D offered little more as the film continued to construct the black community (the B.R.O.T.H.E.R.H.O.O.D serving as a microcosm of such) through deploying a series of stereotypes. Inside the B.R.O.T.H.E.R.H.O.O.D, audiences meet: "Smart Brother" (Gary Anthony Williams), a fat, nonthreatening, asexual, and happy computer geek who helps the cause through his knowledge (of technology) and his brainpower. Not to be outdone, "Conspiracy Brother" (Dave Chappelle), is a walking embodiment of the stereotypical angry and delusional black male. Dressed in the typical revolutionary garb—black beret or skull cap, leather jacket, and Dashiki—he too resembles a throwback to 1970s Blaxploitation films, which habitually ridiculed radicals. Conspiracy Brother, however, takes a modern and comedic twist with his laughable tendency to turn all things, including the most ordinary of issues, into radical conspiracies orchestrated by the all-powerful white male. Throughout the film, he deals the "race card" from both the top and bottom of the deck, questioning the racial implication of the terms "Good morning," and "Hi," the invention of the computer, and the 16-herbs and spices found at KFC, the black man's ultimate vice. "Sistah Girl" (Aunjanue Ellis), the film's third cinematic "sample" of the Blaxploitation era replicates many long-standing stereotypes of black women. She is smart, sexy, and sassy; in the same instance she can seduce a man with her sexuality she can kick his ass, always in the name of black liberation. Without question and reservation, Sistah Girl is down for the black community and its men.

The final member of the B.R.O.T.H.E.R.H.O.O.D that we are introduced to is Lance (Neil Patrick Harris), the lone white member of the underground crime-fighting organization, who the film portrays as timid, awkward, having no rhythm, and clueless. More important, despite working for the B.R.O.T.H.E.R.H.O.O.D, an organization dedicated to truth, justice, and the Afro-American war, Lance, "an expert on white culture" is completely ignorant about racial issues and the black experience. Undercover Brother's introduction to Lance is indicative of his own racial politics:

Lance: Wholly molely, it looks like source awards up in here.

Undercover Brother: Who's that? [Pointing to Lance]

Lance: Whhhaaaaaaaaaattttttttttttttt suuuuuuuuuuuup?

Undercover Brother: How did the white boy get a job at the B.R.O.T.H.E.R.H.O.O.D?

Chief: Shit, man, what can I tell ya, affirmative action.

Lance: Here we go; open up the window its getting racial up in this piece.

Lance is not simply a stereotype of whiteness, but an embodiment of two dominant visions of contemporary racial politics, at least at its surface:

1. Whites can be a minority within certain spaces and situations (see *8 Mile* (2002) or news reports about white athletes in the NBA or those who play at historically black colleges). As the only white person within the B.R.O.T.H.E.R.H.O.O.D, he is the one subjected to mistrust, ridicule, and prejudice.

2. The film uses Lance to articulate dominant beliefs that those who benefit from affirmative action, who take advantage of quota systems, lack the needed qualifications to prosper within those organizations. Despite not initially being for the cause and lacking knowledge about race relations or black history, Lance is able to secure a position in B.R.O.T.H.E.R.H.O.O.D because of his whiteness, affirming widespread and dominant beliefs about affirmative action (only after he watches *Roots* and apologies for his people's past injustices does he deserve to be in the B.R.O.T.H.E.R.H.O.O.D).

"The Chief" (Chi McBride), the stereotypical fearless leader who commands respect through both fear and affection, leads the entire group. He is "an amalgamation of all the overworked, hot-headed but benevolent black law-and-order figures of Hollywood film and television" (Guerrero 7). Each of these characters is limited to his/her stock and stereotypical representations, providing a flat understanding of the complex identities that describe black leaders, black nationalists, or even black intellectuals.

The film's inscription of dominant stereotypes, however, is not limited to those characters within the B.R.O.T.H.E.R.H.O.O.D, as evidence by its construction of the "man" and its depictions of whiteness with Mr. Feather (Chris Katan) and "White She-Devil" (Denise Richards). The man, though never seen, captures the stereotypical essence of a racist whiteness. Not just seeking power and control, the Man is driven by his own racism, his fear of blackness and of cultural and communal integration between different racial communities. Sounding very much like white nationalist thought, which is today so prevalent on the Internet, "the Man," and Mr. Feather denounce and fret the increased influence of the black community on white youth. Mr. Feather, unlike "the Man," has not been able to fully resist the power in the coolness associated with blackness, succumbing to the allure of hip-hop and the power of a black aesthetic. If the "man" represents the stereotypical old guard of racism, Mr. Feather embodies the new manifestation of racism with his fetishization and demonization of blackness. He works for the destruction of blackness based on fear and disdain for the other; yet, he also is influenced by black cultural practices, which in turn fuels his hatred and fear. In one instance, he demands swift action to stop the invasion of blackness into the white community and culture via popular culture. "Little by little we are blending and merging until one day we are going to become one united people living and working and dancing together like the News or Ally McBeal or the people who work at Saturn. We have to stop it until its too late." While at times offering sophisticated understandings of racism based on theories that recognize racism as derived from contempt and love of the other, the surface of *Undercover Brother* reveals a very shallow understanding of contemporary American racism. Irrational and contradictory, the film imagines racism in a very stereotypical, Jerry Springer sort of way, where racism becomes something peripheral and limited to those crazy and delusional individuals.

The final member of their white supremacist team is "White She Devil," the Man's most powerful weapon and the black man's "kryptonite:" a sexy and sexualized white woman. (Not surprisingly, both Sistah Girl and White She Devil use their sexuality for their respective causes replicating societal views about female sexuality. Moreover each uses that sexuality in an effort to win the heart and support of Brother.) White She Devil does not simply embody the stereotypical white women—blond, blue eyes, curvy, wholesome, yet sexual: all-America, but additionally signifies both the historically constructed ideas regarding the ideal white womanhood and the widespread myth regarding black men's inability to resist those ideal white women. Despite his authentic blackness, his resistance to the Man and his Black Nationalist identity, Brother cannot resist the sexuality of a white woman, ultimately succumbing to the Man's ultimate weapon in White She Devil. In falling into this trap, Brother does not merely fulfill the stereotypical narrative of black men's sexual fantasies of white women, but in doing so he looses his true identity. While undercover inside The Man's cooperation as part of "Operation Token," a mission focused on uncovering The Man's plans to control the General and other black leaders, Brother—Anton Jackson—finally meets his match in White She Devil. Although Lance had prepared him for the experience with boy band music, scenes from *River Dance, Leave it to Beaver,* and *Major Dad,* as well as *Friends* trivia, significant amounts of mayo and introduction to "all things white," in an effort to facilitate his cover as a whitewashed black male, he is not prepared for She Devil. Neither Lance nor the B.R.O.T.H.E.R.H.O.O.D had the ability to simulate the allure and intoxicating sexuality of She Devil. Her charm and presumable skills in the bedroom are too much to handle, resulting in Brother trading in his blackness for a whitewashed existence not as part of his undercover work but as his true identity.

With Brother (now Jackson) trading in his leisure suit for khakis, his 1970s R&B for karaoke of "Ebony and Ivory," and his concern for liberation of the black community for material possessions and acceptance, Jackson is the embodiment of a sellout. He loves nonfat lattes, mangos, smoothies, and even mayo. As evident here, *Undercover Brother* is saturated with simplistic renderings of blackness, whiteness, "Oreos," race, and even racism. My initial reaction to the film, especially its beginnings, focused on these aspects, at least until Conspiracy Brother and "The Chief" pushed my thought and the film's message in a new direction with their debate concerning Undercover Brother's turn to the dark side, for example, his transformation into Anton Jackson. As Undercover Brother enters the B.R.O.T.H.E.R.H.O.O.D, his comrades see a new man, dressed in khakis and a sweater, with a voice sounding like stereotypical uptight "whitened" black man.

Conspiracy Brother: Undercover Brother, what happened to you?
Sistah Girl: He had sex with a white girl, that's what happened!
Conspiracy Brother: Was it everything I've dreamed of?

Chief: White girl or no white girl, where the hell have you been?

Undercover Brother: Not there cause that's where people who swear go.

Sistah Girl: You sound like a 14-year-old white chick.

Undercover Brother: I don't think so sisteeerrr girl.

Sistah: It's sistaahh girl, Dude.

Undercover Brother: Maybe on planet Ebonics. But where I come from, we like to pronounce our "Es" and "Rs"." Thank you very much.

Conspiracy Brother: "Es" and "Rs," Ebonics, huh? I be thinking that somebody in this room be sellin out. I say we kill 'em. Shit the door, Nigger. Shhh! It's gonna be alright baby, don't look. I'm sorry, but you need to go [Grabbing the shotgun from Conspiracy Brother's hand].

Undercover Brother: Hey buddy, if I hadn't read that article in *Vanity Fair* on anger management, I'd put away this guava,-mango-broccoli smoothie and put my foot in your ptooty.

Conspiracy Brother: Ptooty?

Undercover Brother: Maybe you guys don't like the new me, but I don't give a gosh darn. . . . Now, if you excuse me, I must get going, Frasier is on.

Sistah Girl: Bajeebies?

Conspiracy Brother: He said he would stick his foot in my so-called ptooty.

Chief: Dammit, you can only keep an agent under cover so long before he loses his identity. Hell, no man can resist low interest loans and non-fat lattes forever.

Conspiracy Brother: And white women!

Lance: Let me get this straight. Whenever a black guy does well, starts wearing Dockers, buys a couple of Celine Dion records and sleeps with a white chick, you automatically say he sold out.

Chief: That's enough Lance.

Lance: Always try to shit the white man down.

Conspiracy Brother: That's right. . . . That ain't right!

Beyond the stereotypes and the surface deployment of black and racial identity, this scene captures the broader racial politics evident in *Undercover Brother.* It challenges assumptions about selling out, situating within larger context of political economy, while challenging viewers to think about issues of assimilation and the privilege that comes with accommodation. This powerful commentary on whiteness as privilege reflects the complex construction of race and identity within *Undercover Brother.* In this instance, it challenges those who see race as a fixed and essential category, who see assimilation as a desire to be white rather than a yearning to taste those privileges confined to whiteness, *Undercover Brother* offers a counter-narrative to dominant racial discourse. Beyond surface and parodic invoking of simplistic representations of blackness and whiteness, *Undercover Brother* ultimately offers a powerful commentary on race and American race relations.

Moreover, as I examined deeper, I saw how the film's use of stereotypical characters and stock representations did not work to legitimize racist ideologies, nor did it attempt to "rob the histories of actual strong black man, intellectual black thinkers and black revolutionaries of their power and significance" (Guerrero 2005, p. 7). Rather, the film, in ironically reducing each character to nothing more than a name and constructing racism as an irrational fear of the other, offers a powerful message regarding stereotypes: as baseless constructions, stereotypes not only deny characters multi-dimensions and depth—realness—but the deployment of stereotype representations robs characters (and the audience) of a history, a sense of individual significance, and overall humanity. *Undercover Brother* is about much more than his leisure suit just as Conspiracy Brother is about more than accusing the white man of committing injustices against communities of color.

The film's implicit racial politics is not limited to its challenge to stereotypes and societal prejudice. It is evident in its vision of post-Civil Rights history and its conception of racism, popular culture, and social movements.

Undercover Brother begins with an insightful commentary of political and cultural progress, so often invoked by teachers, commentators, pundits, and politicians who construct the present moment as one of colorblindness evident in the dramatic improvements in race relations during the last 40 years. While it takes the film a while to make this message clear, *Undercover Brother* makes its opposition to simplistic understandings of racial progress clear. It conceives the past as a time of joy, of communal and cultural power that has subsequently been corrupted by integration, by the "man," facilitated by the induced ignorance of the black community. The film begins with a montage of images of the Civil Rights Movement, including Jesse Jackson's "I am somebody" speech and shorts of *Soul Train* and James Brown singing "I am black and I am proud." Highlighting politically charged social movements and communally grounded black cultural productions as something lost and worthy of celebration today, *Undercover Brother* laments the problems facing the black community in the twenty-first century, evidenced by the popularity of Urkl, Dennis Rodman, and others. Moreover, by positioning today's pop icons in juxtaposition to past leaders, *Undercover Brother* denounces the widespread commodification of blackness that resulted in a depoliticized cultural movement all while the conditions facing African Americans have worsened. "These seemingly random events were orchestrated by the man, a Villain intent on turning back the clock on race relations," the narrator announces above images of mundane black popular culture figures. "Just when it seemed the funky spirit of the 1970s was lost, a new hero emerged and his name was Undercover Brother."

Eschewing the dominant idea regarding the insignificance of racism in the twenty-first century, an often uttered cliché that black participation within industries of popular culture has facilitated a colorblind America, *Undercover Brother* challenges the bulk of black comedic films by maintaining the importance of blackness, whiteness, and race to the film's narrative, comedic elements, and its context of reception. Even Brother himself is an overtly political character, who, as "the spirit of the 1970s," embodies the Afrocentric and Black Nationalist spirit of years past, positioned as a challenge to the Man, to racism. *Undercover Brother,* while clichéd and defined by his stereotypical and flat characters, is conceived as a freedom fighter, as a source of redemption, liberation, and resistance to the corrupting and co-opting forces of the Man. In the end, the film is conscious that race matters not as basis of the joke but within society; it also maintains the importance of the film in challenging those assumptions and prejudices within society.

The theme of co-optation—of the ways in which dominant white America has seized control of black cultural practices and social movements—is also evident in the film's use of General Boutwell, played by Billy D. Williams. Boutwell, a general turned politician, appears to represent the film's vision of a more involved and grounded-in-the-black-community Colin Powell. He is the dream of many within the black community and a perfect candidate to become the first black President of the United States; he is a military officer, good-looking, "well-spoken," and appealing to both the black and white communities. Fearful at the prospect of a black president, "the Man" instructs Mr. Feather to put a stop to Boutwell: "First hip-hop in the suburbs and now him. They are taking over everything." Heeding the calls to keep his culture and society white by preserving white power and leadership, Mr. Feather initiates Operation Whitewash by drugging General Boutwell, putting him under his influence. Rather than running for president, Boutwell, under the control of the Man (like so many others), announced his intent to open a chain of chicken restaurants, which ultimately will be used as part of the Man's plan to control black people throughout the world. "I've thought long and hard about how I can best serve my country, now that I am no longer in uniform. Well, today I am proud to announce that I will be opening a chain of fried chicken restaurants." As reporters initially question Boutwell's decision, asking him why business over politics, and whether he was afraid of backlash from the black community, they too get beyond these issues, asking him instead what sides would be available with the chicken meals.

The film invokes a long-standing stereotype regarding African Americans and chicken and with the General selling "a nappy meal," which comes with a 40-ounce malt liquor and its commercials resembling minstrel shows of the past with explosions and the General's eyes popping out of his face. This gives voice to the ways in which race is constructed (with Boutwell performing a stereotypical racial identity because he was under the control of others), but also serves as a commentary on co-optation, the absence of contemporary black leaders, and the notion of selling out. It is not just Boutwell who is affected by "Operation Whitewash," but black leaders throughout the community, from Jay-Z, who does a cover of Lawrence Welk, and John Singleton, who does a remake of *Driving Miss Daisy.* In each instance, the film gives voice to the construction of race, of blackness, by rendering the possibility of black artists engaging white culture as absurd. Equally important, it adds context and the pulls and demands of racism on people of color. In one instance, Chief challenges Undercover Brother's denunciation of Boutwell as a sellout. "I don't think it's that simple when dealing with the man."

Undercover Brother uses comedy to offer a powerful commentary on contemporary racial politics, but it additionally provides insight into the need for opposition and social movements toward actualizing racial progress. While at times simplistic and clichéd, *Undercover Brother* does proscribe steps toward challenging co-optation and the evil workings of "the Man." As if almost to distance itself from 1970s Blaxploitation films, which often imagine liberation as the result of the heroism of a single black male, and the Hollywood tradition that conceives black salvation coming through the heroism of white men, as evident in films like *Rosewood, Glory,* and *Cry Freedom* (1987), *Undercover Brother* sees hope in multiracial coalitions. Whether with Sistah Girl and White She Devil taking on the Man together or Lance joining the struggle by way of an apology, *Undercover Brother* constructs antiracist work as one of joint action and responsibility. By the film's end, not only has Anton Jackson, with the help of Sistah Girl, transformed himself back into Undercover Brother, but Lance and White She Devil have committed racial suicide, joining the B.R.O.T.H.E.R.H.O.O.D. This illustrates the film's distinct vision of a new racial politics grounded in cooperation and respect. What makes *Undercover Brother* significant and transformative here is constructing those with privilege as having a responsibility to join the fight. In the film's most dramatic (at least satirically) scene, Lance approaches members of the B.R.O.T.H.E.R.H.O.O.D to right his and his community's wrongs, acting as sort of individualized form of reparations.

Chief, various brother agents, I owe all of you a huge apology. I just watched this show, *Roots*, maybe you've heard of it. It taught me such a profound lesson about bigotry. I have sat on the sidelines of race relations long enough. I want to march down that field of oppression and kick that ball of bigotry right over the goal post of intolerance.

Minutes later, responding to Conspiracy Brother's protest about the inclusion of Lance and White She Devil because of their inner knowledge of the Man and their commitment to the mission of the B.R.O.T.H.E.R.H.O.O.D, Undercover Brother reminded him (and the audience) on the importance of cooperation and multiracial community:

Brother, Brother, we all love your solo enthusiasm, but this is about working together. Now I have been a solo star shooting the shots to win the game, but in workin with y'all come to realize only a team wins a championship.

With inscribing notions of teamwork being superior to individualism, the film ultimately proscribes the formation of multiracial coalitions in an effort to rid the world of exploitation and racism. Undercover Brother tells them that their success reaches only as far as the diversity of their community:

It would have been cool to have Latino, Native American, an Asian, and even a Jewish guy in the mix. The point is by working together we got the job done. Not doubt that's what the B.R.O.T.H.E.R.H.O.O.D is about. Solid!

To battle "the Man" and successfully resist cultural and communal co-optation and destruction, coalitions must function as the backbone of the movement. Its celebratory end with Lance, Brother, Sistah, and others defeating Mr. Feather and almost destroying "the Man," who escapes to establish the film's potential sequel and remind the audiences of the difficulty of ridding society of racial tyranny, is emblematic of its call for a new racial politics based in both coalitions and the formation of distinct black, white, Latino, Asian, and Indigenous identities. The film offers additional proscriptive steps, focusing on the black community overcoming its own "self-hate" (introduced and facilitated by "the Man") and the common practice of black youth performing those identities inscribed by popular culture and dominant media. Despite its emphasis on the power of coalitions, *Undercover Brother* rightfully finds loves with Sistah Girl, thereby conquering his own "issues," and the black man's ultimate temptation. Moreover, the film goes to great lengths to chronicle the ways in which "the Man" has brainwashed black men and women (the film despite its strengths is stuck within a black/white paradigm) into hating blackness and self. It ends, however, with James Brown (or an Undercover Brother masked as Brown) resisting the presence of the Man's whitewashing techniques, instead singing "say it loud, I am black and I am proud." Through both collective social action (coalitions) and efforts to affirm a positive and self-affirming black culture, *Undercover Brother* challenges its audience toward action, toward moving beyond the simplistic representations offered from Hollywood and the music industry, all toward battling the Man. Despite its clichéd and Hollywood simplicity, as well as its inscription of stereotypes and a narrative of a heroic black man saving the community, *Undercover Brother* demonstrates the possibilities of using comedy as a powerful instrument within contemporary racial struggles. While unique, *Undercover Brother* is not alone in this regard, replicating the efforts of Spike Lee's *Bamboozled*.

BAMBOOZLED

Bamboozled features Pierre Delacroix (Damon Wayans), an African American network executive who is ordered by his boss Mr. Dunwitty (Michael Rappaport) to come up with a "hot, trend-setting, urban hit." Along with his assistant, Sloan (Jada Pinkett), Delacroix invents "The New Millennium Minstrel Show" casting Manray as Mantan (Savion Glover) and Womack as Sleep N' Eat (Tommy Davidson). The intent of the show was to be controversial and

satirical, poking fun at the racism and negative images of African Americans of
the twentieth century. However, the show lives up to its name and becomes
popularly accepted by most characters in the movie.

The significance of this movie is its portrayal of different forms of modern
minstrelsy. First of all, the movie itself is a parody of minstrelsy. It refers to
Delacroix as an "Oreo"—a Harvard-graduate with a strange made-up accent,
who practices Pilates and leads an upper-class lifestyle. It refers to Mr. Dunwitty
as someone who is "blacker than [Delacroix]" through his marriage to a black
woman, childhood in the ghetto, and his knowledge of black popular culture.
Furthermore, this paradox also carries through the show, as the "New Millennium Minstrel Show" is really about two black characters, with blackened
face and huge red lips, which takes place on a cotton plantation in the 1940s.
Mantan and Sleep N' Eat embody stereotypes, many still alive today, such as
the uneducated, ignorant, lazy, and stupid coon. What is interesting about the
movie is that the audiences, a diverse group of people, do not take offense to
this modern minstrelsy and the public accepts the show without any controversy. Even Delacroix and Sloan, who were originally offended by the script,
end up laughing at the racist performances of Mantan and Sleep N' Eat. As the
movie progresses, Womack, Manray, and Sloan become enraged with the depiction of racism and discrimination against blacks, which leads Womack to leave
the show. In the end of the movie, Manray gets abducted by a group of radical
blacks called "Mau Maus" as they broadcast his murder live on television.

One might ask: "Did Delacroix achieve his goal in producing satirical material aimed at challenging dominant notions of blackness and its stereotypical
representations in popular culture?" In other words, when the audiences in
the movie do not have a grasp of how race, gender, class, and sexuality have
evolved through history, can they really understand the objectives behind the
production of the "New Millennium Minstrel Show?" I believe that *Bamboozled* highlighted for us that when the historicity of race, gender, class, and
sexuality function outside the context of a performance, such as the minstrel show, it reduces the performance to a reenactment of its original form
of entertainment—to reinforce the authority of whiteness. Marvin Carlson
states in his book, *Performance: A Critical Introduction:*

As a critical operation, masquerade performances always run the danger that Derrida
cited in any deconstructive operation, which seeks to turn established structures back
on themselves—that this process may also especially for a conventional audience, simply reinscribe or reinforce those structures. (1996, p. 176)

The "New Millennium Minstrel Show" did not achieve its goal of over-
throwing dominant representations of black stereotypes; instead, it served to
continue the subordination of blackness while at the same time maintaining
white supremacy. At the same time, however, *Bamboozled* was successful in
challenging and unsettling the hegemony of white supremacy inside and outside the entertainment industry.

Like *Undercover Brother, Bamboozled* uses stereotypes and exaggerated racial (racist) caricatures to unsettle, if not destroy, accepted racial representations and practices. From its opening moments, its use of satire, its deployment of grotesque images, and its utilization of potentially offensive representations function in opposition to racism in the entertainment industry, to the widespread and accepted practices of racial commodification, and the violence that emanates from contemporary popular culture.

Bamboozled and the efforts of Pierre de La Coix represent an attempt to expose the racism that defines America's entertainment industries. For example, during a contentious debate between Pierre and Mr. Dunwitty, at which Dunwitty calls on Pierre to use his blackness to develop a show that is both hip and sexy, Pierre is forced to make a decision. Pierre's claim that a show about the black middle class would appeal to average Americans is quickly shot down by Dunwitty, who does not just demand a show about gangstas and hos, or even one that appeals to white sensibilities of blackness (although this is implied). Rather he compels Pierre to develop a show that would appeal to black American because of its realness. "Brotherman, I'm blacker than you," Dunwitty tells Pierre this over and over again, as if to confirm his authenticity and his power in denouncing a show about the black middle class as unappealing and not black enough, especially compared to shows like *The Jeffersons* and *Good Times,* both shows that Pierre and Spike Lee obviously see as little more than coon shows. After their discussion, Pierre heeds Dunwitty's advice, deciding that his only way out of this situation and a racist entertainment industry is to provide them with what they are looking for, to design a show that is so racist, so negative, and so offensive that the network would be forced to fire him while also realizing that it (the network; audiences) wants to see black people on TV as something other than buffoons.

The use of satire in *Bamboozled,* as evident in Pierre's development of the "New Millennium Minstrel Show," goes to great lengths to illustrate the persistence of racism in American entertainment. Ironically, and although Pierre develops the show to resemble *Amos and Andy* and to embody the spirit of Mantan Moreland and Step 'n Fetchit, with shuffling and singing, ignorant and lazy, "real-life coons," the opposite occurs. Dunwitty loves the show, his bosses love the show, fans don blackface to express their love of blackness/ blackface and love for the show, and advertisers join forces with the show. In this way, *Bamboozled* powerfully illustrates not just how racism sells, but the pleasure produced by "real-life coons." In a powerful scene, Lee focuses on the audience when it is first exposed to the "New Millennium Minstrel Show," initially tepidly clapping, only to eventually applaud with great emotion. Interestingly, the extras that made up this scene were not made aware of the content of the film or the nature of this fictitious show, as to elicit an authentic reaction. Their initial horror, the primarily white audience gauging their own reaction from black peers, and the eventual applause are all real and authentic, granting the film significant power in documenting the persistence of racism within the entertainment industry.

The commentary that *Bamboozled* offers challenges those ideologies that have facilitated and given legitimacy to the idea that blackness is transferable—that traits that define blackness can be easily bought, sold, consumed, tried on, and returned if necessarily. Irrespective of skin color, relationship to community, and understanding of history, racial identity, and privileges, anyone can be black. *Bamboozled* successfully challenges contemporary white supremacist logic, while also denouncing widespread practices of commodification and the ubiquitous mocking of contemporary popular constructions of blackness.

Bamboozled does not only limit its condemnation and critique to Dunwitty or the white fans of the "New Millennium Minstrel Show," who in donning blackface are emblematic of processes of commodification. The film also illustrates the ubiquity and complexity of commodification and racial performance through characters such as Big Black African and those who make up the Mau Maus (the revolutionary hip-hop group who protest the racism of New Millennium).. While taking a different form (given that the majority of the Mau Maus are black), the construction of the Mau Maus in *Bamboozled* as performing their own corrupted vision of blackness as being radical in spite of their surface understanding of political struggle and progressive ideologies, further underscores the film's treatment of commodification. Unlike many of the other films discussed here, which celebrate cultural appropriation as a sign of cultural hybridity or progress, *Bamboozled* chronicles the ways in which popular culture robs black identity of its cultural and historical roots, instead mockingly reducing it to a profitable aesthetic in the advancement of white supremacy.

The film's incorporation of "Da bomb," a brand of malt liquor, whose advertisements play on white stereotypes of black sexuality, white imagination of the black phallus (the bottle resembles a large penis), and a ghettocentric (hip-hop) aesthetic, all reflect the film's critique of material culture selling products through racist representations of blackness. In this case and others, blackness embodies a Hollywoodized hip-hop aesthetic and rapacious sexuality, not simply replicating stereotypes, but functioning as a means to sell malt liquor, which the advertisement makes clear will help all who desire to become black. With the "Da bomb," *Bamboozled* illustrates how companies use (pimp) blackness to sell its products, convincing white consumers (as well as others) that the path to securing blackness rests with drinking "Da bomb," objectifying women and wearing Tommy Fieldnigger gear or that of others. Spike Lee's inclusion of commercials and references to Tommy Fieldnigger, as a direct reference to Tommy Hilfiger for all his profiteering of a particularly branded black aesthetic, further emphasizes the film's political statements regarding commodification. This is a process that reduces blackness to a racist caricature that can be bought and sold; a representation that doesn't simply generate profits but also legitimizes white supremacist discourses and practices; a long-standing process of white profiting of an imagined black culture and style; and a process that facilitates racial performance and hegemonic notion that race is meaningless beyond style and consumable goods of differences.

The oppositional politics and complex treatment of black culture and race relations evident in *Bamboozled* penetrates every cinematic sequence. Yet it is unavoidable and clear in the film's final scene. While critics have denounced the film's ending, which has the Mau Maus kidnapping and killing Mantan on national television, Sloan murdering Pierre, and the police shooting the Mau Maus as clichéd and melodramatic, these final moments are crucial to the film's cinematic and political message. In the violent finale, the majority of those guilty of appropriation, commodification, performing a stereotypical blackness, and otherwise functioning as a cog within the racist industry are killed off (except Dunwitty). This ending elucidates Lee's point that only when we completely wipe clean the legacies of minstrelsy, the institutions of racism, and the ideologies/discourse that give meaning and support to racialized commodification, white supremacy and cultural appropriation can the equality of representation and material outcomes be recoded. There is no reform, but a possibility of a new racial and cultural politics through violence.

Bamboozled's glimmer of optimism, ironically deployed in scenes of in-your-face violence is muted by two additional cinematic inclusions in this final scene. As the police surround the safe house of the Mau-Maus, they do not peacefully move in for the arrest, instead moving with the ultimately successful intent of shooting to kill. Of importance, the police spare one body, the lone white member of the Mau Maus, demonstrating that blackness is not simply a commodity or an aesthetic, but a source of life and death. Angered by the decision of the police to spare his life, he screams, "Kill me . . . why don't you kill me. I'm black." In this instance, Lee poignantly illustrates how minstrelsy in all its forms reflects a process where whites except or endure everything but the burden of blackness. The failure of the police to shoot him (which is based on a real incident in Riverside, California, where the police shot several members of a gang, all who were youth of color, sparing the one white participant) not only reveals the privileges of whiteness but the absurdity of the notion that he or Dunwitty or Isaac could be black irrespective of knowledge of black history, African art, or understanding of hip-hop.

This powerful message and that of the violent nature of racial struggle leaves audiences wondering if wiping the racial slate clean is indeed possible. The legacies of racial violence, from lynchings to police brutality, and racist representations, from *Amos and Andy* to the "New Millennium Minstrel Show," remain intact regardless of the appearance of change, especially if changes come through white performances and commodification of blackness. *Bamboozled* works hard to make this point clear, concluding the film with a cinematic montage of past (and future) representations of blackness, illustrating the links between a commodifiable inscription of blackness, its demonization, and persistent levels of individual and state violence.

CONCLUSION

Anthony King criticized Cedric the Entertainer for "his flippant disrespect for our civil rights heroes," denouncing the travesty of *Barbershop* as not an isolated incident but "reflective of a generation that has lost touch with its legacy and lacks cultural respect" (Neal 2005, p.13). In other words, King sees that the only possibility of salvaging the hip-hop generation is through discipline and punishment, which would teach them the unacceptability of mocking sacred history. Beyond the inscription of ideologies and tropes that have long been at the center of efforts to pathologize and demonize youth of color, the hyper-focus on the *Barbershop* controversy, and even protests against the deployment of stereotypes within Hollywood, has come at the expense of a more sustained conversation regarding commodification of blackness, the erasure and/or demonization of the black poor within black films, the deployment of colorblind and conservative ideologies in and around contemporary black films, and overall the efforts of contemporary cinematic projects to legitimize the racist status quo.

More revealing, public discourse has remained fixated on the betrayal of black heroes in *Barbershop*, the negative portrayals of blackness within hip-hop (and not in films like *Soul Plane* or *Bringing Down the House*), or the absence of "respectable" representation, as opposed to calling for action against the prison industrial complex, state violence, or widespread racist policy. According to William Jelani Cobb the controversy surrounding *Barbershop* illustrated how far things have devolved; "faced with unchecked military aggression, a White House that has a renewed and overt commitment to imperialism, a million incarcerated African Americans and a national conscience bereft of moral considerations, Jesse and company were left to film criticism as a form of protest" (Neal 2005, p. 13). Worse, the controversy and backlash missed several issues of how both *Barbershop* films, and many other comedies, legitimize dominant discourses of race, colorblindness, and the American Dream. The Hollywood effort to legitimize calls for African Americans to pull themselves up by their bootstraps, or its teaching about race, culture, and social distance is a much more dangerous affront to the legacy of Martin Luther King Jr. or Rosa Parks. The failure of Jackson and others to denounce *Barbershop* for its deployment of reactionary racial frames, or challenge the racist representations and ideologies that emanate from *Soul Plane, Bringing Down the House, My Baby's Daddy, Love Don't Cost a Thing,* and a host of other comedies is not merely a commentary on how far things have devolved but elucidates who has truly lost touch with the legacy of the Civil Rights Movement.

Amid a series of black comedies that (1) reify colorblind ideologies that ultimately legitimize racism, poverty, and inequality, (2) reduce blackness to a consumable commodity that ultimately legitimizes white supremacy and (3) erase or pathologize the black poor in the advancement of racism, the conversation has remained fixated on notions of positivity and respectability. The problem rests not with airing the dirty laundry of the black community, but on the failure to expose America's dirty laundry that has been soiled by the blood and despair caused by state violence, inequality, and persistent levels of poverty. The failure that came to life only after Hurricane Katrina is that American popular culture, particularly Hollywood and television, is too busy laughing at black people and denying the existence of racism, poverty, and societal problems to facilitate a public discourse and initiate change. Whether the film is *Soul Plane, Bringing Down the House,* or the *Barbershops,* Hollywood ubiquitously legitimizes racism (regardless of embedded contradictions), abandoning the long-standing and less visible (*Bamboozled, Undercover Brother*) tradition of transgressive black comedies for the sake of an even longer and more popular tradition of black comedies that aid in the perpetuation of colorblind and classic white supremacy.

5

MOVING FORWARD WITHOUT MOVING BACK

THE 2005 OSCARS

In the days leading up to the 77th installment of the Academy Awards (Oscars), there was much celebration in the media, as well as from many of my students, for the number of nominations that went to actors and artists of color (Jamie Foxx for *Ray* (2004) and *Collateral* (2004), Don Cheadle and Sophie Okonedo for *Hotel Rwanda* (2004), Morgan Freeman for *Million Dollar Baby* (2004), among others). While many question whether the successes of the 2002 Oscars would translate into increased opportunity for artists and actors of color, and even whether the blackening of the big screen would result in transformative representations, this "sequel" provided evidence to a spectrum of people of a change inside and beyond Hollywood. Michael Sragow, a movie critic for the *Baltimore Sun*, described 2005 as a watershed year, not just for the Oscars, but for black America. "What it means from Ground Zero here in Hollywood is that studios will take more chances on telling stories about African-Americans and then marketing them to everyone," said Kevin Rodney Sullivan, the African American director of the 2004 hit *Barbershop 2,* which grossed $65 million in the United States on a mere $18 million budget (Sragow 2005). Similar rhetoric was evident throughout the media and elsewhere. J. Douglas Allen-Taylor described the 2005 Oscars in more dramatic terms, concluding that the nominations and potential victories for black artists represented a watershed moment in America's racial history:

For many African Americans, however, this year's Oscars will have a far different meaning: the awards will be a symbolic referendum on whether America has finally come to see and accept African Americans—the *real* African Americans, what and who we are when we go back to our communities at night and toss off our shoes and shut out the outside world—or if we will have to wait a little longer. . . . And so, this weekend, even if they do not watch the actual ceremonies, large numbers of black Americans will pay special attention to this year's Academy Awards. In many ways, the results will not matter. The release of the movie *Ray* has already affirmed something for many African Americans—their secret selves, long-nurtured in dark corners, but kept from general public view. In years to come, we are going to see the coming out of this movie as a river crossed, and it is as yet unknown what will be found on the far bank. (2005)

In the estimation of many commentators, the blackening of America's screens and the blackening of the Oscars revealed a dramatic transformation of the representational politics and the racial ideologies emanating from contemporary Hollywood, which in turn embodied the broader racial realities of contemporary America. Of course, these commentators failed to think about the broader questions regarding representation, politics, and the racial state of America. Few people commented on the success of *Ray* and Jamie Foxx within a long tradition of degrading representations of black masculinity, given the film's disproportionate emphasis on the hypersexuality and drug addiction of Ray Charles. Little was made of the way in which *Ray*, like so many films discussed in *Screens Fade to Black*, concretized discourses regarding the American Dream, celebrating racial progress and the ability of one man to pull himself up by his bootstraps with the help of his musical talents and accommodationist politics. The celebration equally erased the buddy aspects of both *Collateral* and *Million Dollar Baby*, where the wisdom of black characters served as the source of redemption for the film's white heroes.

Amid all the many articles concerning progress and representational change supposedly evident in Hollywood and America, few noted the numerous films released this same year, which did not deviate from hegemonic racial representations. Even fewer acknowledged the broader context of American race relations, which renders a celebration of progress either absurd or meaningless, in that is there anything worth celebrating given levels of poverty, AIDS acquisition, rates of infant mortality, incarceration, and unemployment.

Clearly, African American film and the blackening of America's big screen matter, but despite immense celebration, it matters not because of progress inside and especially beyond the worlds of representation, but rather as part of larger new racist politics. And although the importance of contemporary African American cinema rests with the immense amount of financial profits or personal pleasures derived from widespread commodification of blackness, I have attempted to illustrate in *Screens Fade to Black* that the importance of contemporary films is increasingly significant precisely because of the ways it reflects and reinforces dominant modes of production, means of representation, and conventions of hegemonic ideologies of this new racist moment. Indeed, whether suffused with celebrations of the American Dream or constructing American ghettos as spaces of refuge for pathologies or commodifiable cultural practices necessitating control and surveillance, contemporary representations of blackness constitute vehicles and vectors, instruments and powerful teaching tools for the expression and inscription of dominant symbols, preferred sentiments, and hegemonic structures. The celebration of the American Dream and the demonization of those who find its possibility illusive serves the interests of white supremacist discourses and practices that maintain inequalities and privileges.

The task of this book is to shed light on the ways in which contemporary Hollywood, in spite of the increased visibility of black artists and the increased diversity of representations available to communities of color, continues to advance systems of racism and privilege. It seeks to answer important questions beyond those of representation and opportunity for current artists. Notwithstanding the appearance of progress or colorblindness to some, does Hollywood and popular culture in general contribute to a racist state, whether manifested in persistent police brutality, poverty, erosions to social welfare programs, mass incarceration, or other instances of inequality? How do contemporary cinematic representations naturalize inequality and reify claims of colorblindness, which in turn justify inequality or explain away the ample racial gaps that define contemporary America? These questions guide *Screens Fade to Black,* in the end arguing that the ascendance of black artists, the increased commodification of blackness, and the declining visibility of grotesque racial stereotypes, do signify a new era within Hollywood or America. Rather, they reflect new racist sensibilities or politics that mix old and new, offering a new veneer to long-standing color lines and ideologies. As a dominant American institution, Hollywood continues to operate toward the maintenance and perpetuation of racial inequality.

In spite of the celebration of celebrity, of American racial progress toward colorblindness, given the success and adoration afforded to Beyonce Knowles, Denzel Washington, and Michael Jordan, this ubiquity has not ushered in a dramatic shift in America's racial logic. Notwithstanding, celebrations abound about the end of racism as evidenced by trends within popular culture. However, dominant media remains a site of promulgation of hegemonic notions of race, gender, and sexuality. Writing about Destiny's Child, Patricia Hill Collins argues the constancy of hegemonic visions of black female sexuality: "Destiny's Child may not be like the girls next door, but . . . in this new mass media context, Black sexual stereotypes are rendered virtually invisible by their ubiquity" (2004, p. 29). Likewise, Imani Perry, in *Prophets of the Hood,* identifies popular culture not exclusively as a site of stereotypical representations, but a space where "the isolation of black bodies as the culprits for widespread multiracial social ills" becomes commonplace (2004, p. 27). *Screens Fade to Black* has taken a similar approach, illustrating the simultaneity of commodification and demonization, focusing on the ways in which processes of commodification and demonization jointly facilitate a perpetuation of racial inequality and maintenance of white supremacy and privilege.

Building on much of the current academic literature concerned with race and popular culture and popular discourses, *Screens Fade to Black* has eschewed the long-standing binaries that pitted racism against celebrity (representation). Rather, scholars have noted the simultaneity of commodification—a form of embracement—and demonization of both black male bodies and cultural practices (Collins 2004, Watkins 1998, Boyd 1997). "The love of black culture with the simultaneous suspicion and punishment of black bodies is not unusual" (Perry 2004, p. 28). Underscoring the ways in which contemporary films enact this racial logic and the realities of the commodification-demonization-new racism matrix, *Screens Fade to Black,* through its discussion of film and context, makes clear that whether in demonization, commodification, or their simultaneous inscription, contemporary cinematic representations ultimately advances a reactionary politics that deleteriously affects the vast majority of the black community.

In this final chapter, I want to do two things simultaneously. First, I highlight the key features and central principles of the contemporary representations of blackness, that is, the construction, circulation, and consumption of films concerned with both the commodification and demonization of blackness and those that have sought to celebrate racial progress by illustrating the availability of the American Dream. Second, given the constancy of representations of blackness and the inability to discuss every film, I highlight some additional films and themes, pointing to emergent themes and representations within black cinema and their connection to the arguments of *Screens Fade to Black,* ultimately calling for greater critical attention to reflect these emergent issues.

JUST SCENERY: AUTHENTICATING HIP-HOP AND THE AMERICAN DREAM

Building on the successes of ghettocentric films, the popularity of *Grand Theft Auto* and other video game spin-offs, as well as the growing hold of hip-hop on the cultural marketplace, Hollywood is increasingly using the ghetto as mere landscape. Reflecting the discursive tendency that links fetishization and celebration of blackness to colorblindness and racial progress, Dr. Dre, one of the "godfathers of rap," sees the increasing visibility and acceptance of hip-hop as a sign of racial change. He once noted that "people in the suburbs, they can't go to the ghetto so they like to hear what's goin' on. [But] everyone wants to be down" (hooks 1994, p. 152). bell hooks, however, complicates this celebratory reconstitution of hip-hop, situating processes of commodification, fetish, and the pimping of a corporate ghettocentric imagination, arguing that "the desire to be 'down' has promoted a conservative appropriation of specific aspects of underclass black life, who in reality is dehumanized via a process of commodification wherein no correlation is made between mainstream hedonistic consumerism and the reproduction of a social system that perpetuates and maintains an underclass" (hooks 1994, p. 152).

Kevin Powell concurs, describing this phenomenon as a "cultural safari for white people" (Kitwana 2005, p. 53). Hollywood has certainly capitalized on the white yearning for "cultural safari" and conservative desires to maintain the status quo. Whereas previous films, to varying degrees, gave voice to the effects of deindustrialization, poverty, structural racism, and state violence, recent films like *Honey* (2003), *You Got Served* (2004), and *Hustle and Flow* (Craig Brewer, 2005) merely use the ghetto landscape as part of the overall commodification of hip-hop and the "hedonistic consumerism" of "specific aspects of underclass black life," which in turn perpetuates our new racist moment.

In a certain sense, contemporary Hollywood depicts present-day ghettos as safe spaces, to which white and middle-class viewers can safely enter (the danger usually comes from one lone dangerous black male in need of discipline and state surveillance). State violence, poverty, violence, poverty, drugs, and the devastation resulting from America's post-Civil Rights policies are erased from the dominant ghettocentric imagination. Rather the ghetto provides the needed authenticity for each film's use of hip-hop. In other words, the significance of the ghetto resides with the production of hip-hop and the corresponding cultural aesthetic. Focusing on a middle-class, light-skinned black woman living in the ghetto, the ghetto location of *Honey,* directed by Billie Woodruff, seems inconsequential except to authenticate her blackness, its American Dream tale, and the film's use of hip-hop. *Honey* chronicles the story of Honey Daniels (Jessica Alba) in her rise from obscure club girl to budding music video dance star and subsequent fall after she realizes that the industry wants her for her body and sexuality rather than her talent. The plot chronicles her struggles to find her place in the music industry, and her desires to remain connected with the community. Eventually she chooses the community with her efforts to develop a hip-hop dance academy for youth in need of an alternative path to violence and drugs.

Beyond the aesthetic markers—dirty streets, graffiti, gritty skylines, chain link fences, ample noise—that give legitimacy to the film's use of hip-hop and dance (it's real and authentic hip-hop dance because it comes from the streets as Honey even finds inspiration for particular moves from street artists and performers), Honey's ascendance from the ghetto serves as the reason for celebration. She uses her skills, passion, work ethic, and values to elevate her out of the ghetto and help her secure the American Dream. At first, Honey finds financial salvation through the music industry as a video girl; later she turns her back on these riches for the good of the community. By using the connections and financial capital made available because of her talents and success in the industry (as well as her middle-class status and her light skin, both aspects ignored by the film and its critics), she eventually opens up a hip-hop dance academy to push ghetto youth away from crime. Thus the ghetto embodies both the vehicle out of the ghetto, given that it exists as the site for the production of authentic and commodifiable hip-hop, and the space from which youth must exit to secure the American Dream. In the end, the racial implication that gives rise to ghetto communities, and the way in which race affects its daily organization are erased, reducing the black community and blackness to nothing more than a cultural aesthetic.

Similarly, *You Got Served* (Chris Stokes) follows a similar formula in its attempt to capitalize on the cultural popularity of hip-hop. *You Got Served* takes viewers into a world of competitive hip-hop dance (battles), in which artists and their crews challenge one another to determine who reigns supreme on the dance floor. It explores the inner world of street dance, where crews (gangs) don't fight with guns or knives over territory or drug clientele, instead battling for respect and money through their choreography and displays of gritty real hip-hop dance. As with many of the films discussed within *Screens Fade to Black*, *You Got Served* reduces blackness, in its deployment of hip-hop styles, music, and dance, to an easily commodifiable aesthetic. Anyone can be hip-hop regardless of skin color, class, or place of residence; anyone can dance. The cultural or even geographic specificity of hip-hop as a site of resistance for disempowered youth of color is ostensibly erased from the narrative. In fact, the narrative of *You Got Served* constructs hip-hop and its related aesthetic signifiers as something culturally available to all youth without any question regarding power and privilege.

The crew from what appears to be South Central, Los Angeles, which includes Elgin (Marques Houston of IMX) and David (Omarion of B2K) battles a crew from Orange County, although both crews walk, talk and look the same (the OC crew being a little whiter). Both groups are multiracial and equally embodying a hip-hop aesthetic. In the end, audiences are left with a narrative in which the fact that one crew is from South Central and another is from Orange County is relatively inconsequential in terms of cultural styles and life opportunities. As a consequence, residential segregation, poverty, various forms of state violence, dismal schools system, and the place of hip-hop as a vehicle of resistance are erased. Equally important, in its effort to treat South Central Los Angeles as a mere backdrop, *You Got Served* also erases the racial, political, economic, and geographic significance of Orange County, as a place where white privilege is clearly pronounced. In both cases, geography is important, but the film treats these disparate locales as inconsequential.

Another facet of *You Got Served*, as well as *Honey* and several other films that require additional interrogation, is the tendency to imagine America's ghetto as places of play and cultural performance for both the film's characters and those who sit inside America's movie theaters. The poverty, mass unemployment, heightened levels of incarceration, policing, and degradation cause both despair and resistance, which ranges from single mothers working three jobs to support their families to community activists forming organizations that seek to empower their community by providing job training or after-school programs.

Writing about shoe commercials, Robin Kelley asserts that popular images of street basketball "romanticize the crumbling urban spaces in which African American youth play" (1998, p. 197). As inner city spaces are glamorized and commodified for their seedy and dangerous elements, structural shifts continue to worsen these spaces. The process of commodification is not limited to the generation of pleasure for players; it is evident in the usefulness of black bodies and imagined urban spaces to contemporary cinematic representations of blackness. Reflecting the hypervisibility and glorification of the deindustrialized inner city community, this recent wave of hip-hop ghettocentric films reflect the commodification of African American practices of play within popular culture.

Nike, Reebok, L.A. Gear, and other athletic shoe companies have profited enormously from postindustrial decline. Television commercials and print ads romanticize the crumbling urban spaces in which African-Americans play, creating demand for the sneakers that they wear. Marked by chain-link fences, concrete playgrounds, bent and rusted netless hoops, graffiti-scrawled walls, and empty buildings, these visual representations of "street ball" have created a world where young black males do nothing but play and enjoy doing so in a post-industrial wasteland. (Kelley, 1998, pp. 195–196)

One result of this is that those living outside such communities often refuse to engage "ghettos" at a political, economic, or social level because they are content to enjoy consuming and gazing at inside those spaces from the safety of a suburban Cineplex or the privacy of their own home.

Moreover, the ideological trope of limiting discussions of ghetto communities to the play that transpires within such communities obfuscates the daily struggles and horrors endured in postindustrial America. The realities of police brutality, deindustrialization, the effects of globalization on job prospects, and the fact that many parents work three jobs just to make ends meet are all invisible because the dominant image of street basketball continues to pervade American discourses about inner-city neighborhoods.

You Got Served shows black youth dancing, playing basketball, and merely hanging out, only taking a break from play to help out the local drug dealer as part of their effort to secure enough money for the battle against the Orange County crew. In *Honey,* the youth who are eventually saved by Honey Daniels are always at play, whether dancing in the community center or in the streets.

In both these films, as well as others like *Hustle and Flow* and *Get Rich or Die Trying* (2005), Hollywood is attempting to capitalize on a commodifiable hip-hop, thereby erasing the historical, geographic, cultural, and racial specificity of this cultural practice. Through each film, viewers are provided with a safe entry into a world of hip-hop, in its most authentic form, given its ghetto orientation, so that audiences can sample and even don the cultural styles of "the other" —as if mandated by a new racist logic that has systematically reduced blackness to hip-hop and hip-hop to blackness, and in doing so has reified dominant arguments regarding race being nothing more than commodifiable cultural difference. As reflective of larger new racist discourse, such films, as noted by hooks, legitimize reactionary politics and perpetuation of the hegemonic racial order that demonstrates, despite the blackening of the screens, that power continues to reside in white hands.

One of the central themes of *Screens Fade to Black* is the ways in which contemporary African American films construct and deploy dominant understandings of the American Dream. In both celebrating the achievement of the American Dream with the black middle class and demonizing/pathologizing the black underclass for the illusiveness of their American Dream, contemporary African American films reflect a new racist moment. This pattern has continued in recent years. *Honey* and *You Got Served* tells the stories of black men and women, reaching their talents as hip-hop artists or dancers. In other words, each fulfills narrow dominant representations regarding the limited avenues of securing financial success and cultural assimilation all while erasing the ways in which racism and state violence limit other opportunities. More important, each of these films focuses on discipline and hard work as the keys to securing success in contemporary America, offering a powerful articulation of long-standing notions of bootstrapism.

In *Honey,* Honey Daniels secures her dreams—opening a studio to provided the needed discipline for them to secure their dream—through her own hard work, her discipline, and her positive outlook, which in the context of the film cannot be detached from her presumably middle-class status and her mixed-race identity. In a sense, because of Honey's discipline and moral values, she successfully secures her American Dream, which revolves around uplifting and pulling-up those within her community. *You Got Served* follows a similar template, with choice, discipline, and moral values being the keys to battle against the Orange County crew. Only when David and Elgin start making "positive choices," reflecting their discipline and their willingness to play by society's rules, are they able to "make it." Bootstraps and discipline both play a prominent role in both *Hustle and Flow* and *Get Rich or Die Trying,* embodying the prominent themes of contemporary African American films. Beyond discipline and bootstraps being the path to securing the American Dream, each constructs hip-hop as a way out of a life of crime and desperation. Their simplistic constructions of crime and the reduction of criminality to cultural values and discipline are not just problematic cinematic tropes but reflective of a larger cultural trend inside and outside Hollywood—the simultaneity of commodification and demonization of black bodies toward the celebration of the availability of the American Dream for all and the maintenance of the contemporary racial order.

In no other recent film is this more evident than in Thomas Carter's *Coach Carter* (2005), which tells the story of Ken Carter, who in 1999 returned to Richmond High School, where he was a former star athlete, to coach a basketball team. The film celebrates his arrival and his implementation of a series of strict policies, ranging from a dress code to a written contract mandating certain behaviors and good grades, which eventually leads him to cancel the season because of player failures in spite of their success on the floor.

Coach Carter does not construct the ghetto as peripheral, as a mere backdrop. Instead the film uses the ghetto as a signifier of what the boy's basketball team at Richmond High School must overcome. Nevertheless, it does resemble other films in its erasure of contemporary color lines and persistent state violence. According to Jared Sexton in "The Field of Fantasy and the Court of Appeal: On *Friday Night Lights* and *Coach Carter*," this film erases the realities of contemporary white supremacy and strategies of resistance: "Despite clear evidence that the troubles Carter finds at Richmond High are institutional and, moreover, ordered unambiguously by broader political, economic, and social contexts, questions of systemic change encouraged by collective political struggle." Instead of giving voice to contemporary racial policies and racial realities, *Coach Carter* constructs the ghetto as a space of cultural pollution, as a production site for violence and faulty values that results in an absence of discipline, which the film links to the prevalence of single mothers and welfare. Coach Carter addresses these problems as any good black father would, proving that the solutions to today's problems don't reside with collective mobilization or struggle, but with cultural change, discipline, and "proper" basketball. As such, Coach Carter, who like Captain Davenport, Dr. Lee, and even Melvin teach their "black sons" how to behave and act like men, embodies the path to achieving the American Dream.

Coach Carter, whose discipline allowed him to leave the ghettos of Richmond for a successful business career, returns to help the next generation, one far worse off because of the failures of the community. He uses basketball as a vehicle of instilling the needed discipline and values to secure American success. "Coach Carter embeds a conservative ideology of individual achievement (which for the players is also the pathway to their rescue and/or/as escape) within his promotion of team spirit," writes Sexton. "Achievement becomes available to any and all that demonstrate the requisite traits: work ethic, respect for authority, obedience, lawful behavior, and self-discipline. Discipline, as we have seen already, is the key issue and its constant repetition across all of the films mentioned thus far is telling. The boys must be brought under control wherever we find them, but it is only in the case of *Coach Carter* that the force of law—the police, the prison—is a real and present danger, is, in fact, omnipresent and immediate" (2005). Reflective of the discursive orientation of new racism, *Coach Carter*, like so many other contemporary films discussed here, erases racism while reducing race to the cultural deficiencies, thereby celebrating the possibility of the American Dream through choosing a path of hard work, discipline, and the adoption of mainstream cultural values.

What is most interesting about this recent wave of hip-hop ghettocentric films that reflect a difference from its predecessors (except for *Antwone Fisher*) is their attempt to create kinder and gentler cinematic ghettos. They take America's poorest communities that house a disproportionate number of Latino and black families and construct them as idyllic places where with the right guidance and discipline, full participation in American life is not only possible but also likely. Although pushing violence and poverty into the background, none of these films fully displace these social problems from the contemporary imagination, rather solidifying claims and discourses that blame the poor and communities of color for persistent inequalities in telling stories of these more "positive" individuals. The "positivity" in these narratives emanates from a dominant understanding of the failures of their brothers, sisters, and neighbors. The happiness of the narratives and the celebration of these films as innovative or a "breath of fresh air" reflect the hegemony of demonizing those who do not succeed or secure their dreams.

Of equal importance, these films construct a more "positive" ghetto experience (according to critics and their fans) through the complete erasure of poverty, police brutality, deindustrialization, mass incarceration, and violence. The reconstitution of the ghetto as such a space of happiness and play continues a pattern established by the films discussed in *Screens Fade to Black*, in that these films likewise erase the significance of race as reflective of larger discourses of colorblindness. The role of these films in perpetuating persistent inequality and hegemonic understanding of ghetto communities—as the outgrowth of post-Civil Rights policies—necessitates continued analysis, given the cultural, financial, political, and ideological success of Hollywood's current ghettocentric imagination.

WHITE STORIES, BLACK FACE: *MY BABY'S DADDY* AND *LOVE DON'T COST A THING*

Recycling is nothing new for Hollywood. Each year, many films are recycled using today's stars to bring to life old stories. Whether the remake is of *Miracle on 34th Street* (1947), *Ocean's 11* (1960), *The Manchurian Candidate* (1962), *Planet of the Apes* (1967), and *Willie Wonka and the Chocolate Factory* (1971), there is a proven market and formula of success for "updated" and redone old films. More common is the practice of sampling storylines and recasting old tropes as to not only capitalize on market trends while relying on safe narratives, in both an ideological and financial sense. For example, two recent African American-centered films, *My Baby's Daddy* (2004) and *Love Don't Cost a Thing* (2003) merely recast black bodies (literally with the later film) in previously successful films, transforming 1980s films about white anxiety to projects attempting to capitalize on the aesthetic and cultural popularity of hip-hop in the twenty-first century.

My Baby's Daddy was directed by Cheryle Dunye, whose previous films (*Stranger Inside* [2001] and *Watermelon Woman* [1996]) offered two powerful narratives of rupture to dominant representations. However, this film recycles the narrative of *3 Men and a Baby* (1987), merely replacing soon-to-be white fathers (Ted Danson, Steve Guttenberg, and Tom Selleck, who by happenstance found themselves looking after a little girl) with three black men—Eddie Griffin, Anthony Anderson, and Method Man. Each of them have to confront their manhood, irresponsible lifestyle, after getting their girlfriends pregnant. In fact, the film marketed itself as *Boyz N the Hood* meets *3 Men and a Baby,* demonstrating how *My Baby's Daddy* sought to capitalize on the dominant and acceptable sensibility of blackness, masculinity, and fatherhood in a hip-hop context. More important, the film's comedic elements work from the hilarity of a hip-hop generation, of those who might be boys in the hood, of black men becoming fathers. The mere premise of fatherhood and (blackness) hip-hop coexisting not only reflects the film's narrative approach and its connection to those other films discussed in *Screens Fade to Black* but the larger representational strategies of this new racist moment. Writing about *Daddy Day Care* (2003), Mark Anthony Neal surmises the discursive and ideological messages (and context) of *My Baby's Daddy* and the wave of black children's comedy (*Are We There Yet?* [2005] and *Johnson Family Vacation* [2004]), each of which uses long-standing stereotypes of black masculinity in a hip-hop representation moment:

The very reason we all found a film like Eddie Murphy's *Daddy Daycare* so damm funny was because the idea that group of [black] men would run a childcare facility is utterly preposterous to our sensibilities. Yes, the men in the film were challenged to run a daycare facility, as any novice childcare worker would be regardless of gender [and race], but the subtext of the film was that we found these [black] men incapable of engaged fathers. (Neal, 2005, p. 108)

As evident here and with the previous discussion, the recycling of dominant narratives in blackface relies on accepted racial tropes that not only play on cultural differences (deficiencies) as a basis of laughter and pleasure, but also the supposed interchangeable nature of racialized narratives (i.e., the erasure of racism) and the profitability of commodifiable black narratives.

Love Don't Cost a Thing goes to greater extremes, directly copying the script of *Can't Buy Me Love.* Like these other films, it seeks to capitalize on the popularity of hip-hop and particularly inscriptions of blackness. More important, although *Love Don't Cost a Thing* tells the same story through black characters and the inclusion of black cultural practices, the racial shift has little other effect on the narrative and the film's story. As with predominant discourses, *Love Don't Cost a Thing* legitimizes claims that race is meaningless except as a marker of difference. We see no evidence of racism inside and outside the school, no black community, no cultural practices (beyond hip-hop), and no historical significance in the blackness of Alvin Johnson (Nick Cannon) or Paris Morgan (Christina Milian), but rather an effort to tell universal story of American elites, who happen to be black.

Such films must be understood as part of a larger project of colorblindness, one that reduces race to an aesthetic, a style, to something that can be bought, sold, and tried on without any thought, so that the narrative of *Can't Buy Me Love* can be recycled in blackface without any change in plot, narrative, character development, or reception. The trend of telling stories through upper-middle class black bodies, who also embody a hip-hop aesthetic, in once-white narratives is a profound illustration of this current Hollywood (American) racial moment that seeks to capitalize on a safe inscription of blackness. In so doing it legitimizes dominant understandings of the American Dream, cultural differences, and the meaning of race in the twenty-first century. However, such a trend is not limited to middle-class narratives that illustrate racial transcendence as the American Dream through recycled narratives, but are equally narrative in other types of films such as *The Longest Yard*.

THE LONGEST YARD

During the summer of 2005, *The Longest Yard* took America by storm. Although not written or directed by a black director, I think it is important to use this film as a springboard to a discussion of other remakes to emphasize the ways in which Hollywood is using particular representations of blackness to sell its products. It also demonstrates the links between dominant discourses (in this case that of sports and that of criminality) and cinematic representations of blackness.

Replicating the narrative of its original (1974), where Burt Reynolds plays a prisoner/quarterback who organizes a game against the guards, the newer version replaces Reynolds with Adam Sandler in the same role, transforming the primarily white prison population in the original version to one of all black males in the 2005 version. This shift not only seeks to capitalize on the popularity of Chris Rock (who plays Caretaker) and hip-hop, but plays to hegemonic visions of sport, crime, and blackness. In other words, this change forces us to think about the meaning and significance of even the "slightest" alteration to the original film. Whereas colorblind discourses wish us to think that the increased visibility of bodies of color within *The Longest Yard* is either an insignificant change or a marker of progress, we see it otherwise. Given the fact there are currently 1 million African Americans in prison and the ubiquitous merging of the athlete and criminal into a single body of color, conversations are needed to think through the meaning and significance of a blackface remake like *The Longest Yard*. Given that Harry Edwards predicted in 1998, that eventually America's prisons will have their own teams to compete in the NBA or NFL and given the mass incarceration of people of color, the changes to this film are not inconsequential.

The issues concerning the remake of *The Longest Yard* are not limited to the ways it (and Hollywood) increasingly relies on its version of blackness, often codified through sports, music, and hip-hop culture, as aesthetic markers of difference/coolness, but the ways diversity dramatically alters the meaning of this (as well as other) film. The current version of *The Longest Yard* moves beyond guard/prisoner division of the original to one marked by racial strife: the-not-just white but Aryan guards versus the primarily black prison population. The film, however, doesn't blacken Paul Crewe, reserving the quarterback, leader, and coach positions for Sandler. As the great white hope, Crewe helps. With the assistance of his own "ghetto pass" (Caretaker), the prisoners exert revenge on the racist guards.

In the tradition of several racialized sports film (*Hardball, White Men Can't Jump* [1992], *Wildcats* [1986], *Sunset Park* [1996] and *Coach Carter*), *The Longest Yard* doesn't limit the saving and redeeming to Crewe, chronicling how Crewe's interaction with prisoners of color contributes to his own growth and redemption, from selfish, point-shaving athlete to one for and about the team. *The Longest Yard* is as much a story about Paul Crewe's transformation from "made white boy to earnest, responsible and righteously vengeful white man" (Fuchs). The changes from original to "modern" version are not inconsequential. They are fundamental to the film's place within the blackening of America's big screens and the racial, ideological, and political context of both production and consumption.

ERASING RACE AND WHITENING PICTURES

Two other films further capture Hollywood recycling, especially as it relates to processes of commodification and new racist cinematic representations. In 2000, MTV released *Carmen*, starring Beyonce Knowles and Mekhi Phifer, a remake and modernized version of the 1954 classic, *Carmen Jones*, which starred Harry Belafonte and Dorothy Dandridge. To reach new audiences, particularly America's urban youth, the operatic original was transformed into a hip-hop musical. Embodying the widespread commodification of hip-hop, this film merely tried to capitalize on the popularity of Beyonce and hip-hop, not just disgracing the original film, but drastically transforming its narrative and message. I say this not because of its poor acting and clichéd, recycled narrative, but because of its erasure of the cultural, historical, and racial significance provided in *Carmen Jones*. Despite its many faults, the original film offered a powerful glimpse at the experiences of black men and women during World War II, giving voice to their contributions to the war effort and the immense contradictions of America during the 1930s and 1940s. Likewise, while following in the footsteps of a wave of postwar tragic mulatto films, in its portrayal of Carmen, the original at least elucidates the powerful place of mixed race identity within and beyond Hollywood. The effort to bring *Carmen Jones* into a hip-hop world was not unique, as evident in the attempt to remake other classic films.

In early 2005, Sony Pictures released *Guess Who* (Kevin Rodney Sullivan), a modernized version of Stanley Kramer's 1967 classic, *Guess Who's Coming to Dinner*. The original, not without its own problems, tells the story of John Prentice (Sidney Poitier) and his introduction to the parents (Katharine Hepburn and Spencer Tracy) of his white girlfriend Katharine Houghton. It attempts to give voice to the problems of American racism, albeit through a story of interracial relationships and the unwillingness of parents to accept racial change into the next generation. In an attempt to update this film, *Guess Who* tells an entirely different narrative with a white male (Ashton Kutcher) playing the role once played by Poitier. Such a reversal of racial roles is not insignificant. *Guess Who* treats prejudice and family resistance to an interracial relationship as interchangeable. In effect, the efforts to recycle and modernize this older narrative results in a dramatically changed narrative and racial commentary, which is both disturbing and reflective of dominant racial discourses that argue "we're all prejudiced" at the expense of any discussion of power and privilege.

In each of the films discussed here, we see a common trend of Hollywood's efforts to recycle and blacken old films—the commodification of blackness in such a way that each of the films reifies common understandings that race is little more than a culture or aesthetic marker. Worse, each of these films treats race as relatively meaningless in that one can blacken a character or a screen without dramatically altering the narrative, reflecting the nature of new racist (and colorblind) discourses. Whether in blackening once white films without any substantial narrative revisions or the mere erasure of race from a particular film, this pattern reflects widespread practices of Hollywood and the realities of new racism within contemporary cinematic representations of blackness.

Inquiry and analysis into racialized remakes necessitate more than analysis of Hollywood's money-making schemes, or discussions of how the film has changed (as evident with discussion of *The Longest Yard, Carmen,* and *Guess Who*). What is required is a reflection on the ways in which long-standing and newly conceived racial, gender, sexual, and class-based tropes function within older narratives, and how these new films reflect older and newer understandings of racism. Moreover, there needs to be greater inquiry into how the use of racial tropes and how the blackening of white narratives and characters and the erasure of the racial commentaries provided by previous films reflect this new racist moment. I certainly hope future work accepts this challenge and avoids conversations about films that at first glance don't appear to be in the African American film tradition, yet contribute to hegemonic representations and hegemonic understandings of race and racism in the twenty-first century.

As mentioned in Chapter 2, interracial buddy films have long been a predominant narrative trope in the history of Hollywood. Although they are not new, (for example, *In the Heat of the Night* [1967], *Silver Streak* [1976], *48 Hours* [1982], and *Lethal Weapon* [1987]), the recent wave of buddy films reflect both the old and new elements of new racism within the cinematic representations of blackness.

The initial emphasis on buddy pictures in Hollywood was on societal discourses regarding integration, which emphasized not just the potential for racial harmony in breaking down social distance between the races, but the mutually redemptive process available in interracial cooperation. Regardless of the specifics, a vast majority of past films told narratives of interracial cooperation that ultimately resulted in personal and communal growth. Not surprisingly, a vast majority used middle-class black characters as the key player in most of these relationships, with this almost perfect black man teaching and helping a troubled white character grow, while the white character offers friendship and access to institutional power not otherwise available to black men and women.

In recent years, a similar if not more exaggerated form of this scenario has taken place, which Donald Bogle describes as Hollywood's contemporary Huck Finn fixation. Rather than offer narratives that celebrate the mutually redemptive relationship between black and white middle-class males, these recent films focus on the ghetto as a space for interracial harmony. In each case, the hardships and struggles of African Americans, often youth, are constructed as powerful lessons or teachable moments concerning values and morals that can ultimately enhance the life opportunities for troubled white individuals. For example, in *Hardball* (Brian Robbins, 2001) Conor O'Neill (Keanu Reeves) faces an uncertain future because of his gambling addiction, his lack of work ethic, and his inability to commit to work, family, or relationships. Only through his relationship with a group of black kids, who he is forced to coach in order to make ends meet, does he grow as a man. These black youth teach him about authentic struggle and real-life fears, which include issues of life and death. Throughout the film, it is he who learns from the wisdom of the youth on his baseball team. In the end, he finds happiness, direction, and a girlfriend, all of which is typical of a Hollywood happy-ending that erases the persistence of violence and poverty facing contemporary black youth.

Similarly, in *Save the Last Dance* (Thomas Carter, 2001), Derek Reynolds (Sean Patrick Thomas), a savvy, soon-to-be upwardly mobile black youth living in the inner city, proves to be a source of growth and redemption for Sara Johnson (Julia Stiles). An aspiring dancer, Johnson gives up on her dreams of becoming a professional dancer after the death of her mother, only to rekindle her passion through her relationship with Reynolds. More important, he does not merely help her overcome the displaced pain of losing her mother by encouraging her to start dancing again, but introduces her to hip-hop, to this previously uninhabitable black world. His efforts—teaching her about blackness—propel her to the next level with her dancing, aiding her efforts to secure admission into a prestigious dance school.

In film after film, from *Monster's Ball* (2001) and *Green Mile* (1999) to *Radio* (2003), *Men of Honor* (2000), and *Finding Forrester* (2000), black characters, so often inner-city black youth, assist in the personal, professional, spiritual, and racial growth of a white counterpart. In effect, these films construct these black characters as noble savages, whose experiences with violence, poverty, despair, and otherwise uncivilized living conditions have left them with an unusual amount of wisdom, insight, and understanding of the world that proves beneficial to whites—those with privilege, who did not have to fight to survive. The mythologizing process here, reflective of a widespread fetishizing discourse concerning the black underclass, celebrates injustice not only as an instrument of character building but as something that is ultimately beneficial to whites and American progress. To begin to challenge societal injustices and the hegemony of new racism necessitates analysis of these films within a broader context of African American cinematic representations and the blackening of contemporary Hollywood screens in a new racist era. To deny their significance because of a white director or an interracial cast not only falls into an essentialist trap that obfuscates the ideological, representational, political, and discursive connection between a spectrum of films, but aids in perpetuating a new racist moment. *Screens Fade to Black* does not take up these films, but it examines their ideological and political kin, illustrating the importance of future work in examining the ways in which each contributes to contemporary racial discourses and practices, each of which facilitates persistent inequality and a perpetuation of institutionally bound white privilege. The possibility of any sort of oppositional politic rests with critical inquiry, collective struggle, sustained analysis, and oppositional representational politics.

CROSSOVER APPEAL: TRANSCENDING AFRICAN AMERICAN CINEMA

Although relatively uncommon, the recent efforts of Spike Lee and John Singleton to create crossover or mainstream films not specific to either a black cinematic tradition or invested in telling "black stories," deserves thought and future analysis as well. Some people may want to cite *25th Hour* (2002) or *Four Brothers* (2005) as evidence of progress inside Hollywood and American popular culture, given that two of America's most prominent black filmmakers of the last decade have written and directed films that don't seem invested in race or the African American experience, but neither film avoids race or racism in a contemporary context. On the surface, both films deviate from the previous works of Lee and Singleton to a certain degree, signifying a certain amount of progress and increased power for Lee and Singleton, who have been able to transcend the limitations established by a Hollywood that seeks out black filmmakers to tell commodifiable black stories, neither effort replicates the ideologies or politics of those new racist cinematic productions discussed throughout *Screens Fade to Black*.

As we look beyond the surface, we see two films that were not commercial successes, in spite of critical praise and their star-studded casts. For example, *25th Hour*, notwithstanding the casting of Ed Norton (Monty Brogan) and Rosario Dawson (Naturelle Riviera), earned only $13 million at the box office. Although *Four Brothers* amassed almost $70 million, significantly more than Singleton's other 2005 project, *Hustle and Flow* ($22 million), which he produced, the success of *Four Brothers* illustrates the power of a crossover film that deemphasizes race and focuses on racial harmony via violence. Some want to cite racial progress and a new racial moment in Hollywood, but the specifics of each film, their varied casts (Mark Wahlberg and Tyreese Gibson were crucial to success of this film as marketable commodities of hip-hop), and their politics reveal that we are not witnessing some racially transcendent moment but one defined by continued interest and support for films that reify white privilege and hegemonic racial discourses.

The limited success of *25th Hour* compared to the popularity of *Four Brothers* reveals how audiences continue to seek out films that present a stereotype, commodified and converting inscription that legitimizes predominant American discourses and the existence of white privilege. To think about what and who is celebrated, and why certain artists and films receive praise and audience support, is tremendously revealing on a number of levels.

Another important facet here is the tendency of critics to celebrate Lee's foray into a "non-African American" cinematic landscape. Notwithstanding the appearance of a film or one that departs from the narrative tradition, politics, or ideology of Lee's previous films, *25th Hour* is very much in line with Lee's filmography. In telling the story of Monty, a white yuppie living in Manhattan, New York, and his arrest for drug distribution, Lee offers a powerful commentary on the privileges of whiteness, especially in the context of America's Jim Crowed criminal justice system. Despite being a major player in New York's drug economy, one that connected Monty to the Russian mob, Monty enjoyed the privileges of whiteness from his arrest right up until his day of incarceration: Monty is freed on bail, allowed to enjoy his freedom while awaiting the beginning of his incarceration. He even gets to drive himself to prison. Juxtaposed against *Clockers* (1995) in which Lee shows the unrelenting policing of black youth and inner city communities as part of the war on drugs, the casual treatment of Monty embodies Lee's profound commentary on race in America in the twenty-first century.

In a sense, Lee uses the presumption of a universal story where whiteness is conceived as outside a racial context as a means to offer a powerful commentary on race and racism. Both these films reveal a potential powerful trend of filmmakers challenging racial and reactionary orthodoxy through narratives that appear to be "universal," and that centers whiteness as a point of analysis and/or critique. Likewise, scholarship needs to avoid the simplistic definitions of African American film that limit conversations to those films that tell "black stories," or are marketed as glimpses into black life because of an all-black cast or setting within the black community. A film like *25th Hour* offers an important and sometimes powerful commentary on race, blackness, commodification, representation, the American Dream, materialism, and whiteness, all through a "universal narrative" and the directorial voice of an important black artist. Given the hegemony of reactionary and new racist cinematic productions, these efforts and those of other filmmakers need to be celebrated, highlighted, and hopefully emulated in future years.

CINEMATIC OPPOSITION IN A BARREN MARKETPLACE

After several hundred pages of unrelenting critiques centering on the new racism of contemporary African American films, I can imagine readers thinking that I don't like anything. Friends and family members have long questioned me about my criticisms of film, telling me not to hate so much and just watch the movies. Given the consequences and context of production and consumption, there is little choice but to critically engage contemporary films.

All that being said, it should be clear that with rare exceptions, I don't hate any of the films discussed in *Screens Fade to Black*. Despite my desire to provide in-depth criticisms and analysis, some of these films have made me laugh, and others have elicited tears and joy. The tendency to establish a binary between criticism and analysis and enjoyment is a problem that necessitates intervention, for the unwillingness to critically engage spheres of entertainment because popular culture serves the interest of injustice.

Second, *Screens Fade to Black* is not a collection of denouncements against a series of films that I don't like, but rather an effort to talk about representation politics and ideology. I do, however, hate oppression and white supremacist discourses and practice—I loathe violence, poverty, and despair. In this sense, *Screens Fade to Black* is not so much about film but about the ways in which films aid and abet structural inequalities. Whether I like or enjoy these films is insignificant, which, like my analysis, reflects my position as a white male ethnic studies scholar, given the guiding question—how do these films assist with racial formation and distributions of power and privilege within contemporary America? It is not even so much about whether the films discussed are "good films," but how the films contribute to the current racial order whether in celebration of the American Dream or the reduction of race to cultural differences.

Third, as evident in the conclusion of each chapter, it is important to highlight those films that not only challenge the accepted narratives and representations of Hollywood, but also exist as a voice to opposition. Given the hegemony of contemporary representations of race and racism, which saturate a spectrum of institutions and spaces, interventions and ruptures within contemporary Hollywood are key to the fulfillment of any oppositional politics.

Beyond the films already discussed, there have been many others, most of which were never released into theaters, that offer counter-narratives, alternative representations, and antinew racist politics. For example, *Shackles* (Charles Winkler, 2005) and *Animal* (David Burke, 2005) offer powerful glimpses into America's prisons, avoiding the common traps of fetish and demonization. Rather, each offers narrative regarding the effects of the prison industrial complex and the spectrum of resistance from those caught up in American's matrix of incarceration.

Not all these counter cinematic focus on the ghetto centric imagination. *Brother to Brother* (Rodney Evans, 2004), for example, tells the story of the Harlem Renaissance, documenting this powerful movement in black cultural history. Additionally, it brings the often neglected and ignored history of black gays onto the screen, illustrating the importance of films and analysis that explores the intersections of race, gender, and sexuality. In fact, over the course of completing this book, I thankfully came across several recently release films—*George Washington* (David Gordon Green, 2000), *Commitments* (Carol Mayes, 2001), *All About You* (Christine Swanson, 2003)—each touching on a different aspect of contemporary black life, providing depth and humanity while constructing blackness as historically, culturally, politically, and socially relevant in contemporary America.

Although a vast majority of films that deviate from the Hollywood narrative and the dominant racial discourse have never been released to the big screen and never entered the popular cultural landscape, there have been certain Hollywoodized interventions. In 2004, *Hotel Rwanda* (Terry George) garnered immense critical praise, eventually receiving several Oscar nominations. Although it earned only $23 million in box office receipts (it cost 17.5 million to make), most of which resulted from the publicity generated by Oscar coverage, *Hotel Rwanda* made an important contribution to contemporary representations of blackness.

Hotel Rwanda tells the true-life story of Paul Rusesabagina (Don Cheadle), a hotel manager, who, in the midst on the 1994 civil war in Rwanda, provided refuge to more than 1,000 Tutsi refugees (he was Hutu) during their struggle against the Hutu militia. As the world turned a blind eye to Hutu-initiated genocide, Rusesabagina risked his life to protect his national brothers and sisters. The film provides a cinematic glimpse of this history and the complex dialectics of race, nation, and global politics through its moving narrative. Its importance rests with its effort to bring the scope of the cinematic representation of blackness to films that transcend U.S. boundaries. Given the extent of globalization, the cultural and political significance of the Black Diaspora, as well as the links between racial formation across various geographies, *Hotel Rwanda* was a needed intervention to the current trajectory of African American representation.

The film also challenges long-standing Hollywood representations of Africa as a place of uncivilized savagery (*Black Hawk Down*, 2001, Ridley Scott), revealing the humanity and complexity of war-torn Africa. It also disrupts the hegemony of claims concerning U.S. interventions and concerns for global inhumanity. *Hotel Rwanda* reveals not only the inaction of the U.S. government during the war but also the hypocrisy and racism of U.S. policy toward Africa. The importance of *Hotel Rwanda* ultimately rests with its disruption of both dominant representations of blackness and the larger discourses regarding race (blackness) in a global context.

The challenges to hegemonic blackness of contemporary screens is not limited to foreign films, those located outside the U.S. independent black films and those that went straight to DVD, as evident with Spike Lee's 2003 release of *She Hate Me*. An immensely complex film, Lee mixes black sexual politics, issues of commodification, same sex marriage, corporate greed, and the sexuality of black male and female bodies inside a story of a black man trying to make it inside American big business. *She Hate Me* offers two distinct, but interconnected, narratives, demonstrating the intersections of race, gender, sexuality, class, and the American dream:

1. John Henry Armstrong (Anthony Mackie) is a black Harvard-educated biotech executive working at one of America's top pharmaceutical companies. His conscience leads him to blow the whistle on his company, resulting in an investigation from the Securities & Exchange Commission into the legality of its business practices (think Enron). His efforts, driven partially by the company failures to fulfill its promises to the nation regarding an AIDS vaccine, results in his firing, his being labeled unemployable from corporate America, and his eventual arrest.

2. Armstrong, in need of cash, agrees to provide Fatimah (Kerry Washington)—his ex-girlfriend and a now lesbian—and dozens of lesbians with his sperm in exchange for $10,000 dollars. As part of his effort to maintain his American Dream (his material possessions) and their desire to start their own families (their American Dream), Armstrong's life spirals from one defined by a traditional path to the American Dream to something far from conventional.

She Hate Me successfully links together its multiple narratives through its understanding of race. It convincingly challenges widespread celebrations of the American Dream and those who claim racial transcendence for the black elite, demonstrating the powerful ways race—as detriment, as source of community, and as basis of cultural identity—continues to operate within contemporary contexts. Likewise, although less successful and not without problems, it also demonstrates the importance of intersectional understandings of race whether in black male heterosexuality or black lesbianism. In fact, the biggest disappointment with the film rests with Lee's sexual politics, a common theme throughout his career, given the propensity of *She Hate Me* to fetishize black lesbianism and its reduction of black female sexual identities to pornographic male fantasies, with Armstrong able to sexually satisfy the most unattainable women—the lesbian (somewhat reminiscent of long-standing ideas of both black male and female hypersexuality). Likewise, the film inscription of patriarchy and the importance of the nuclear family—albeit with a man and two women—undermines the oppositional potential of the film, which at times seems too invested in fetishizing black lesbian sexuality all the while maintaining the importance of men and masculinity (as well as their sperm).

Unfortunately, and probably not due to these problems, *She Hate Me* did not attract audiences (it amassed only $365,124 at the box office compared to *Soul Plane, Bringing Down the House,* and *Barbershop,* which generated $14 million, $133.5 million, and $75 million, respectively). Nor did it win over critics, given its challenge to the hegemonic denials of racism, widespread commodification and demonization of blackness, and the celebration of the American Dream.

Although others want to celebrate Oscars or the increased visibility of artists of color, we need to pay tribute to those films that challenge the hegemony of Hollywood representations and those films that advocate for a new racial politics. We need to acknowledge films such as *She Hate Me* or *Hotel Rwanda,* which not only challenge the narrow set of representations and racial politics available within contemporary Hollywood, but work to disrupt those injustices that continue to plague minority communities.

CONCLUSION

In this final chapter, as in the rest of *Screens Fade to Black,* I have sought to demonstrate the importance of contemporary representations of blackness, as important vehicles for the demonization and commodification of blackness. I have called not simply for more creative and critical engagements with contemporary representations, with the cultural instruments of this new racist moment, but for a new understanding of its content and form. More than a merely pleasurable or profitable "cultural safari" into the black community, contemporary African American cinema reminds us what is possible and powerful, who is a failure and unworthy. They encapsulate the central tensions structuring racialized communities and social relations. They trace the limits of "common sense," cataloging the (not so) sincere fictions through which most Americans engage—or rather avoid engaging the world. The contemporary blackening of America's representational field signifies not a new colorblind racial politics, but the contours of new racism, embodying the dominant ideological preoccupations and presuppositions, articulating the social problems and moral panics projected upon the screen and America's racial reality.

The films discussed in *Screens Fade to Black* use and refuse the intersections of race, class, gender, and ability to entertain and instruct, deploying long-standing racial tropes even as the films and the broader discourse of reception denies the importance of race and racism in the twenty-first century. Reflecting shifts within globalized commerce and technology, the power of these films foreshadow increasingly interpenetrated media worlds that interpolate subjects with greater and greater ease. In the end, contemporary representations of blackness—whether through processes of demonization, commodification, or their likely combined efforts—matter because race and racism matters and because popular culture matters in the creation, construction, dissemination, and articulation of dominant tropes and discourses of race, gender, class, sexuality, and nation. It matters because the contours and vectors of the dominant understandings of race, blackness, whiteness, and the current racial politics emanate from film and its representational field, increasingly serving as a vehicle for the celebration of the American Dream as evidence of racial progress, and as a representational space for the demonization of black and brown youth. In this way it replicates discourses that take place within the dominant media, political circles, and public discourse. It matters because of the many issues that continue to plague our society.

It matters because in 2005, the year many celebrated as the greatest in the history of black film, the number of black men incarcerated reached over 1 million. Its significance resides with George W. Bush's continued refusal to meet with the Congressional Black Caucus, as a symbol for the declining political power available to the black community. Its importance rests in the simultaneity of the blackening of these screens, and Bill Bennett's calls for abortion as a method of crime prevention; the ample amount of racial discourse, and the persistence of color lines, inequalities, violence, death and despair, all of which embodies a continuation of America's old racial politics, even as we see changes to the surface. It surely matters because of the devastation caused by and visible with Hurricane Katrina, the troubled response of a nation and its leaders, as well as what this "natural disaster" revealed about contemporary America. Even as films highlight progress and the America Dream, thereby erasing the millions of impoverished African Americans, Hurricane Katrina provided the most powerful rupture to this representational field. In the context of contemporary representations, one has to wonder if the effects of colorblind discourses and the vectors of contemporary representations of blackness in the American imagination, which had all but forgotten the black poor before this hurricane. African American films matter because they exist along side these tragedies and the violence that defines our present moment as either diversions or sites of pleasure, or ideological projects that garner consent for the hegemonic order. They matter because despite the ubiquity of happy endings, despite the universality of making the final shot or securing success, our real world is without a happy ending, at least for the great majority of its inhabitants.

As in *Screens Fade to Black,* these films matter because racism kills. The celebrations and demonizations of blackness jointly facilitate the hegemony of new racism, which in the end maintains color lines and white privileges, whether manifesting in the perpetuation of the prison industrial complex or systemic poverty that reared its head in wake of Hurricane Katrina. It matters because social justice—the ability of all people to live their lives free of oppression based on race, class, gender, sexuality, and ideology—is a goal that U.S. society has long forgone for profit at any cost. It has never been "just a movie." It has always been lives, livelihoods, injustice, and a desire for much, much more.

Appendix

A POINT OF DEPARTURE:
THE LITERATURE OF
AFRICAN AMERICAN CINEMA

As this text avoids the discursive and intellectual debates that define much of today's academic debates concerning representations, African American cinema, and race and popular culture, it is important to explore the existing literature. Although reviewing this body of work is helpful and significant in discussing the history of African American cinema, it has often neglected its place within a larger cultural and racialized landscape toward critical and textual analysis.

The African American film literature is vast, but the focus, approach, and style of this project sets it apart from its competitors, in terms of focus on contemporary popular films, its broad definition of African American cinema, its orientation to themes, and its accessibility. Although it is impossible to review every book, I will provide a brief discussion of some of the representative texts here, highlighting the significant differences between these texts and *Screens Fade to Black: Contemporary African American Cinema*.

Donald Bogle, with *Toms, Coons, Mulattoes, Mammies, and Bucks: An Interpretive History of Blacks in American Films*, offers the most comprehensive examination of the history of African American cinema. Arguing that this history is defined by five distinct stereotypes, Bogle's work is exhaustive. However, as with much of the literature (Thomas Cripps, *Slow Fade to Black: The Negro in American Film, 1900–1942;* Cripps, *Making Movies Black: The Hollywood Message Movie from World War II to the Civil Rights Era;* Nelson George, *Blackface: Reflections on African-Americans in the Movies;* James Snead, *White Screens Black Images: Hollywood from the Dark Side*), the focus lends itself to the history of black performers and their place in the history of Hollywood. What is important for this project is that Bogle neither critically engages the films as texts (he talks about every film, so it is impossible to provide any depth) nor covers recent cinematic productions. The absence of films like *Barbershop, Antwone Fisher,* or *Training Day* reflects its ideological project, narrative strategy, and date of publication. Moreover, its orientation toward films produced and written by white directors and long-standing traditions of racist stereotypes from Hollywood limits understanding of the powerful ways in which new racist codes, ideologies, and tropes infect a vast majority of today's films, regardless of author.

A vast majority of the literature dealing with African American film locates theoretical discussions at the center of its work. Primarily geared toward academic discourses surrounding representation, intersectionality, appropriation, black independent films, and the connection between culture and power, these books (Manthia Diawara, *Black American Cinema;* Gladstone Yearwood, *Black Film As a Signifying Practice: Cinema, Narration and the African American Aesthetic Tradition;* Mark Reid, *Redefining Black Film;* Vincent Rocchio, *Reel Racism: Confronting Hollywood's Construction of Afro-American Culture*) don't necessarily help the lay reader understand the issues surrounding African American cinema. Issues of language, accessibility of theories used, and the overall purpose of these texts limit its audience to academic circles. As with the historical works, this section of literature ignores both the most recent offerings in African American film and much of the academic and communal debates concerning the manifestations of racism in the contemporary moment.

Likewise, several more recent texts (Sheril Antonio, *Contemporary African American Cinema;* Krin Gabbard, *Black Magic: White Hollywood and African American Culture;* bell hooks, *Reel to Real: Race, Sex, and Class at the Movies*) have interrogated contemporary representations of blackness emanating from Hollywood. Their focus on specific films, however, limits their discussion to the films themselves and their inscription of dominant understandings of blackness, rather than the larger discursive or cultural landscape.

Since 2000, several texts that look at the representations of inner-city communities have been published. The work of Craig Watkins (*Representing: Hip Hop Culture and the Production of Black Cinema*), Paula Massood (*Black City Cinema: African American Urban Experiences in Film*), Norman Denzin (*Reading Race: Hollywood and the Cinema of Racial Violence*), Valerie Smith (*Not Just Race, Not Just Gender: Black Feminist Readings*), Norma Manatu (*African American Women and Sexuality in Cinema*), and Jesse Rhines (*Black Film/White Money,* Rutgers University Press) all provide examples of a needed direction in the field. Each, to different degrees, successfully situates their discussion of film within a larger political/social/economic context. Watkins, for example, spends almost half of his book talking about political and economic shifts of the 1980s. Moreover, each of these authors offers narratives that are both accessible and sophisticated. Their focus, however, is significantly different to that of *Screens Fade to Black.* Watkins and Denzin focus on the social/political relevance of the "ghettocentric genre," essentially discussing only *Menace II Society* and *Boyz n the Hood*. Rhines centers on economics, whereas Massood provides a historical treatment of the city on film. The focus of these of monographs and their scope of inquiry ending in the mid-1990s leaves room for future projects.

As the majority of the literature is geared toward academic audiences, many are narrowly focused. In a sense, the bulk of the literature is very niche-oriented. The aforementioned films dealing with ghetto representations are just as narrowly focused, in terms of themes and films discussed and their time periods, as much of the feminist scholarship (Lisa Anderson, *Mammies No More: The Changing Image of Black Women on Stage and Screen;* Jacqueline Bobo, *Black Women as Cultural Readers;* the work of bell hooks and Valerie Smith). The narrowness of these texts and their orientation toward academic debates further separate them from this project, which attempts to cover a broad range of films that are linked by their time of release.

Last but not least is Ed Guerrero's *Framing Blackness,* a text that stands alone. Its approach (theme-based), its mixed methodology (cultural studies and history) and focus (multi-film, genre, and period), and its accessibility provide a template worth following. Unlike virtually every other piece of literature within this canon, Guerrero talks about those films that are widely accepted as part of African American cinema, as well as numerous films that center or deal with issues pertinent to the African American community. Although a potential source of competition, in that both texts work from similar approaches, *Screens Fade to Black* begins where Guerrero ends *Framing Blackness,* by critically engaging the ways these films teach race, racism, and racial politics. Focusing on *Barbershop, Antwone Fisher, Brown Sugar,* and others, this project will serve as a sequel or a companion to Guerrero's work, moving beyond textual utterances toward a greater emphasis on the historical moment of production and consumption of these films.

The existing literature contains a number of insightful treatments of the history and cultural relevance of African American cinema; there are numerous works chronicling the history of struggle and of racist images; there are even more that unpack particular films, dissecting meaning from these cinematic texts. However, no text has accepted the challenge of examining the recent wave of African American films, or exploring what this period says about the state of Hollywood and American race relations.

BIBLIOGRAPHY

Alexander, Bill. "Barbershop." *USA Today,* September 25, 2002, http://blackvoices. aol.com/black_entertainment.

Allen-Taylor, J. Douglas. "Race and 'Ray.'" Alternet.com, February 25, 2005, http://www.alternet.org/movies/21352/.

Anderson, Lisa. *Mammies No More: The Changing Image of Black Women on Stage and Screen.* New York: Rowman & Littlefield, 1997.

Antonio, Sheril. *Contemporary African American Cinema.* New York: Peter Lang Publishers, 2002.

Associated Press, "'Barbershop' Brouhaha." CBS News, September 26, 2002, http:// www.cbsnews.com/stories/2002/09/25/entertainment/main523269. shtml.

Barkley, Charles, and Michael Wilbon. *Who's Afraid of a Large Black Man?* New York: The Penguin Press, 2005.

Berlant, Lauren. *The Queen of America Goes to Washington City: Essays on Sex and Citizenship.* Durham: Duke University Press, 1997.

Bobo, Jacqueline. *Black Women as Cultural Readers.* New York: Columbia University Press, 1995.

Bogle, Thomas. *Toms, Coons, Mulattoes, Mammies, and Bucks: An Interpretive History of Blacks in American Films.* New York: Continuum Publishers, 2001.

Bonilla-Silva, Eduardo. *Racism without Racists: Color-Blind Racism and the Persistence of Racial Inequality in America.* New York: Rowan and Littlefield, 2003.

———. *White Supremacy and Racism in the Post-Civil Rights Era.* Boulder: Lynne Rienner Publishing, 2001.

Boseman, Keith. "'Brown Sugar:' Simply Too Sweet for Hip-Hop Beats." *Hyde Park Citizen,* October 24, 2002, p. 16.

Bourdieu, Pierre and Jean Claude Passerson. *Reproduction in Education, Society and Culture.* Beverley Hills, Calif.: Sage Publishers, 1977.

Boyd, Todd. *Am I Black Enough for You: Popular Culture from the 'Hood and Beyond.* Bloomington: Indiana University Press, 1997.

Caputo, Angela. "Alumni's 'Barbershop' Reels in both Money and Debate." *Columbia Chronicle,* September 30, 2002, http://www.ccchronicle.com/back/2002_fall/2002–09–30/campus4.html.

Carlson, Marvin. *Performance: A Critical Introduction.* London: Routledge, 1996.

Cashmore, Ellis. *The Black Culture Industry.* New York: Routledge, 1997.

Cole, C.L., and David L. Andrews. "America's New Son: Tiger Woods and America's Multiculturalism." In *Sports Stars: The Cultural Politics of Sporting Celebrity,* ed. David L. Andrews and Steven J. Jackson (pp 70–86). New York: Routledge, 2001.

Cole, C.L., and David L. Andrews. "Look—It's NBA Show Time!: Visions of Race in Popular Imaginary." In *Cultural Studies: A Research Volume,* ed. Norman Denzin, Vol. 1 (pp. 141–181). New York: Routledge, 1996.

Collins, Patricia Hill. *Black Sexual Politics: African Americans, Gender and the New Racism.* New York: Routledge, 2004.

Crenshaw, Kimberle. "Mapping the margins: Intersectionality, identity politics, and violence against women of color." *Stanford Law Review* 43 (1991): 1241–99.

Cripps, Thomas. *Slow Fade to Black: The Negro in American Film, 1900–1942.* Oxford: Oxford University Press, 1993.

Cripps, Thomas. *Making Movies Black: The Hollywood Message Movie from World War II to the Civil Rights Era.* Oxford: Oxford University Press, 1993.

Cripps, Thomas. *Black Film as Genre.* Bloomington: Indiana University Press, 1978.

Cross-White, Agnes, and Sherman R. White, Jr. "Cut the Controversy over 'Barbershop,'" October 2002, Project 21, http://www.nationalcenter.org/P21NVWhiteBarbershop1002.html.

"Cruel and Invisible," *Los Angeles Times,* December 16, 2003, B8.

Davis, Angela. *Are Prisons Obsolete?* New York: Open Media, 2003.

Denzin, Norman. *Reading Race: Hollywood and the Cinema of Racial Violence.* Thousand Oaks, Calif.: Sage Publications, 2002.

Diawara, Mantia. *Black American Cinema,* Newark: New York: Routledge, 1993.

Dillon, Monica. "What's Wrong with Antwone Fisher?," February 3, 2003, http://www.blackliving.com/forums/index.php?showtopic=2204.

Du Bois, W.E.B. *The Souls of Black Folk.* New York: Penguin Reprints, 1996, 1903.

Fanon, Frantz. *The Wretched of the Earth.* New York: Grove Publishers, 1965.

———. *Blacks Skins, White Masks.* New York: Grove Publishers, 1967, 1991.

Feagin, Joe, and Melvin Sikes. *Living with Racism: The Black Middle Class Experience.* Boston: Beacon Press, 1995.

Ferguson, Robert. *Representing "Race": Ideology, Identity and the Media.* New York: Oxford University Press, 1998.

Fiske, John. *Understanding Popular Culture.* New York: Routledge, 1989.

Fuchs, Cynthia. "Doing Time: The Longest Yard." Popmatters.com, May 28, 2005, http://www.popmatters.com/film/reviews/l/longest-yard-2005.shtml.

———. "Chemical Reactions: Conversations with Charles Stone III." *Reel Images Magazine,* http://www.reelimagesmagazine.com/txt_features/conversations/reel_conversation_charles_stone_iii.htm.

———. "Ya Don't Stop: Brown Sugar." Popmatters.com, October 10, 2002, http://www.popmatters.com/film/reviews/b/brown-sugar.shtml.

———. "Love and Basketball." Popmatters.com, 2000, http://www.popmatters.com/film/reviews/l/loveandbasketball.shtml.

Gabbard, Krin. *Black Magic: White Hollywood and African American Culture.* New Brunswick, N.J.: Rutgers University Press, 2004.

George, Nelson. *Blackface: Reflections on African-Americans in the Movies.* New York: Cooper Square Press, 2002.

Giroux, Henry. *The Abandoned Generation: Democracy Beyond the Culture of Fear.* New York: Palgrave Macmillan, 2003.

Goldberg, David Theo. *The Racial State.* New York: Blackwell Publishers, 2001.

Goldberg, Eve, and Linda Evans. "The Prison Industrial Complex and the Global Economy": A Pamphlet. Berkeley: Prison Activist Resource Center, 1998, http://www.prisonactivist.org/crisis/evans-goldberg.html.

Grant, William. *Post-Soul Black Cinema: Discontinuities, Innovations, and Breakpoints, 1970–1995.* New York: Routledge, 2004.

Gray, Herman. *Cultural Moves: African Americans and the Politics of Representation.* Berkeley: University of California Press, 2005.

———. *Watching Race: Television and the Struggle for Blackness.* Minneapolis: University of Minnesota Press, 1995.

———. "Television, Black Americans and the American Dream." In *Gender, Race, and Class in Media: A Text-Reader,* ed. Gail Dines and Jean M. Humez (pp. 430–37). Thousand Oaks: Sage Publications, 1995.

Guerrero, Ed. *Framing Blackness: The African American Image in Film.* Philadelphia: Temple University Press, 1993.

Guerrero, Lisa. "Racial Representation and the Ironic Response in African American Popular Culture," Unpublished Paper Presented at Department Colloquium, Washington State University, Spring 2005.

Hall, Stuart. *Representation: Cultural Representations and Signifying Practices.* Thousand Oaks: Sage Publications, 1997.

———. "What Is This 'Black' in Black Popular Culture." In *Black Popular Culture,* ed. Gina Dent (pp 21–36). Seattle: Bay Press, 1992.

Hall, Wiley A. "Urban Rhythms: 'Barbershop' an Unusually Good Movie about Blacks." *The Baltimore Afro-American,* October 4, 2002, p. A2.

Harrison, Eric. "'Baby Boy' Is Passionate and Disturbing." *Houston Chronicle,* June 27, 2001, p. 1.

hooks, bell. *We Really Cool: Black Men and Masculinity.* New York: Routledge, 2004.

———. *Reel to Real: Race, Sex, and Class at the Movies.* New York: Routledge, 1996.

———. *Outlaw Culture: Resisting Representation.* New York: Routledge 1994.

———. *Black Looks: Race and Representation.* Boston: South End Press, 1992.

"Is Everything Funny to Black People? 'Barbershop' Proves Love of Money Comes Before Love of Self." *Chicago Weekend,* September 19, 2002, p. 1.

James, Joy. *Shadowboxing: Representations of Black Feminist Politics.* New York: St. Martin's Press, 1999.

———. *Resisting State Violence: Radicalism, Gender, and Race in American Culture.* Minneapolis: University of Minnesota Press, 1996.

Jarrett, Vernon. "Why Pay for Insults? Say NO to 'Barbershop.'" *Chicago Defender,* September 21, 2002, p. 3.

Johnson, Allan G. *Privilege, Power and Difference.* New York: McGraw-Hill Publishers, 2001.

Johnson, James Weldon. *The Autobiography of an Ex-Colored Man.* New York: Dover Publishers, 1995, 1912.

Kelley, Robin. "Playing for keeps: Pleasure and profit on the postindustrial playground." In *The House that Race Built,*" ed. Wahneema Lubiano (pp. 195–231). New York: Vintage, 1998.

———. *Race Rebels: Culture, Politics, and the Black Working Class.* New York: Free Press, 1996.

Kellner, Douglas. *Media Culture: Cultural Studies, Identity, and Politics Between the Modern and the Postmodern.* New York: Routledge, 1995.

Kellner, Douglas. "Reading Images Critically: Toward a Postmodern Pedagogy." In *Postmodernism, Feminism, and Cultural Politics,* ed. Henry Giroux (pp. 60–82). Albany: State University of New York, 1991.

King, C. Richard, and Charles Fruehling Springwood. "Body and Soul: Physicality, Disciplinarity, and the Overdetermination of Blackness." In *Channeling Blackness: Studies in Television and Race in America,* ed. Darnell Hunt (pp. 185–206). New York: Oxford University Press, 2005.

King, C. Richard, and Charles Fruehling Springwood. *Beyond the Cheers: Race as Spectacle in College Sport.* Albany: State University of New York, 2001.

Kitwana, Bakari. *Why White Kids Love Hip Hop: Wankstas, Wiggers, Wannabes and the New Reality of Race in America.* New York: Basic Books, 2005.

Kong, Deborah. "'Barbershop' Controversy Mocks Civil Rights Icons." *The Miami Times,* October 8, 2002, p. 1A.

Liptsitz, George. "The Possessive Investment in Whiteness: Racialized Social Democracy and the 'White Problem in American Studies," *American Quarterly,* 47, September (pp. 369–87), 1995.

Manatu, Norma. *African American Women and Sexuality in Cinema.* London: McFarland Publishers, 2003.

Marable, Manning. "Black America: Multicultural democracy in the Age of Clarence Thomas and David Duke" *(Pamphlet Series No. 16).* Westfield, N.J.: Open Magazine, 1992.

Marriott, David. *On Black Men.* New York: Columbia University Press, 2000.

Massood, Paula. *Black City Cinema: African American Urban Experiences in Film.* Philadelphia: Temple University Press, 2003.

McIntosh, Peggy. "White Privilege: Unpacking the Invisible Knapsack." In White Privilege: Essential Readings on the Other Side of Racism, 2d ed., ed. Paula Rothenberg (pp. 109–113). New York: Worth Publishers, 2005.

Mercer, Kobena. *Welcome to the Jungle: New Positions in Black Cultural Studies.* New York: Routledge, 1994.

Moorti, Sujata. *Color of Rape: Gender and Race in Television's Public Sphere*. Albany: State University of New York Press, 2002.

Neal, Mark Anthony. *New Black Man*. New York: Routledge, 2005.

Omi, Michael, and Howard Winant. *Racial Formation in the United States: From the 1960s to the 1990s*. New York: Routledge, 1994.

Parenti, Christian. *Lockdown America: Police and Prisons in the Age of Crisis*. New York: Verso Publishers, 2000.

Perry, Imani. *Prophets of the Hood: Politics and Poetics in Hip-Hop*. Duke University Press, 2004.

Pough, Gwendolyn. *Check It While I Wreck It: Black Womanhood, Hip Hop Culture, and the Public Sphere*. Boston: Northeastern University Press, 2004.

Reid, Mark. *Black Lenses, Black Voices: African American Film Now: African American Film Now (Genre and Beyond)*. New York: Rowman and Littlefield, 2005.

———. *Redefining Black Film*. Berkeley: University of California Press, 1993.

Rhines, Jesse. *Black Film/White Money*. New Brunswick: Rutgers University Press, 1996.

Richards, Cindy. "The Problem Isn't the Breast, Its Violence against Women," *Chicago Sun-Times*, February 8, 2004, http://www.suntimes.com/cgi-bin/print.cgi.

Riley, Clayton. "Forward." In *Find an Image: Black Films from Uncle Tom to Super Fly*, by James Murray. Indianapolis: Bobbs-Merril Company, 1973.

Rocchio, Vincent. *Reel Racism: Confronting Hollywood's Construction of Afro-American Culture*. Boulder, Col.: Westview Press, 2000.

Rothenberg, Paula. *White: Essential Readings on the Other Side of Racism*. New York: Worth Publishers, 2005.

Sailer, Steve. "Barbershop." UPI, September 12, 2002, http://www.upi.com/inc/view.php?StoryID=20020912–085147–1675r.

Saltman, Kenneth, and David Gabbard, eds. *Education as Enforcement: The Militarization and Corporitization of Schools*. New York: Routledge, 2004.

Sexton, Jared. "The Field of Fantasy and the Court of Appeal: On *Friday Night Lights* and *Coach Carter*." In *Visual Economies of/in Motion: Sport and Film*, edited by David J. Leonard and C. Richard King. New York: Peter Lang Publishers, 2006.

———. "The Ruse of Engagement: 'Black Cinema' and the New American Century," Unpublished Paper Presented at University of California Riverside, December 2, 2003.

Smith, Valerie. *Not Just Race, Not Just Gender: Black Feminist Readings*. New York: Routledge, 1998.

Snead, James. *White Screens Black Images: Hollywood from the Dark Side*. New York: Routledge, 1994.

Sragow, Michael. "A Watershed for the Oscars," Baltimore Sun, January 26, 2005, http://www.baltimoresun.com/features/lifestyle/bal-te.to.barrier26jan26,1,907447.story?coll=bal-artslife-today.

The Diva, Bams, & Cass. *3 Black Chicks Review Flicks: A Film and Video Guide with Flava!* New York: Rose Cooper, 2002.

Watkins, S. Craig. *Hip Hop Matters: Politics, Pop Culture, and the Struggle for the Soul of a Movement*. Boston: Beacon Press, 2005.

Watkins, S. Craig. *Representing: Hip Hop Culture and the Production of Black Cinema.* Chicago: University of Chicago Press, 1998.

West, Cornel. *Race Matters.* New York: Vintage Press, 1994.

White, Sherman R. "Cut Controversy over 'Barbershop.'" *New York Voice,* November 6, 2002, p. 4.

Williams, Linda. *Playing the Race Card: Melodramas of Black and White from Uncle Tom to O.J. Simpson.* Princeton: Princeton University Press, 2001.

Williams, Patricia. *The Alchemy of Race and Rights.* Cambridge: Harvard University Press, 1992.

Williams, Rhonda. "Living at the Crossroads: Explorations in Race, Nationality, Sexuality, and Gender." In *The House that Race Built,*" ed. Wahneema Lubiano (pp. 136–56). New York: Vintage, 1998.

Winant, Howard. *The World Is a Ghetto.* New York: Basic Books, 2002.

Wynter, Leon. *American Skin: Pop Culture, Big Business & The End of White America.* New York: Crown Publishers, 2002.

Yearwood, Gladstone. *Black Film As a Signifying Practice: Cinema, Narration and the African American Aesthetic Tradition.* New York: African World Press, 1999.

Zook, Kristal Brent. "Rocking The Cradle: John Singleton Pulls the Pacifier from Men Who Won't Grow Up." *The Washington Post,* June 20, 2001, p. C.01.

INDEX

About the Author

DAVID J. LEONARD is Assistant Professor of Comparative Ethnic Studies at Washington State University. He is a past contributor to Greenwood's *Martin Luther King: An Encyclopedia*.